OOPS!
The PC Problem Solver Anybody Can Use

Mike Miller

que

OOPS! The PC Problem Solver Anybody Can Use, Third Edition

Copyright © 1994 by Que® Corporation

Library of Congress Catalog No.: 94-67362

ISBN: 1-56529-918-3

97 96 95 94   4 3 2 1

Interpretation of the printing code: the rightmost double-digit number is the year of the book's printing; the rightmost single-digit number, the number of the book's printing. For example, a printing code of 94-1 shows that the first printing of the book occurred in 1994.

Screen reproductions in this book were created using Collage Complete from Inner Media, Inc., Hollis, NH.

Publisher: David P. Ewing

Associate Publisher: Michael Miller

Managing Editor: Michael Cunningham

Marketing Manager: Greg Wiegand

Credits

Publishing Manager
Don Roche, Jr.

Acquisitions Editor
Thomas F. Godfrey III

Product Director
Joyce J. Nielsen

Production Editor
Jeanne Terheide Lemen

Copy Editors
Kelli M. Brooks
Lisa Gebken
Patrick Kanouse
Lynn Northrup
Maureen Schneeberger

Technical Editor
Randall G. Bryant

Illustrator
John Alberti

Book Designer
Paula Carroll

Cover Designer
Jay Corpus

Production Team
Troy Barnes
Cameron Booker
Trudy Coler
Amy Cornwell
Anne Dickerson
Maxine Dillingham
DiMonique Ford
Daniel Kidd
Bob LaRoche
G. Alan Palmore
Kaylene Riemen
Nanci Sears Perry
Hilary Smith
Mike Thomas
Tina Trettin
Donna Winter

Indexer
Charlotte Clapp

Acquisitions Coordinator
Deborah Abshier

Editorial Assistant
Jill L. Stanley

Composed in *ITCGaramond* and *MCPdigital* by Que Corporation.

Dedication

To friends and family, especially my father and mother, for their love and support.

Acknowledgments

Thanks to:

Don Roche, Tom Godfrey, and the rest of the gang at Que, for suffering through the awkward situation of managing their boss on this project.

John Alberti, as always, for his marvelous illustrations.

Trademarks

About the Author

Mike Miller is Director of Strategic Planning for Macmillan Publishing, and author of over a dozen best-selling computer books. Mike has been a part of the computer book industry since 1987, and has been involved with computers even longer—since the days of KayPro portables and dBASE II software. In spite of this grizzled history, he helps his colleagues live life vicariously by driving fast cars, listening to very loud movies on his home theater system, and collecting various pieces of animation and comic book art.

Contents at a Glance

III A Quick Course in Problem Solving

Contents

II Figuring Out What Went Wrong

III A Quick Course in Problem Solving

INTRODUCTION

OOPS! is a book for people with problems.

Computer problems, that is.

You don't have to be a computer nerd to have computer problems. And you're not a dummy if you can't figure them out on your own.

This book was written to help you—a normal, average, non-geek, non-dummy computer user—find and fix common computer problems. Nothing too complex is presented, and the solutions are easy enough for people like you and me to try.

In short, if you want to attempt some simple solutions for common problems, this book is for you.

My personal background probably helps to make *OOPS!* useful. You see, even though I like computers, I'm not a techno-nerd—I'm a normal guy, just like you. But for some reason, throughout my career, I've been the guy people come to if they have computer problems—neighbors, friends, coworkers, you name it. I'm not sure why, but I think it has something to do with the fact that I take the time to figure out what's wrong and then show people how to fix the problem themselves. Or maybe, I'm just a soft touch. Whatever the case, I have a lot of experience helping people through the rough times with their computer systems— and that experience can help you through the rough times when you have a problem with your computer system.

Why OOPS! Was a Hit

This is the third edition of this book. When I began writing the first *OOPS!* book, I never thought that it would be the first "troubleshooting" book to sell 100,000 copies.

But OOPS! wasn't —and isn't—a normal troubleshooting book.

OOPS! is written for my father and my brother and other "average" computer users. Once or twice a year I get a call from my father or brother, along the lines of: "Mike, this computer is doing something kind of funny. Could you come out and take a look at it?" More often than not, I can figure out what's wrong over the phone and describe the steps to make things right. That's why this book has sold so well—nothing fancy, nothing overly technical, just good old-fashioned problem solving on a level normal folks can understand.

Who Should Read This Book?

This book is designed to be used by "normal" computer users. You don't have to be a technical expert to read this book, because I don't go into a lot of technical mumbo-jumbo. I help you cope with common computer problems and figure out how to get things back to normal. My comments and advice mix common sense with some tricks regular computer users might not be aware of. The goal is to get you back up and running in the shortest possible time with the least possible fuss.

Why should you read this book? Obviously, you should read this book if you're having trouble with your computer hardware or software. In addition, reading this book *before* you experience trouble can help you *avoid* problems in the future. You'll be surprised at the simple steps you can take to minimize the chances of things going wrong with your computer system.

What Does This Book Discuss?

OOPS! is divided into three major sections.

I recommend that everyone read Part I, "Start Here Before Things Go Wrong." This section contains a lot of useful information for anyone wanting to get the most out of their computers and protect themselves from possible problems.

Part II, "Figuring Out What Went Wrong" is the "What To Do When..." section, which gets down to the core of the matter, offering specific solutions to specific problems you may encounter.

Part III, "A Quick Course in Problem Solving," serves as a reference in helping you track down the causes of many common problems.

I think you'll find Chapter 30, "The Great Troubleshooting Road Map," to be particularly helpful in narrowing your search through this book for the cause of your problem.

What's New in This Edition?

If you've read a previous edition of *OOPS!*, you're probably wondering what's new this time around. Well, in addition to some new problems (and hopefully better advice—I'm a little bit smarter and more experienced now than when I wrote the previous editions!), you'll find these new chapters:

- **The Do's and Don'ts of DOS**, which leads you through DOS basics (Chapter 3)

- **The Why's and Why Not's of Windows**, which explains basic Windows stuff (Chapter 4)

- **Staying Alive: How To Keep Your System in Tip-Top Shape**, which tells you all about basic system maintenance (Chapter 5)

- **What To Do When... Your CD-ROM Doesn't Spin Right**, which tackles tricky problems with CD-ROM drives (Chapter 18)

- **What To Do When... Your Sound System Doesn't Sound Right**, which sounds off on problems with sound cards and speakers (Chapter 19)

- **What To Do When... Your New Software Causes New Problems**, which leads you through common problems when you update the software on your computer (Chapter 24)

- **What To Do When... Your Hardware Upgrade Downgrades Your System**, which addresses problems you can encounter when you add new hardware and accessories to your system (Chapter 25)

- **Windows Error Messages... What They Mean and How To Deal with Them**, which lists common Windows error messages (Chapter 27)

- **Getting It Right—Common System Settings**, which lists all sorts of system information you might need in the course of dealing with your computer system (Chapter 29)

In addition, I've changed the focus of the book to deal more with Windows-based systems, since Windows seems to be the operating environment of choice these days.

A Message to All My Old Readers

If you purchased a prior edition of *OOPS!* and liked it enough to also purchase this new edition, I only have one thing to say to you: THANKS! I really appreciate your feedback and comments, as well as your support. You folks keep me going!

Conventions Used in This Book

While reading *OOPS!*, you should note the following conventions that will help you more easily understand the text:

UPPERCASE letters are used for file names and DOS commands—for example, COPY, COMMAND.COM.

Italic text indicates words or phrases introduced and explained for the first time—for example, *hard boot*.

Words and keys that you press or type are indicated in bold—for example, **CD C:\DIR01**.

On-screen prompts and messages (including error messages) are indicated by a special typeface—for example,

```
File not found.
```

Keyboard keys are usually represented as they appear on your keyboard—for example, Tab.

Key combinations are represented with the plus sign and indicate that you press and hold one key while you also press the other—for example, Ctrl+Shift.

The Last Word in the Introduction

I hope this book helps you correct whatever is currently wrong with your system and, in the process, makes you feel more comfortable with your computer. There's really little to be afraid of inside that ugly beige box, once you know how things work. If I do my job right, your job will be easier and less stressful—because you'll have fewer computer problems to bother with!

Mike Miller
August, 1994

Start Here Before Things Go Wrong

The 10 Most Common Computer Problems

What Causes Most Problems?

We all know how mischievous your personal computer can be sometimes. That's why I'm starting this book with a list of the ten most commonly encountered computer problems. In this chapter, I describe what causes these problems and how you may be able to fix them. Chances are that you can find your current problem on this list. So if your computer is misbehaving, look here before you read any further.

Now, I don't mean that you shouldn't read the rest of the book. I especially recommend chapters 2 through 9, which teach you how to prepare for and protect yourself from many problems.

Although there are literally thousands of potential computer problems, most stem from one of three causes:

- *You did something wrong, such as typing a command incorrectly or accidentally hitting the wrong button.*

- *Your equipment is not turned on, plugged in, or connectedcorrectly.*

- *Your software is not installed or set up correctly.*

So when you encounter a problem and feel moved to exclaim, *"Oops!"* following these simple steps could very well resolve the situation:

1. Try the procedure again.

2. If the problem persists, make certain that your equipment is turned on and that all cables are connected correctly.

3. Try the procedure *one more time*.

What Are the Most Common Problems?

If one of these three steps doesn't alleviate the problem, take a look at the following top 10 list. Most computer users can find their solutions right here; if you don't find yours in this list, read the rest of the book!

1. Your Computer Won't Start

If your computer doesn't start when you flip on the power, check first for some obvious causes. First, make sure that you turned on the *power switch* and not some other switch on the computer. (On many computers, the *turbo switch*, which lets your computer run at a faster or slower speed, is right next to the power switch.)

Next, make certain that your computer's power cord is plugged in. Now, make sure *again* that it's plugged in—both into a power outlet *and* into the back of the computer. (You'd be surprised how easy it is to jiggle the power cord loose from the back of your machine!)

Then make certain that the power outlet has power. (Do you see a trend here?) Make sure that the wall switch, if any, is turned on and that all fuses and circuit breakers are securely in place. If you use a surge suppresser, check that it, too, is turned on.

If none of these methods work, you really *do* have a problem. Just look at the potential causes for a dead computer:

- *The cord from your computer to your power outlet may be bad.* (Try replacing your power cord with a cord from another computer.)

- *The power supply transformer in your computer may be faulty.* (Call a technician and get prepared to write a big check.)

- *If your computer makes noise but nothing appears on your screen, something may be wrong with your monitor.* (Try replacing your monitor with a monitor from another computer system.)

- *You may have a damaged sector on your hard disk that prevents your computer from booting—which is the hard-core computer user's term for "starting a computer."* (Call a computer technician for help on this one.)

A "dead" computer is the most common ailment that plagues PC users and may result from any number of nasty causes. Turn to Chapter 10 for a multitude of possible solutions to get you back in shape and ready to roll.

2. Your Computer Locks Up While Running

Sometimes your computer comes on and runs perfectly—then it suddenly just freezes up. Your keyboard doesn't work, nor does your mouse. In fact, repeatedly pressing keys on the keyboard elicits nothing but a series of obnoxious beeps. What gives?

This problem most commonly results from a loose cable between your keyboard and your system unit. Try unplugging and replugging the keyboard cable to see if that fixes the problem.

Sometimes, however, your software is the culprit, not your hardware. Programs can occasionally become stuck in endlessly repeating loops that make your system appear to lock up. Try pressing the **Esc** key a few times; with most programs, this cancels the operation in progress. If that doesn't work, try the **Ctrl+C** or **Ctrl+Break** key combinations. Again, pressing these keys often interrupts any software operation in progress, breaking the loop.

If none of these methods does the trick, you may just have to reset your computer and start over again. Press the **Ctrl+Alt+Del** key combination to perform a *soft boot* of your system. (This works 88 percent of the time.) If your system is *really* locked up, however, even this won't have any effect. The only solution may be what hard-core techies call a *hard boot*: use the Reset button or the main on/off switch to turn off your PC. Then turn the machine back on.

When Your Windows Are Locked

If you're running Windows and your computer freezes up, you may have a completely different set of problems (and solutions). If you're in Windows, however, you can still reboot a particular application—or Windows itself, if it is frozen—by pressing Ctrl+Alt+Del. Turn to Chapter 22 for more Windows-specific advice.

After you *reboot*, you'll probably discover that you've lost any data you entered after you last saved your file to disk. (If so, let this hard-earned lesson encourage you to save your data frequently while working at the keyboard.) Fortunately, rebooting without first exiting a program does not usually damage the program files themselves. Just to be safe, however, make sure that you try every other option *before* you reboot your computer.

3. A Program Locks Up While You're in Windows

Sometimes, when you're working under Windows, a program just seems to stall—it locks up, and just won't do anything, either with the mouse or the keyboard. You can change to other programs (by using the mouse to click on another window, or by pressing **Alt+Tab** to manually switch to another open program), but this particular program just isn't moving. What can you do?

First, you may want to give it a few more minutes. Sometimes, when Windows is low on memory (or disk space) and/or you're working with a particularly big file, Windows gets a little pokey. Your program may actually be working fine, but just working slow!

If your patience begins to wear thin, however, you'll want to close the program and get on to other things. Make sure that the offending program is the active program (by clicking anywhere in the program's window), and then hit the **Ctrl+Alt+Del** keys simultaneously. You should see a Windows message informing you that proceeding will close the listed program. Press Enter to close the program and return to Windows.

Once you're back in Windows, you probably want to exit Windows, reboot your machine, reenter Windows, and then restart the program in question—just to make sure all used memory has been freed, and to prevent any additional system problems from developing.

4. Your Printer Won't Print

The most common printer problems also are the simplest to solve. If your printer refuses to print, make certain first that it is plugged in. Then make sure that the printer cable is plugged firmly into both your printer and your system unit. Next, make sure that the machine is ready to print—check that you turned your printer on and that it is toggled into the on-line position. Finally, confirm that your printer has plenty of paper and that none of it is jammed in the mechanism. If you've just run out of paper and added more, you may need to turn your printer off and back on again to reset the printing process.

One more thing—if you're using Windows, make sure you have the right printer selected, which is normally done in a Printer Setup option in your software program. You can also check your printer selections by clicking on the Printer icon in the Windows Control Panel.

If you check all these factors and your printer *still* doesn't work, turn to Chapter 15 for more detailed troubleshooting information. The software you're using may not have been installed correctly for operating your particular printer, or your printer might really be out of whack. If it's the latter, get ready to spend some bucks—printer repair isn't cheap.

5. You Accidentally Delete a File

Nothing is more frustrating than realizing that you've just deleted a file you didn't want deleted. Fortunately, there are methods for recovering deleted files from among the dearly departed.

If you're running Windows and DOS 6, Microsoft includes a neat little Windows version of the UNDELETE utility. Just open up the Microsoft Tools program group and launch Microsoft Undelete for Windows (by clicking on the little trashcan icon). Switch to the directory that holds your deleted file, and then click on the deleted file name. When this file is highlighted, click on the Undelete button. When the Enter First Character dialog box appears, replace the "?" with the real first character of the deleted files name. When you then click OK, your deleted file will be automatically undeleted.

If you're not running Windows, you can use the UNDELETE utility included with DOS 5 or DOS 6. All you need to do is type the following at the DOS prompt:

UNDELETE FILENAME.EXT

If you can't remember the file's name, you can undelete all the deleted files in the current directory. Just use the UNDELETE command with the /ALL switch, like this:

UNDELETE *.* /ALL

Undeleting with Older Versions of DOS

If your version of DOS is older than DOS 5, you don't have access to the UNDELETE utility. You can, however, use a utility program that performs essentially the same operation. (Norton Utilities and PC Tools are two such utilities.) See Chapter 20 for more

If you use this method, DOS replaces the first character of the deleted file with a question mark. You'll have to supply the real first character before DOS can undelete the file.

6. You Accidentally Reformat a Disk

All brand-new disks must be formatted before they can be used by your system. After a disk is formatted, however, you don't want to reformat it; reformatting a disk destroys all the files that are on it. (This means that if you're using a disk, you don't have to—and don't want to—format that disk again.)

Fortunately, DOS 5 and 6 include an UNFORMAT utility, similar to the UNDELETE utility. To unformat a disk, simply type the following command (with X representing the drive letter of the newly formatted disk):

UNFORMAT X:

Be aware, however, that this command does have limitations. It won't unformat disks that haven't been formatted a certain way, for example. And like UNDELETE, UNFORMAT is not available in older versions of DOS. See Chapter 17 for more details.

7. You Receive a Windows Error Message

There are a few common error messages that Windows generates when it runs into problematic situations. Here are some of the most common, and how to deal with them.

General protection fault or Unrecoverable application error

These are the most common Windows error messages. A General protection fault (or GPF) is generated under Windows 3.1 when a serious system problem has occurred—like when something big crashes. When you encounter a GPF, you are most often presented with the option to close down the offending application. Do this, and then exit Windows and reboot your computer. This will clean things up and let you get restarted with whatever it is you were doing.

An Unrecoverable application error (or UAE) is the Windows 3.0 equivalent of the Windows 3.1 GPF. Unlike a GPF, a UAE message is generally followed by an automatic shutdown of Windows which leaves you back at the DOS prompt. If this happens, reboot your computer, restart Windows, and go back to your previous task.

Application execution error

This message occurs when Windows tries to load a program that either doesn't exist (maybe you erased it from your hard drive?) or isn't located where Windows thinks it is. Check your drive and directories to make sure you're loading a program that really exists and is located where you think it is.

Cannot find file

This message is similar to the previous message—Windows can't find what it's looking for. Check to see if everything is where you think it is before proceeding.

Insufficient memory or Out of memory

These error messages result from a low memory condition. You may need to close some open programs, or even close and then restart Windows to free up any lost memory. If you get these messages often, you probably should add extra memory to your system.

System Error

This message occurs when some part of your system—that is, part of your hardware—stops working. Check your disk drives, sound card, etc., to find the source of this problem.

8. You Receive a DOS Error Message

DOS generates error messages when you do something wrong, or when something peculiar is going on with your system. Here are some of the most common error messages, and how to deal with them.

```
Abort, Retry, Fail?
```

When FAIL Means IGNORE

If you're using DOS 5 or 6, you'll receive the Abort, Retry, Fail? message as described. If you're using a version of DOS prior to DOS 5, however, you'll receive a different, but similar message: Abort, Retry, Ignore? In this case, Ignore is the same as Fail and gives exactly the same results. Why Microsoft changed this, I don't know—so don't ask!

You encounter this message when DOS tries to carry out a command but can't. Usually, another message precedes the Abort, Retry, Fail? message, and you may be able to determine the problem from the first message.

Pressing **A** (for Abort) tells DOS to cancel the operation in progress. Pressing **R** (for Retry) instructs DOS to attempt the operation again. (Use Retry if you can figure out a simple fix, such as closing the drive door or inserting a disk into the drive.) Pressing **F** (for Fail) causes DOS to skip the error and continue with the rest of the operation, although you may experience errors or file damage.

If you choose Fail after the Abort, Retry, Fail? message, then the Current drive no longer valid message appears. You should type another drive letter followed by a colon and press Enter.

```
Bad command or filename
```

The error message Bad command or file name results when DOS doesn't understand what you just typed. More often than not, you simply mistyped a DOS command.

Correcting the error that caused the bad command/file message is simple (most of the time): retype your last command. If you encounter this error message regularly, consider typing your commands *more slowly* to improve your accuracy.

You also should check all the little things in the command—make sure that you have your slashes and backslashes right, don't insert spaces where they don't belong, and don't forget to use colons where appropriate. (If in doubt on how to use a command, refer to one of Que's many DOS books, such as *Using MS-DOS 6.2,* Special Edition.)

If you are sure that you are typing the command correctly and still get the Bad command or file name message, DOS probably can't find the program you are trying to invoke. You need to tell DOS where to find it. First, locate the disk directory that contains the program. Then use the CD command to change to that directory—or type the path as part of the command.

    File not found

The File not found message appears when DOS cannot find a file you try to invoke. This message is often caused by the same error as that of the preceding error message: you mistyped the name of a file. The solution also is the same: retype the file name.

The possibility does exist, however, that you've typed the file name correctly and DOS really cannot find the file. You can always include the directory path for the file in the command itself. For example, if you want to delete a file in directory DIR01, you would word the command this way:

> ### Finding Your Path
>
> You also can tell DOS where to find a program by editing a specific line in the AUTOEXEC.BAT file that is run when you first start your system. This line includes the PATH command and establishes a path that DOS uses to look for commands and files. After you add a directory to the path, you no longer have to refer to that directory; DOS knows where it is, automatically. See Chapter 10 for more details on the AUTOEXEC.BAT file.

DEL C:\DIR01\FILENAME.EXT

You also could just change to the directory before you issue the command, using the CD (change directory) command, like this:

CD C:\DIR01

When you're in the right directory, you can issue the command without having to type the entire path to the file name.

It's possible, too, that you're trying to access a file that has been deleted from your disk. If so, issue the UNDELETE command to recover the file, as discussed in Chapter 20.

> ### What "Bootable" Really Means
>
> When computer nerds use the word "bootable," they mean a disk that can be used to start your system. For your system to start, it must access certain system files (explained in Chapter 7) contained on a disk. If a disk doesn't contain these files, then DOS can't use the disk to start up and the disk is regarded as "nonbootable." A bootable disk won't give you the Non-system disk or disk error message; a nonbootable disk will.

`Non-system disk or disk error`

If you see a `Non-system disk or disk error` message on your screen, you probably need to remove a floppy disk from drive A. This message appears when you first turn on your computer. Because your computer always looks for a bootable disk in drive A before proceeding to your hard disk, a nonbootable disk causes your system to freeze and forces DOS to generate the error message. Simply remove the disk, and press Enter to restart the booting procedure.

If drive A is empty, your hard disk must be the source of the problem. Turn to Chapter 17 for more information.

`Not ready reading drive X`

This error message appears when you attempt to access a floppy disk drive that has no disk in it. You solve this problem simply by placing a disk in the specified drive. The `Not ready reading drive X` message also can appear if a disk is in the drive, but the drive door is not fully closed. Close the door and the message disappears.

If this message is displayed when a disk is in the drive and the drive door is closed, you may have either a bad disk or a faulty disk drive. See Chapter 17 for more information.

9. You Have Problems Installing New Software

More often than not, these days, installing new software is a breeze. But you can still run into problems, especially when upgrading your existing software to a new version. Just take a look at these common problems and solutions:

- *Your new software doesn't work.* This is either due to bugs in the new software, a bad or incomplete installation, some sort of incompatibility with your system, or an error (probably on your part) in starting the program. Starting with the last problem first, make sure you're in the proper directory to start the program, and that you're using the right command and/or file name to launch the application. If so, you may want to try reinstalling the program, just in case something went wrong with the initial installation.

- *Your new software causes your old software not to work.* Some new programs alter your CONFIG.SYS and/or AUTOEXEC.BAT startup files; it's possible your new software did this in a way that affects your older programs. It's also possible that your new program has some sort of memory conflict with an older program. Examine your startup files and make any changes necessary; you can also try launching your programs in a different order to see if that improves the situation.

- *The upgraded version of your old software doesn't work with your old files.* This used to be a common problem; a lot of software publishers didn't ensure perfect compatibility between different versions of their own programs! You may need to contact the publisher of your software to obtain some sort of conversion program. Of course, it's also possible that the new version of your program simply doesn't know where your old files are; you may need to change some program option settings to direct the new software to your old directories.

See Chapter 24 for more information on software upgrading/installation problems.

10. You Have Problems Upgrading Your Hardware

Major changes to your system can cause major problems—even if you seem to be doing everything just right. The most common problems are either that your new hardware doesn't work, or that your old hardware doesn't work after you've installed your new hardware. While you can find a more detailed analysis of this situation in Chapter 25, here are a few things to look for:

- *Your new hardware isn't properly installed.* Check all your connections, make sure that all boards are properly seated and that all cables are firmly connected.

- *Your system isn't configured properly for your new hardware.* Most systems need to be told that something new has been hooked up. Check your installation instructions to make sure you've installed the proper software drivers and changed the appropriate software switches to recognize your new hardware. In some instances, you may also need to reconfigure individual programs to work with your new hardware.

- *Your system has an interrupt conflict.* This happens when two different parts of your system try to use the same interrupt, or IRQ, setting. The easiest fix for this is to change the COM port setting for your newest component; note that some devices (such as mice and modems) don't work well together if they share even- or odd-numbered ports. (For example, avoid hooking a mouse to COM1 and a modem to COM3— you're better off using ports 1 and 2 or 1 and 4, if possible.) If this doesn't work, then you'll have to reconfigure the IRQ settings for one or more of your hardware devices. (This is sometimes done via software programs, and sometimes via switches located on the boards themselves.)

Other Problems

If your specific problem isn't addressed in this chapter, don't panic! This book contains 29 additional chapters, one of which undoubtedly holds the key to improving your current situation. If you can isolate the general cause of your problem (keyboard, printer, etc.), turn to the chapter that addresses that topic. If you can't determine even the general problem area, go directly to Chapter 30, "The Great Troubleshooting Road Map," to help you track down the likely culprit.

Don't worry if some of the information presented in this chapter seems foreign to you. Just turn the page and proceed to Chapter 2, where you receive a refresher course on the computer basics you need—to get (and keep) yourself out of trouble.

Computer Basics for the Technically Timid

Before you begin unformatting disks, editing startup files, and checking printer ports, it might be a good idea to take a quick refresher course in computer basics. The best way to start is by examining each component of your system—what that part does and what problems it could experience.

Don't let all this initial attention to technical detail disturb you, however. This book is written for *you*, the average computer user, not some techno-dweeb who carries a screwdriver set in a pocket protector.

By the way, if you want more details about DOS and Windows, read ahead to chapters 3 and 4. In this chapter we'll stick pretty much to hardware and system basics. So turn the page, and let the class begin!

All About Your System Hardware

Computer *hardware* comprises those parts of your system that you can actually see and touch. (Contrast this to your computer software, which consists of data stored in magnetic form on your disks. You can see and touch the disks, but not the actual data they store.)

Getting Really Technical

If you're *really* interested in the technical mumbo-jumbo about computer hardware that I *don't* cover in this book, there's help in the form of another fine Que book. Check out *Upgrading and Repairing PCs*, now in its third edition; it's a really comprehensive book about almost everything you can find inside your computer.

Your hardware, therefore, includes your *system unit* (that big ugly box that houses your disk drives and many other components) and all the parts inside it. Anything connected to your system unit also is called hardware, including your monitor, your printer, your keyboard, and your mouse. Always keep your system unit in a well-ventilated location free of excess dust and smoke. (The moving parts in your computer don't like dust and dirt and any other such contaminants that can muck up the way they work.)

Because your computer generates heat when it operates, you must leave enough room around the system unit for the heat to dissipate. *Never* place your computer in a confined, poorly ventilated space; your PC may overheat and shut down if it isn't sufficiently ventilated.

For extra protection to your computer, connect the power cable on your system unit to a surge suppressor rather than directly into an electrical outlet. A *surge suppressor*—which looks like a power strip with multiple outlets—protects your PC from power line surges that could damage its delicate internal parts. When a power surge temporarily "spikes" your line voltage (causes the voltage to momentarily increase above normal levels), a surge suppressor shuts down power to your system, acting like a circuit breaker or fuse.

When You Don't Want To Use a Surge Suppressor

A surge suppressor does what it does by shutting down your system when a power spike occurs. While this protects your computer, you do lose any data you were working on when the surge suppressor did its job. Of course, this is better than losing your entire hard disk to a voltage spike. But if you use your PC for applications in which you can't afford even a momentary shutdown (on-line in a retail store, for example), you may want to invest in a battery-operated backup power supply. These devices send auxiliary power to your PC during power outages—and, when used in conjunction with a surge suppressor, give you *complete* power protection.

All the different components of your computer system connect to one another through various cables and adapters. These cables can be a source of trouble if they're not connected correctly. Make sure that you plug all cables securely into their sockets; in fact, screw them into place if you can. Make certain, too, that the cables don't have abrupt bends or kinks in them. If your cables aren't as straight as possible, the wires inside them may break or become damaged.

Under the Hood

When you open up the case on your system unit, you see a myriad of computer chips and circuit boards. The really big board located at the base of the computer is called the *motherboard* because it's the "mother" for your microprocessor and memory chips, as well as for the other internal components that enable your system to function. (Microprocessors are described in the section "The Brains Behind It All," later in this chapter.)

Your PC—The Inside Story

Opening up your computer's system unit is not for the faint of heart. Not only is it terribly intimidating, but you stand a good chance of breaking something if you really don't know what you're doing. So if you're the least bit unsure of whether you should be poking around inside your PC—*don't poke*! Let someone more technically qualified do the dirty work so you can get back to your keyboard and mouse that much faster.

The motherboard contains several slots into which you can plug additional *boards* (also called cards) that perform specific functions. A *disk drive controller card*, for example, enables disk drives to "talk" to your microprocessor. A *video card* enables your microprocessor to transmit video signals to your monitor. Other available cards enable you to add sound, modem, and fax capabilities to your system.

Most PC motherboards contain six or more slots for add-on cards; if you try to add too many cards to a low-end system, however, you may run out of slots! If that happens, either reevaluate your need for some of the cards, or consider buying a new system with enough slots to hold the additional cards.

Getting Carded

For instructions on how to insert specific cards (such as sound cards, video cards, and so on), refer to the detailed documentation that comes with each specific card. You also might want to check out a wonderful Que book on step-by-step upgrading for normal users, *Upgrading Your PC Illustrated*. This book includes everything you need to know to add cards and other peripherals to your computer system.

How To Add New Cards

To add new cards to your motherboard, first open up the case of your system unit. Then plug the new card securely into an open slot and fasten it in place with a securing screw. Many cards protrude out of pre-punched holes in the back of your system unit, enabling you to connect other devices (called *peripherals*) to the board. (The video card, for example, has connectors that enable you to plug in a cable to run from the card to your monitor.)

What Can Go Wrong with Add-On Cards

If add-on cards aren't inserted correctly, your entire system may fail to function. Some cards, too, contain physical *switches* that must be configured for your system. Set these switches in the wrong positions, and that card—or your entire system—may seriously malfunction. Some cards also require you to run software-based "setup" programs to configure parts of your system. Whatever the case, always be sure to consult the instructions that come with each card to make certain everything is set correctly before you button up the case and turn on the power again.

You may even find it necessary to make adjustments to your operating system or to specific software programs so that you can use your new cards. Check each program to determine whether it must be adjusted or set up individually to operate with your new card.

The Brains Behind It All

Deep inside your system unit lurks the one component that controls your entire system: the microprocessor chip. The *microprocessor* (also called the *central processing unit*, or *CPU*) chip resides atop the motherboard, surrounded by many other chips and transistors that help it do its job.

The microprocessor really is the brains inside your system. It processes all the instructions necessary for your computer to perform its duties. The more powerful its microprocessor chip, the faster and more efficiently your system runs.

Microprocessors carry out the various instructions that enable your computer to compute. Every input and output device hooked up to a computer—the keyboard, the printer, the monitor, and so on—either issues or receives instructions that the microprocessor must process. All your software programs also issue instructions that must be implemented by the microprocessor. This chip truly is the workhorse of your system because it affects just about everything your computer does.

Types of Microprocessors

Several different types of microprocessor chips currently exist. All IBM-compatible computers use chips originally designed by Intel. Other types of computers use other kinds of chips; the Apple Macintosh chips, made by Motorola, for example, are of a totally different design than Intel's.

Over the years, Intel has produced various chips for IBM-compatible computers. The different Intel chips vary primarily in the number of instructions per second that each type of chip can imple-

Mutant Chips

Intel also produces "hybrid" chips with the SX designation. These chips—such as the 80386SX and 80486SX—work much like the normal chips (which are sometimes called DX chips) but with slightly slower performance.

ment. The original IBM PC used an 8088 chip. Since then, Intel has produced more powerful chips under the 80286, 80386, and 80486 designations. The higher its model number, the more powerful the chip. The more powerful the chip, the faster it works.

The newest chip from the Intel stable, however, doesn't have a number. (Intel discovered that it couldn't trademark numbers, so it decided to give the chip a distinctive name instead.) This chip, which probably would have been the 80586, is called the *Pentium*. While Pentium computers were quite

The Powerful PowerPC Chip

Motorola has recently introduced a new type of chip called the *PowerPC* chip. This microprocessor is bunches faster than even an Intel Pentium, and is thought by many to be part of the future of personal computing. Today, PowerPC chips have been introduced for use in Apple Macintosh computers. IBM and other companies are expected to introduce PowerPC-powered machines that are IBM-compatible in the near future.

expensive—and quite rare—just twelve months ago, today you can buy a Pentium-based system for less than $2000.

Certain program types require certain chips to run on a particular system. You can't run Windows Version 3.1 on a computer with an 8086 or 8088 chip, for example. If your PC contains an older chip, make sure that you buy only software that can run on your system. (Chip requirements usually are listed on the software package itself.) If you own a computer with an 80386, 80486, or Pentium chip, the chances are good that just about any software can run on your machine.

Microprocessor Speed—The Faster, The Better

Even within the same chip family, different chips run at different speeds. CPU speed is measured in megahertz (MHz); a CPU with a speed of 1 MHz can run at one million clock ticks per second! The higher its megahertz, the faster the chip runs. You can buy 80486 chips, for example, that run at 25 MHz, 33 MHz, 50 MHz, 66 MHz, and even *100MHz*! When you purchase a new PC, look for one with the combination of a powerful microprocessor and a high clock speed for best performance.

What Can Go Wrong with Your Computer's CPU

Not much can go wrong with a microprocessor, short of it failing altogether. And microprocessor failure is normally pretty rare if you keep your PC in a well-ventilated place. You may, however, notice that some software programs run very slowly on underpowered machines—that is, machines with slower chips. If you own an older PC that is equipped with an 8086 or 80286 chip, you may not be able to run some of the newer programs sold today. If in doubt, check the software's packaging or documentation, or ask the software publisher (or your dealer) if a particular program is designed to run on your PC. You may just have to avoid purchasing certain programs—or else upgrade to a newer, more powerful computer that can run all the programs you want it to.

Memory—The Temporary Storage in Your System

Before your CPU can process any instructions you give it, your instructions must be stored somewhere, in preparation for access by the microprocessor. These instructions—along with other data processed by your system—are temporarily held in the computer's electronic *memory*. All computers have some amount of memory, which is created by their memory chips. The more memory that's available in a machine, the more instructions and data that can be stored at one time.

Why Your Computer Needs More Memory

Memory is measured in terms of *bytes*. One byte is equal to approximately one character. A unit equaling approximately one thousand bytes (1,024, to be exact) is called a *kilobyte* (K), and a unit of approximately one thousand (1,024) kilobytes is called a *megabyte* (M).

Most computers today come with at least 4M of memory, and some of the more expensive machines have 8M or more. To enable your computer to run as many programs as quickly as possible, you need as much memory installed in your system as it can accept—

Cashing In the Chips

If you're adding memory to your PC, make sure that you get the right kind for your system. There are actually different types of chips (which go by names like *SIMMs* and *DIPs*), as well as chips that contain different amounts of RAM. The instruction manual for your PC should tell you what kind of memory you need to add; if not, a good computer technician can figure it out for you.

or that you can afford. Extra memory can be added to a computer either by installing a plug-in card or by adding new memory chips directly to the motherboard. Installing additional memory chips is not a task for the average user, but it can easily be performed by a qualified computer technician.

What Can Go Wrong with Your Computer's Memory

If your computer doesn't possess enough memory, its CPU must constantly retrieve data from permanent storage on its hard disk. This method of data retrieval is slower than retrieving instructions and data from electronic memory. In fact, if your machine doesn't have enough memory, some programs will run very slowly on it (or you may experience random system crashes when running them), and other programs can't run at all!

Thanks for the Memory

To operate correctly, many software programs require a minimum amount of memory beyond the normal 640K. Microsoft Windows, for example, really needs 4M to run at a decent speed—and likes 8M of memory a lot better. If you're using high-end programs, the increased performance you gain is definitely worth the relatively minimal expense of adding extra memory.

You'll also have to make sure that your system is set up properly to maximize its use of memory. You can set all sorts of system options by inserting commands into your CONFIG.SYS and AUTOEXEC.BAT files. If you get these commands wrong, however, you could lock up your entire system!

DOS 5 and 6 include some really neat features that make it easy to get the most from your system's memory. See Chapter 3 for more information.

Data Central

The second main physical component inside your system unit is the *hard disk drive*. The hard disk *permanently* stores all your important data. Some hard disks can store more than 200M of data. (Contrast this to your system's memory, which stores a much more limited amount of data only temporarily; your computer's memory often acts as a short-term storage bin for data that's been read from its hard disk but not yet fed into its microprocessor.)

How a Hard Disk Works

A hard disk consists of numerous metallic platters. These platters store data *magnetically*. Special read/write *heads* realign magnetic particles on the platters, much like a recording head records data onto magnetic recording tape.

Data is recorded on your hard disk in circular *tracks*, which are much like the tracks on a record album or compact disc. Each disk is further divided into *sectors*. Your computer uses the intersection of track and sector as a sort of electronic road map to locate individual pieces of data on the disk. This tracking data is stored in a special section of the disk, called the *file allocation table* (*FAT*). Your system refers to the FAT data to determine where to find specific files on your hard disk.

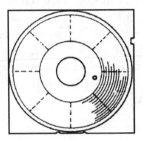

Before data can be stored on any disk, including your system's hard disk, that disk must first be *formatted*. A disk that has not been formatted cannot accept any data. When you format a hard disk, your computer prepares each track and sector of the disk to accept and store data magnetically and, in the process, creates a blank FAT on the disk. You use the DOS FORMAT command to format both hard and floppy disks.

What Can Go Wrong with Your Hard Disk

Your hard disk can cause you a great deal of trouble if you don't treat it right. Because a hard disk is a physical device that spins at a high rate of speed, it can actually wear out over time. The disk may start spinning at the wrong speed, or the platters that make up the disk may themselves become damaged. If your system is located in an area with too much dust or smoke, the disk platters can become contaminated; a contaminated disk may not read or write data correctly. Eventually, too, the platters and the read/write head may become misaligned. When this happens, consult a technician. Your disk may be salvageable, or it may have to be replaced.

The data on your hard disk also can be subject to various problems, many of which have human causes. If you accidentally format a hard disk that has data on it, for example, you lose all that data. You can accidentally erase varying amounts of data on your hard disk, too, if you're careless in deleting files. What's more, if computer viruses manage to infect your system, they can scramble your valuable data, making your hard disk function abnormally, if at all. So always take extra care when working with your hard disk; if you don't, all its megabytes of data can very suddenly—and quite painfully—become inaccessible.

Data To Go

Along with its hard disk drive, every computer has one or more *floppy disk drives*. (In fact, most early computers didn't even have hard disks; they relied totally on floppy drives to store their data.) These drives accept floppy disks of one of four types: 3 1/2-inch double density, 3 1/2-inch high density, 5 1/4-inch double density, and 5 1/4-inch high density. Floppy disks work much like hard disks except that they consist of thin sheets of a magnetic-tape-like material instead of hard metallic platters. (That's why they're called floppies; the material is fairly flexible—or floppy—compared to that used in a hard disk.)

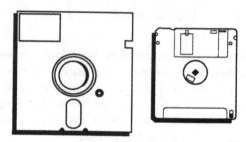

Floppy disks store varying amounts of data, ranging from 360K (in the 5 1/4-inch double-density variety) to 1.44M (the 3 1/2-inch high-density variety). Because floppy disks are more portable than hard disks, the former are used to store data that's transported physically from PC to PC. And floppies are useful, too, for storing backup copies of the data on your PC's hard disk.

How Floppy Disks Work

Better Safe Than... Well, You Know

For extra safety, you may want to store your backup diskettes in a different location from your computer system, such as in a safe deposit box at your bank. This way, if your computer is damaged by fire, your backup data is still safe.

The heads in floppy disk drives work just like the read/write head of a hard disk drive. The only difference is that the floppy disk drives are not sealed from the elements as are hard disk drives. Floppy disk drives, therefore, are even more susceptible to dirt, dust, and smoke than are their "hardier" cousins. If you seem to encounter more than a few read/write errors when you use different floppy disks, the disk drive itself might require realignment or even replacement.

What Can Go Wrong with Floppy Disks

Floppy disks are susceptible to every ailment that can possibly befall a hard disk—and then some. Because disks are portable, they can become damaged during transit. And because data is stored on floppies magnetically, placing a disk too close to a magnetic source (such as a stereo speaker or a ringing telephone) can erase its data.

The main warning to heed is to be as careful with your floppy disks as you would with any other computer part or peripheral. Don't assume that just because they are made of flexible material they can't be seriously harmed. And always make sure that you have copies of any important files

> **Monitoring Your Disk**
>
> Remember that your data is stored on your disks. Remember, too, that your computer monitor—just like a television set—radiates a certain amount of magnetic interference. Add these two factors together and you come to the startling realization that, if you leave your disks too close to your monitor, they can be erased! *Never* leave your disks sitting on top of or directly beside your monitor—or a magnetic catastrophe may result!

stored on disk as well as on your hard disk—just in case. (In fact, making an extra floppy copy of your really vital files couldn't hurt either!)

Data from a Laser

There's a third type of disk that is becoming quite popular among computer users. This disk is called a *compact disk-read-only memory*, or *CD-ROM* for short. (The ROM part means that you can only read data from the disk; unlike normal hard or floppy disks, you can't write new data to a CD-ROM.)

How a CD-ROM Works

CD-ROM disks look just like the compact discs you play on your audio system. In fact, they're very similar in the way they contain data (audio data in the case of regular CDs, and computer data in the case of CD-ROMs). Information is encoded at a disk-manufacturing plant, using an industrial-grade laser. This information takes the form of microscopic pits below the disk's surface. Like hard and floppy disks, the information is arranged in a series of tracks and sectors, but the tracks are so close together that the disk surface is highly reflective.

Data is read from the CD-ROM disk via a drive that uses a consumer-quality laser. The laser beam follows the tracks of the disk and reads the pits, translating the data into a form your system can understand.

While a normal floppy disk can hold only 1.44M of data, the dense storage capabilities of a CD-ROM enable it to hold over *600M* of data! Because of this vast storage capacity, CD-ROMs are used to store data that just won't fit on traditional storage media. For example, you can find CD-ROMs with vast databases of information, CD-ROMs that hold multiple programs that would otherwise use dozens of disks, and CD-ROMs that combine audio and video data in multimedia applications.

What Can Go Wrong with a CD-ROM

Most CD-ROM problems have to do with dirty disks or dirty laser assemblies. Cleaning a disk is easy—just use a soft cloth. If the lens that focuses the laser gets dirty, however, the laser can become unfocused and have difficulty reading the information from the CD-ROM disk. This argues in favor of using a commercial laser lens cleaner (that you insert just like you do a CD-ROM disk) from time to time.

Another major CD-ROM problem concerns the setup for your particular system. Most CD-ROM drives, whether internally or externally installed, require that a *device driver* be loaded into memory before the drive can work. (Device drivers are small files that control peripheral devices, such as video cards and sound cards.) If you don't have a driver installed—or don't have the *correct* driver installed—your CD-ROM drive won't work at all.

Finally, some older CD-ROM drives don't work well on newer computers. If the drive is too slow and the computer too fast, the drive may start giving you trouble. If you suspect this is the case, use the "Turbo" button on the front of your PC to switch to a slower operating speed that your CD-ROM can handle.

Keys to Success

Computers receive data by reading it from disk, accepting it electronically over a modem, or receiving input directly from you, the user. Users provide input by way of what's called, in general, an *input device*; the most common input device you use to talk to your computer is the *keyboard*.

More Keys Than a Mortal Typewriter!

A computer keyboard looks and functions just like a typewriter keyboard, except that computer keyboards have a few more keys. Some of these keys (such as the arrows, PgUp, PgDn, Home, and End keys) enable you to move around within a program or a file. Other keys provide access to special program features. (These include the *function keys*, located on the left side or top of the keyboard, depending on whether it's a regular or enhanced model.)

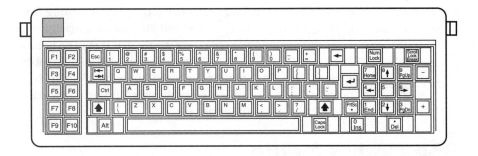

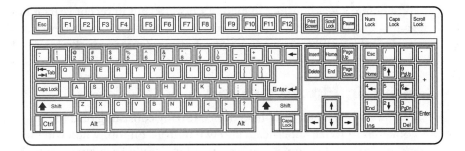

What Can Go Wrong with Your Keyboard

When you press a key on your keyboard, it sends an electronic signal to your system unit that tells your machine what you want it to do. If, for any reason, the system unit doesn't receive this signal, your keystrokes do absolutely nothing (except perhaps exercise your fingers). The most common keyboard problems can usually be traced to some sort of obstacle that's preventing the signals from reaching your system unit. The culprit may be a loose connection, excess dirt or dust—or maybe even a crumb from that Twinkie you ate while working with your files the other night.

To avoid loose connections that could interrupt signals from your keyboard, always make certain the keyboard is securely connected to your system unit. Try also to keep your keyboard free of dust, dirt, and other foreign matter that could block signals to the system unit. And always take care when handling or transporting your keyboard so as not to damage it.

Food and Keyboards Don't Mix

Unfortunately, because computer keyboards do consist of complex electronic components, damaging one can sometimes be far too easy. That's why you never want to eat or drink around your computer. Spilling food and beverages on the keyboard can short out its electronic circuits and wreak havoc on your entire system.

Some "third-party" keyboards (such as those from Northgate and Keytronics) feature unique key configurations that might not work with some PCs. If you're experiencing difficulty inputting data manually into your machine and you think that it may be because your keyboard is incompatible with your computer, try using another keyboard. If the different keyboard works, your problem almost certainly lies within your original keyboard, which means you probably should replace it.

The Mighty Mouse

At one time it was considered merely a novelty, but in recent years it has gained in importance to computer users as a must-have input device so that it now rivals—and for some functions, has supplanted—the keyboard. "It" is the mouse.

How To Mouse Around

The mouse is a small hand-held device usually consisting of an oblong case containing a roller underneath and two buttons on top. When you move the mouse along a desktop, an on-screen pointer (called a cursor) moves in response. When you click (press and release) a mouse button, this motion initiates an action in your program. Many graphically oriented programs now use the mouse; many depend on it in order to function at all. The Windows operating environment is among the latter.

What Can Go Wrong with Your Mouse

Just as with the keyboard, the most common mouse problems result from loose connections. These usually occur when the mouse somehow becomes unplugged from the computer (such as when you tug too hard on it or accidentally roll it off the desk). Because the mouse is a mechanical device, its roller ball can eventually wear out with use, making cursor movement difficult. The constant movement of the mouse across a desk surface can often damage the mouse cable, too. If your mouse's behavior becomes too erratic, it may be time to replace the little rodent.

Sounding Off

Every PC comes with its own built-in speaker. Now, it's true that this is a tiny little thing with really poor sound quality, but it is a speaker. When your computer beeps at you, obnoxiously or otherwise, this is where the sound originates.

PC speakers, like most other types of speakers, seldom go bad. If your PC goes silent, the problem often lies in a specific program rather than with the speaker itself. Many software programs, in fact, enable you to temporarily disable the PC speaker while you use that program. (Refer to the software's documentation for more information.)

You can improve your computer's sound, however, by adding a sound board to your system unit. These boards—like the SoundBlaster board—let you tune in to higher-quality sound produced by those programs that support it, such as many games programs. For a sound board to function to

Add a Sound Board for Multimedia

If you have a CD-ROM drive attached to your PC and you want to try one of those neat new all-singing, all-dancing multimedia applications, you really need to add a sound board to your system. Most multimedia applications require a sound board to operate, since they incorporate really high quality audio.

its fullest potential, you usually need to hook up external speakers to your machine. Several firms sell small self-powered speakers that you can attach right to the output jacks of your sound board and set on top of (or next to) your system unit.

What You See Is What You Get

It would be difficult to operate a computer if you didn't constantly receive visual feedback showing you what your machine is doing. This vital function is provided by your computer's monitor.

The monitor is very much like a little television set. Your microprocessor electronically transmits to your monitor words and pictures (*text* and *graphics*, in PC lingo) in some approximation of how these visuals would appear on paper. You view the monitor and respond according to what you see on-screen.

I'd Like To Make a Resolution...

The monitor itself does not generate the images it displays. These images are electronically crafted by a *video card* installed inside your system unit. To work correctly, both video card and monitor must be matched to display images of the same resolution. Resolution refers to the size of the images that can be displayed and is measured in pixels. (A pixel is a single dot on your screen; a full picture is composed of thousands of pixels.)

You can install video cards that display text and graphics at varying resolutions. You can install cards that display strictly monochrome (black-and-white) images or cards that display color images.

Early PCs could not display graphics at all. They were strictly *character-based* and could display only text. Several years ago, however, an operating standard was developed to display graphics. This was called the CGA standard. CGA cards and monitors are capable of displaying images 320 pixels wide by 300 pixels tall. Next came the EGA standard, which displays images at 640 x 400 pixels. Many current PCs use the VGA standard; it is capable of displays of 640 x 480 pixels. The newest standard is called *SuperVGA*, which really isn't a standard since SuperVGA cards can display images at either 800 x 600 pixels, 1,024 x 768 pixels, or even higher resolutions. As you probably guessed, the higher the resolution, the better and more colorful the picture.

What Can Go Wrong with Your Video Setup

Sadly, your system's video setup can be the source of numerous problems. If your card and monitor are mismatched, for example, you may receive distorted images on your monitor—if you can get anything at all. (You may have to reset the switches on the video card itself to establish the correct setup for your system.) Having software programs that aren't configured for your particular video card can result in display problems, too. And, as with most peripheral-based problems, a loose connection between the monitor and the system unit is Public Enemy Number One behind your most common display glitches. So, to ensure great reception on your monitor, just as you would with your television, make sure that everything is plugged in, set up, and adjusted correctly.

All That's Fit To Print

Your monitor displays images in real time, but in a transitory manner. For permanent records of your work, you must add a printer to your system. Printers create *hard copy output* from your computer programs.

A printer connects to your system unit via a *port*. Port is just a fancy name for the connectors in the back of your system unit. Printer ports are either parallel or serial; serial connections use a single wire to transmit data in one direction at a time, while parallel connections use multiple wires to transmit data in both directions, from computer to printer and back, at the same time. Parallel connections, therefore, are usually faster than serial connections. You can connect your printer to either type, as long as your printer is configured for that particular port.

The Different Types of Printers

You can locate various types of printers for your system, depending on your exact printing needs. The two main categories of printer are *impact* and *nonimpact* printers.

Impact printers are so named because they put ink on paper by some sort of impact. The most popular type of impact printer is the *dot-matrix printer*. Dot-matrix printers employ tiny *print heads* that strike an ink ribbon, pressing it against your paper to leave an image. Dot-matrix heads consist of many individual wires, called *pins*, that create a pattern of dots on your paper. The more dots a printer can create, the better the printed image it leaves. Standard dot-matrix printers range from those with only nine pins up to 24-pin models.

The most popular type of nonimpact printer is the *laser printer*. These printers work much like copying machines, applying toner (powdered ink) to paper by using a small laser. Laser printers, unlike dot-matrix models, can reproduce very detailed graphic images as well as text. (Although dot-matrix printers can print graphic images, too, the details are far less sharp than those produced with a laser printer.)

What Can Go Wrong with Your Printer

All printers can cause you trouble. Not only are the usual problems with hookup and setup to be expected, but printers also require constant maintenance to stay in top operating condition. The ink ribbons of dot-matrix printers must be changed and their heads cleaned regularly to maintain sharply printed images; their paper paths must be kept free of paper shavings to avoid paper jams. Laser printers, though consisting of fewer moving parts than their dot-matrix cousins, require regular replacement of their toner cartridges as well as frequent paper-path cleaning.

Talking to Other Computers

On the Home Font

Incorrect printer setup is a major cause of PC problems. Many new software programs include complex setup procedures to configure a program to match a specific printer for optimal output. In fact, many programs include built-in *fonts* that provide better print quality from certain types of printers. (Fonts are specific typefaces and type sizes for alphanumeric characters.) Many users cry *OOPs!* if their fonts aren't installed and set up properly—if they have one font for display and a different one for printing, for example.

The last major peripheral you may consider adding to your PC system is a *modem*. Modems allow your computer to connect to telephone lines and transmit data to and from other computers, commercial on-line services (such as Prodigy or CompuServe), or the Internet.

Modems come in either internal (board-based) or external (hooking up to an open port on the back of your system) models. Internal modems usually fit into a slot on your motherboard and connect directly to a telephone line. External modems are free-standing devices that connect to your system unit by cable and hook directly to a phone line.

When you connect a modem to your system, take care that all its settings are configured correctly for your computer. You also must install a telecommunications software package to make your modem work, and this software must be correctly configured both for your modem and for the various on-line services you want to access.

If all this sounds somewhat complex, well, that's because it is. I don't mean to scare you away from the joys of on-line communications, but you should be made aware that modems can cause you some headaches. Getting everything hooked up and configured correctly *can* be a chore. Add in the potential for *port conflicts* (when your modem actually interferes with other parts of your system), *dirty telephone lines* (which interrupt data flow), and protocol mismatches (resulting from incompatible configurations between your system and the system you're trying to reach), and many users just decide to chuck the entire idea of using a modem to avoid these hassles. That's really a shame, because after you get a modem set up and running, you'll find the capability of talking to other computer users across the globe worth whatever initial headaches you may encounter.

All About Your System Software

Okay, so you have your hardware set up, your cables connected, your power cords plugged in, and your wall switch turned on. Now what? It's time to try out some of your software.

Operating Your System with DOS

The most essential program on your computer is its *operating system*. If you own an IBM-compatible computer, your operating system is most likely to be *MS-DOS*—usually referred to simply as *DOS*.

DOS is the one piece of software you must have to run all the rest of your software. In fact, DOS must be installed on your system for it to start at all! For this reason, many new PCs come with DOS already installed on the hard disk; those that don't often include the operating system on disks that you install yourself.

DOS Clones

MS-DOS is so named because it is developed and sold by Microsoft (hence the "MS"). There are other variants of DOS put out by other manufacturers. IBM puts out its own version of DOS called either PC DOS or IBM DOS, depending on the version. Novell distributes another version of DOS called either DR DOS or Novell DOS, again depending on the version. On the whole, however, all these DOSs are pretty much the same; feel comfortable applying the MS-DOS advice in this book to any other DOS version you may be using.

To get the most out of your computer system, you need at least a working knowledge of DOS. Chapter 3 gives you some DOS basics, but if you're a total DOS novice, you may want to check out one of Que's many dedicated DOS books for more information. I recommend the following:

- *Easy DOS*, Second Edition, a full-color guide to DOS basics.

- *MS-DOS 6.2 QuickStart*, a step-by-step tutorial on DOS operations.

- *Using MS-DOS 6.2*, Special Edition, Que's most comprehensive DOS book with lots of intermediate and advanced information.

Opening New Windows

Those who prefer not to deal directly with DOS in any form may find another type of shell program that operates on top of DOS useful. *Microsoft Windows* (or just Windows) is such a shell.

Actually, Windows technically is an *operating environment*. It employs a *graphical user interface* (abbreviated *GUI* and sometimes pronounced "gooey") to shield you from the often bewildering world of DOS. Windows features a series of pull-down menus to display its various commands and operations. It uses icons to pictorially represent programs and operations on-screen. Windows also can perform multiple operations simultaneously; this *multi-tasking* capability enables Windows to run more than one program at a time.

One drawback to Windows is that it doesn't operate on all systems. You need an 80286, 80386, 80486, or Pentium system to run this operating environment. You also need at least 4M of RAM in your system for Windows to run at all and 8M to run Windows at its most efficient. Of course, you need a mouse, plus a monitor, and a video card capable of at least VGA resolution—in color. If your system fails to meet these minimum requirements, forget Windows and stick to DOS.

Just as this book can't teach you all about DOS, it can't teach you all there is to know about Windows either. (Although Chapter 4 is a good primer on Windows basics.) If you're a complete Windows novice, I recommend that you examine one of the following excellent Que books on the subject.

- *Easy Windows 3.1*, a good step-by-step, full-color, visually oriented introduction for beginning users.

- *Windows QuickStart, 3.11 Edition*, a step-by-step tutorial on Windows basics.

- *Using Windows, 3.11 Edition,* Special Edition, the comprehensive reference that tells you everything you could ever want to know about Windows.

Filing Your Data

For the past several sections, I've talked a lot about files. DOS features many commands to enable you to manipulate your files. Windows even offers its own separate mini-application—File Manager—to help you manipulate your files. Great! But what exactly is a file, and how does it work?

Identifying Files

Your computer system uses *files* to store data; all electronically generated data is, in fact, organized into files. Files can consist of documents created by your word processor, listings of fields created by your database, or even the core codes of your applications programs themselves. To operate your computer at all, you must know how to work with its files.

In the worlds of both DOS and Windows, every file has its own unique name. A defined structure exists for naming files, and its conventions must be followed for DOS to understand exactly what file you want when you try to access one. Each file name must consist of three parts, as described in the following table.

Name	The first part of the file name consists of up to eight characters, which can include either letters or numbers.
Period	The period following the file's name acts as a divider between the name and the extension.
Extension	This last part of the name consists of up to three characters, again including either letters or numbers, and is used to denote various types of files.

Putting it all together, you get DOS file names that appear on-screen something like the following:

```
FILENAME.EXT
```

So that you don't have to type in individual file names whenever you want to work with more than one file, DOS enables you to enter *wild card characters* to identify multiple files. The two wild card characters DOS recognizes are the * (asterisk) and the ? (question mark). When you are searching for particular types of files, you can substitute a wild card in place of one or more characters in either the file's name or its extension. DOS then

The Name Game

When you type a file name, it really doesn't matter whether you use upper- or lowercase letters; DOS and Windows are programmed to accept either version. The period and extension often are optional when naming a file. Some software programs even add their own unique extensions onto the files they create. (Excel uses files with XLS extensions, for example, and Microsoft Word appends its files with DOC extensions.)

identifies all the files with names that match the characters represented by the wild card.

Using the * wild card results in a match to any character or group of characters, from its particular position in the file name to the end of that part of the file name. So, to identify all files with the BAK extension, for example, place the * before the period in the file name, as shown in the following example:

    *.BAK

The ? wild card results in a match to any single character at that particular position in the file name. To identify files that could have a WK1 or WKS extension, for example, type the following file name:

    *.WK?

What You Can Do with Files

Efficiently manipulating your files is the key to maximizing the overall efficiency of your computer system. Depending on the operating system installed in your machine, you can manipulate files either by using DOS commands or the Windows File Manager. In this book, I concentrate on DOS commands; nearly everything you can do from the DOS prompt, however, can also be done with the DOS Shell or the Windows File Manager.

And just what can you do with your files? The following short list of commands and procedures should give you at least a few ideas.

BACKUP	Creates a backup copy, on another disk, of selected files from your hard disk
COPY	Copies files from one location to another
DEL	Deletes files from your disk
DIR	Shows a listing of all files in the specified directory
REN	Renames files
RESTORE	Restores backed-up files to your hard disk
TYPE	Types the contents of a file to your screen

You can even run programs from the command line by typing an abbreviation of the program's name (such as 123 or WP) and then pressing Enter. If the file has an extension of EXE, COM, or BAT, the program loads and begins running.

When Files Get Vile

Many things can go wrong with files, but, fortunately, you can prevent most of them yourself. (This is mainly because you cause most of the problems in the first place!) Potential user errors involving files include simply typing a file name or command incorrectly, using the wrong syntax, or forgetting to include a command parameter. Make any of these errors, and DOS will tell you about it in no uncertain terms—via an error message. (All DOS error messages, by the way, are explained in Chapter 28, "DOS Error Messages— What They Mean and How To Deal with Them.")

As if these types of user errors aren't bad enough, you can accidentally delete a file you really didn't want deleted. (If you do, you can usually undelete the file as well, as explained in Chapter 20, "What To Do When... Your Files Are Funky.") Or you can inadvertently copy one file over another existing file, which erases the latter. (There's not much you can do about this one, I'm afraid.) In fact, if you try hard enough, you can even sabotage your entire hard disk by using DOS file commands incorrectly. (Scary thought, isn't it?)

> ### File Referrals
>
> Remember that I can't teach you everything you need to know about files in this book. Try one of Que's DOS books for a more in-depth discussion of files and file operations.

But before you become too frightened to use DOS file commands at all, take heart in the knowledge that DOS normally gives you ample warning before it carries out most of these commands. If you heed DOS's on-screen warning, you can halt any such operation before it destroys your files.

> ### Screen Your Mistakes
>
> You can prevent a lot of mistakes by the simple method of *watching your screen for DOS comments!* Nearly all of the most potentially damaging operations are preceded by a DOS message that asks, in essence, if you really want to do this. Look on these messages as your last chance to back out of an ill-conceived operation—and use that opportunity to get out while the getting's good!

Hard disk problems also can inflict severe damage on your files. Bad sectors on a hard disk, for example, can scramble the data in affected files, making them unreadable. And, of course, computer viruses can cause the same type of damage to your files—and in many cases, even worse. Because all your efforts at your computer depend on the integrity of your files, it's imperative that you understand how fragile their existence can be.

But don't worry—many ways exist for you to protect your files from potential catastrophes. That's why you bought this book, isn't it? Make sure that you carefully read Chapter 20 for detailed instructions on how to prepare for and prevent unwanted problems with your files.

Adding Software to Your System

After you've hooked up your hardware, formatted your disks, and installed your operating system, you're ready for the productive part of your computing experience. It's time to add software!

How To Install New Software Programs

Most software programs come with their own installation programs. These are most often started by switching the DOS prompt to the drive containing the software disk and typing INSTALL or SETUP. (If you're installing a Windows program, you need to pull down the File menu, select the Run option, and then type in the name of the installation program on the floppy disk—again, normally INSTALL or SETUP.) Usually, the installation proceeds on its own, with some input from you required to tell the program about your particular system. Make sure that you read the installation instructions for all programs you intend to add to your computer before you begin installation.

Before you install any program, always make *backup copies* of your program disks. That way you retain a spare copy of your program in the event the original disks become damaged. Read Chapter 7, "Preparing a PC Survival Kit," for details on how to do this.

Problems with Your Software Programs

What can go wrong with software programs? Where do I start? As with all aspects of computer operation, the most common problems in working with software are caused by you, the user, making an error (typing in a wrong command, for example), or result from the individual program having been installed or configured incorrectly. See chapters 23 and 24 for specific problem-solving hints for several popular software programs.

Another major software problem you may encounter concerns programs that are actually incompatible with each other. This sometimes occurs when two programs attempt to access the same peripheral device (printer, modem, etc.) or write to the same memory space at the same time. The most perplexing problems you may ever encounter usually involve incompatible programs. The services of a trained computer guru invariably are required to track down this type of problem.

If you suspect that your system is experiencing program conflicts, the best method of identifying the offending program or programs is to run only one program at a time. If each program runs fine separately, try running them together. If conflicts result, try loading the programs in a different order. If you always load Program A before Program B, for example, try loading Program B first this time. If that doesn't fix the problem, you may just have to give up on running the two programs together. It's not a perfect solution, but this isn't a perfect world either.

The Last Word on Computer Basics

This chapter is intended as a crash course in everything that comprises your computer system and how all its parts fit together. Look at what you've learned so far:

Your system unit contains your computer's microprocessor, memory, disk drives, and add-on cards; connected to the system unit are your machine's keyboard, mouse, monitor, and printer. Your computer's operating system is installed on its hard disk and facilitates communications between all parts of the system. Finally, software programs are installed on the hard disk and "talk" to your computer by way of its operating system.

If any of these parts fails to work or communicate with the other parts, your system itself ceases to function normally. On the other hand, if you type a command, file name, or anything else incorrectly, or you connect any of its cables to the wrong port, *you* can be the cause of your system's failure. What all this should suggest to you is always to take the utmost care with your computer system, either when initially installing its various parts or when operating it on a daily basis.

The Do's and Don'ts of DOS

CHAPTER THREE

If it was just you and your computer hardware, life would be difficult. You see, you don't know how to talk its language, and your computer certainly can't speak or understand English. Yep, we would definitely have a major communications problem—if it weren't for *DOS*.

DOS (which stands for *Disk Operating System*, in case you wondered) is the system software that communicates with your system hardware. You and your software programs communicate with DOS, and DOS translates that into commands your hardware understands. In short, DOS operates your computer system for you.

It's important to know a little bit about DOS before you start to troubleshoot your system problems. So read on, and get a *very* basic DOS primer!

DOS Basics for the Technically Timid

The most essential program on your computer is DOS, your computer's operating system. If you own an IBM-compatible computer, your operating system is most likely to be *MS-DOS*, sold and distributed by Microsoft. (That's the MS in MS-DOS, by the way.)

DOS is the one piece of software you must have to run all the rest of your software. In fact, DOS must be installed on your system for it to start at all! For this reason, all new PCs come with DOS either preinstalled on the hard disk or in the box on a set of diskettes.

Taking DOS Apart

DOS is not just a single piece of software, but actually consists of four separate components. These components perform their own distinct duties, but all work together to form the complete operating system. The four layers of DOS are as follows:

- *The basic input/output system (BIOS).* This part of DOS actually interacts with your computer hardware. It's something like a language translator that takes commands from the command interpreter and translates them into a "language" form that your computer hardware can understand.

- *The command interpreter.* Often referred to as the "DOS prompt" or the "command line," this part of DOS enables you to input specific commands, one line at a time, which are then fed by DOS into the BIOS. The BIOS, in turn, translates them into a form understandable by your computer hardware.

- *The DOS utilities.* These special miniprograms can be run either from the DOS command line or from the DOS Shell (see following). They enable you to perform certain tasks, such as formatting disks, and are the keys to your everyday use of DOS.

- *The DOS Shell.* This is the friendly face of DOS, available with DOS versions 4, 5, and 6—but *not* with DOS 6.2 and later versions! (Microsoft discovered few users used the shell, and took it out of the basic package!) The Shell provides access to most common DOS functions from pull-down menus instead of the command line.

In effect, each layer of DOS works as a "shell" to shield you from the complexities of the next lower level—and of the complexity of dealing directly with your computer hardware. To work directly with your hardware, you'd have to speak to it in what is called *machine language* or *assembly language*, which is similar to a series of 0s and 1s. DOS acts as a translator, speaking for you to your hardware in its native tongue.

How DOS Works

Unlike other software programs, DOS starts automatically when you first turn on your system. DOS reads two files that provide it with essential startup information (the CONFIG.SYS file and the AUTOEXEC.BAT file) and then loads itself into your system's memory. These startup files contain technical information necessary for system configuration (such as what drivers to load, how to configure your system's memory, where to look for specific files, and how to display the DOS prompt).

After DOS loads itself into your system's memory, it clears the screen and displays the *DOS prompt*. This prompt tells you what drive you're currently logged on to. Because most software programs reside on drive C, the DOS prompt is often called the *C prompt*. The C prompt usually appears on-screen as follows:

```
C:\>
```

(Some C prompts may look a little different; if yours does, don't worry—it functions the same way.) When you see this prompt, you must type in a specific DOS command, using its correct syntax (how the command must be worded). If you type something incorrectly, DOS displays an error message. If you type nothing, DOS does nothing. (It continues to patiently await your commands.)

DOS offers a complete set of commands that enable you to perform various tasks on your computer: for example, the COPY command copies files, the DEL command deletes files, a REN command renames files, the BACKUP command backs up files, a DIR command lists all the files on a disk, and the TYPE command displays the contents of a file. And these are only a few examples of the DOS commands available to you. Most DOS commands are file-related, as you probably noticed, because manipulating files usually is your main reason for working with DOS.

The DOS Shell

That Old Shell Game

Some people configure their computers to load the DOS Shell when they turn the machine on, without it ever displaying the DOS prompt. To do this, insert the line DOSSHELL at the end of the AUTOEXEC.BAT file. If your system doesn't load the DOS Shell automatically, you can load it manually by typing the following line at the DOS prompt:

DOSSHELL

When you hit the Enter key, the DOS Shell loads into your system.

With DOS versions 4, 5, and 6 (but *not* 6.2 or later, remember!), you don't have to deal exclusively with the DOS command line. These versions of DOS include a feature called the DOS Shell. Using the DOS Shell, you can perform most DOS operations by selecting items from pull-down menus; you may never again have to face the DOS prompt (unless, of course, you want to).

All About DOS Commands

Need More Help with DOS?

Obviously, since this isn't a dedicated DOS book, I can't tell you *everything* you need to know about DOS here. If you want more DOS information, look for one of Que's outstanding DOS

Because DOS is the very core of your computer system, imagine the problems you may encounter when trying to invoke various DOS commands (and doing so incorrectly). Nearly all DOS-related problems result from human error.

Each command must be issued in a certain way, using various switches and parameters. If this format—called *syntax*—isn't followed exactly, the command does not execute and you receive a DOS error message on-screen. To get the desired results from your computer, you must therefore follow all DOS rules to the letter, being especially careful not to mistype anything. As the old saying goes: *garbage in, garbage out*. This is never more true than when dealing with DOS.

The Different Versions of DOS

DOS has been through a lot of changes over the years. Each new change is called a *version*, and the latest *major* version is called DOS 6. (Previous versions were DOS 5, DOS 4, and so on.) DOS 6 builds on previous versions by keeping the same core operations, but adding some new operations and utilities to make your life easier.

Note, however, that Microsoft also releases *point upgrades* in between major upgrades. For example, about six months after the release of DOS 6, Microsoft released DOS 6.2. This point upgrade fixed a few bugs in the initial 6.0 release, as well as eased the installation of a few features. Then, about six months

> ### Then There Are the Non-Microsoft Versions of DOS...
>
> Just to make things even more confusing, Microsoft isn't the only manufacturer of DOS. (It is the *leading* manufacturer, though, with more than 90% of the market.) Both Novell (with Novell DOS) and IBM (with either PC DOS or IBM DOS) market their own versions of DOS. All of these non-MS-DOSs work pretty much like MS-DOS, even though some of the utilities are a bit different. If you have a version of Novell or IBM DOS, you can still follow along with the advice in this book—you just may have to adapt a few things for your specific system.

after that, Microsoft got sued by a company providing disk compression, and had to *remove* DoubleSpace disk compression! This new, DoubleSpace-less version was called DOS 6.21. Shortly after this, Microsoft redid its disk compression (changing its name from DoubleSpace to DriveSpace) and released DOS 6.22. (It's tough to keep up with all this, isn't it?)

What's New in DOS 6

If you have an older version of DOS, you'll really like some of the major utilities and minor commands added to DOS 6 (and 6.2—we'll refer to all the 6.X versions generically as "DOS 6" throughout this book). The basic operation is the same, but look for these new items:

MemMaker	A utility for automatically maximizing your system's memory via configuration of the CONFIG.SYS and AUTOEXEC.BAT files.
DoubleSpace	A utility that compresses the data on your hard disk to give you more usable disk space. (Note that this utility is only available in DOS 6.0 and 6.2; it was *removed* from DOS 6.21!)
DriveSpace	Effectively the same type of disk-compression utility as DoubleSpace; included in DOS 6.22.
Defragmenter	A utility that defragments fragmented data on your hard disk.
UNDELETE	An enhanced version of the DOS 5 utility that "undeletes" deleted files; available in both DOS and Windows versions.

continues

continued

Microsoft Backup	A special stand-alone utility that works in place of the normal BACKUP command to automate your backup operations; available in both DOS and Windows versions.
Microsoft Anti-Virus	A utility that protects your system from computer viruses; available in both DOS and Windows versions.
Microsoft Diagnostics	A utility that analyzes your system and reports on its configuration.
SCANDISK	A disk-checking (and fixing, for some simple problems) utility; included in version 6.2 and later.
INTERLNK	A utility that makes it easy to transfer information from one computer to another.
INTERSVR	A utility (related to INTERLNK) that makes it easy to exchange information between two computers.
MOVE	A command that allows you to move files from directory to directory (or disk to disk) without using the COPY and DELETE commands.
DELTREE	A command that allows you delete entire directories from your disks.
POWER	A utility that minimizes power use on portable computers.
SmartDrive	An advanced disk-caching utility to maximize extended memory use.
SmartMonitor	A Windows-based utility that monitors the use of SmartDrive.

Read on for more detailed information about the most important of these new features.

Maximizing Memory with MemMaker

MemMaker is a new DOS 6 utility that automatically determines your system setup and makes changes to your CONFIG.SYS and AUTOEXEC.BAT files to maximize your system's use of memory. MemMaker loads as many devices as possible into upper memory, so that conventional memory is free for normal program use. It also maximizes the use of

Upper Is Better

If you have more than 640K of memory on your system, the balance is part of some sort of upper memory. You can have memory allocated for upper memory blocks, the high memory area, extended memory, and expanded memory. (The first 640K, by the way, is called *conventional memory*.) Generally, you want to move as much stuff as possible into some form of upper memory so that you'll have more conventional memory for your programs to use. MemMaker optimizes your setup by moving device drivers, terminate-and-stay-resident programs, and other small utilities into upper memory.

upper memory by specifying specific addresses for your drivers (a really technical trick that you could do if you knew as much about your system as MemMaker does, but you probably don't), thus packing things together in memory in a highly efficient manner.

You should use MemMaker whenever you want to maximize your system's memory. This means you should run it when you first set up your computer, after you change operating systems (like upgrading to DOS 6), and after you add new programs or devices to your system. Using MemMaker is infinitely preferable to making all these changes yourself!

Defragmenting Your Hard Disk with Defragmenter

Over time, your hard disk gets all fragmented. This means that little chunks of programs get added and deleted so that there's very little *contiguous* free space on your disk. In other words, your hard disk looks a little like Swiss cheese. The bad thing about a Swiss-cheesed hard disk is that it slows down disk access—and therefore all your system operations.

To get your hard disk back in tip-top shape, you need to *defragment* it. With DOS 6, you have a new utility, Defragmenter, that automatically unSwiss-cheeses your disk.

Compressing Your Hard Disk with DoubleSpace and DriveSpace

If you're like a lot of computer users, your hard disk just isn't big enough. Wouldn't it be nice to make your hard disk bigger?

Well, with DOS 6.0, 6.2, and 6.22 (*but not 6.21!*) you can—sort of. DoubleSpace is a new utility (with versions 6.0 and 6.2) that compresses the data on your hard disk so that it takes up less space, in effect giving you a bigger hard disk drive. Version 6.22 includes a similar utility called DriveSpace; it works pretty much the same as DoubleSpace.

MS-DOS 6.21: Less is More?

Due to a lawsuit from a major supplier of disk-compression technology, Microsoft was forced to remove DoubleSpace from its version of DOS. This resulted in the release of MS-DOS 6.21, which is essentially MS-DOS 6.2 *without* DoubleSpace. Fortunately for all concerned, Microsoft figured out a way to rejig its disk compression while avoiding legal difficulties; it released version 6.22 with a new compression utility called DriveSpace. In any case, if you have MS-DOS 6.21, you *don't* have disk compression—and you should upgrade to version 6.22 to get DriveSpace compression!

This compression takes place in advance of normal operation; the compressed data is decompressed on the fly, as you need it. On most computers, DoubleSpace and DriveSpace work invisibly, without a noticeable slowdown in disk access.

When you install DoubleSpace or DriveSpace, it sections off part of your hard drive and creates a large *compressed volume file* called DBLSPACE.000. This file contains all the compressed information and is seen by DOS as a new "virtual" drive on your system. (If your hard disk was drive C, the compressed drive is drive D.)

Taking a Virtual Drive

A *virtual drive* is something that acts like a drive but isn't really there (kind of like virtual reality—the new reality doesn't *really* exist).

When you run your system subsequent to DoubleSpace or DriveSpace installation, a special device driver is loaded into your system's memory. This driver manages the flow of data to and from the compressed volume file, compressing and decompressing the data in real time.

After you've installed DoubleSpace or DriveSpace, you probably won't even notice that you're using a compressed disk. You should be able to access all your data as easily and as quickly as before. There are some DOS commands that don't work anymore, however—essentially any that need direct access to data on your disk. Take note of the following DOS command changes:

- The DIR command won't always accurately represent the amount of remaining free space on your compressed disk.

- CHKDSK doesn't work on a compressed drive. You need to run the DBLSPACE /CHKDSK [/F] command. (This command is DRVSPACE /CHKDSK [/F] in DOS 6.22.)

- DEFRAG won't defragment a compressed drive. You need to run the DBLSPACE /DEFRAGMENT command. (Again, in DOS 6.22, the command is DRVSPACE /DEFRAGMENT.)

- FORMAT won't format a compressed drive. You need to run the DBLSPACE /FORMAT X command, where X is the drive to format. (Use DRVSPACE /FORMAT X in DOS 6.22.)

- You can't delete a compressed drive via normal commands. You need to run the DBLSPACE /DELETE X, where X is the drive to delete. (Use DRVSPACE /DELETE X in DOS 6.22.)

However, if you want to use DoubleSpace or DriveSpace, there are some things you want to keep in mind to prevent any possible problems:

- *Back up your hard disk completely before running DoubleSpace or DriveSpace.* That way, if you run into DoubleSpace or DriveSpace problems, you can always restore your disk to its pre-compressed condition.

- *Run CHKDSK [/F] from the DOS prompt before running DoubleSpace or DriveSpace, and then delete any files created with the CHK extension.* This will find and eliminate any lost clusters, freeing up valuable disk space.

- *Run Defragmenter before running DoubleSpace or DriveSpace.* Disk compression works best on a defragmented drive.

- *Free up all unused disk space before running DoubleSpace or DriveSpace.* These utilities won't work best if your disk is completely full beforehand. Give yourself some extra free disk space; DoubleSpace and DriveSpace will be happier.

Undeleting Files with UNDELETE

If you have DOS 5, you know all about UNDELETE (which is discussed in more detail in Chapter 20). The DOS 6 version of UNDELETE works just like the older version, but better.

The key improvement in UNDELETE is the addition of a Windows-based Undelete utility. You can run this utility from within Windows because it's a Windows application. Using Windows UNDELETE is as easy as choosing the file to undelete and pressing the right button—that button being the UNDELETE button. The utility will do the rest, in much the same way as the DOS version works.

Backing Up Your Data with Microsoft Backup

While DOS 6 retains the BACKUP command you've all come to know and love, it also includes a new backup utility that works better and easier, called Microsoft Backup. Microsoft Backup is available in both DOS and Windows versions.

Both the DOS and Windows versions of Microsoft Backup work in a similar fashion. You select the drive (and files) to back up, set some basic configuration options, and click to Start. You can select either full or incremental backups; you also use Microsoft Backup to restore files to your hard disk.

Protecting Against Viruses with Microsoft Anti-Virus

Since computer viruses are becoming more pervasive (as explained in Chapter 9), Microsoft thought it best to include an anti-virus utility in DOS 6. Microsoft Anti-Virus is available in both DOS and Windows versions, just like Microsoft Backup.

Microsoft Anti-Virus works to detect, disinfect, and protect your system from computer viruses. DOS 6 also includes VSafe, a memory-resident program that continually scans your system for new viruses. (VSafe is loaded as part of your AUTOEXEC.BAT file.)

See Chapter 9 for detailed instructions on how to use Microsoft Anti-Virus and VSafe.

Microsoft Diagnostics

The final major addition to DOS 6 is Microsoft Diagnostics, a little DOS-based utility that reports on how all the pieces and parts of your system are working. If you're ever in doubt about what you do or don't have hooked up to or set up on your system, Microsoft Diagnostics is the way to find out the straight scoop.

To launch Microsoft Diagnostics, type the following line at the DOS prompt, and then press Enter:

MSD

You can then check out your system to your heart's content, if you're so inclined. (Even if you're not inclined, you may need to print out some of this information for a technician if you ever run into major systems problems.)

The Last Word on DOS (Almost...)

Actually, this chapter *isn't* the last word. As you no doubt gathered as you read this chapter, DOS is a pretty complicated thing—and complicated things can cause complicated problems! So if you're having problems with DOS, you need to turn to Chapter 21, "What To Do When...Your DOS Doesn't." That chapter is the last word on DOS—especially if you're having problems.

The Why's and Why Not's of Windows

Since computing with Windows is different from computing in the plain vanilla DOS environment, you may find it useful to take a quick refresher course in Windows basics. After all, Windows is just another part of your system that can cause you problems!

That said, you need to know a little about Windows before you can fix any Windows problems. This chapter covers the bare necessities of Windows, but if you need to know about how to use Windows, I recommend one of Que's wonderful Windows-specific books, such as *Using Windows,* 3.11 Edition, Special Edition, available at fine retailers everywhere.

Windows Basics for the Technically Timid

Windows technically is an *operating environment*. It employs a *graphical user interface* (abbreviated *GUI* and sometimes pronounced "gooey") to shield you from the often bewildering world of DOS. Windows, like the DOS Shell, features a series of pull-down menus to display its various commands and operations. Windows differs from the DOS Shell, however, in its use of icons to pictorially represent programs and operations on-screen. Windows also can perform multiple operations simultaneously; this *multitasking* capability enables Windows to run more than one program at a time.

One drawback to Windows is that it doesn't operate on all systems. You need an 80286, 80386, 80486, or Pentium system to run this operating environment. You also need at least 4M of RAM in your system for Windows to run at all and 8M to run Windows at its most efficient. Of course, you need a mouse, plus a monitor, and a video card capable of at least VGA resolution—in color. If your system fails to meet these minimum requirements, forget Windows and stick to DOS.

How Windows Works

Windows does an excellent job of shielding you from the DOS prompt. To perform most operations in Windows, all you need to do is use the mouse to pull down a menu or click an icon.

When you use Windows to perform common operations, such as copying files, the program actually tells DOS to do the dirty work for you. When you use the Windows File Manager to copy a file, for instance, the File Manager actually instructs DOS to use the COPY command to duplicate the file. It's all invisible to you.

Windows functions as its own environment, however, and as such uses a great deal of your system's resources: Windows consumes large amounts of hard disk space and requires a good chunk of your system's memory to operate. Although Windows is generally easier to use than DOS, you pay for that ease with a sizable portion of system resources. If your PC's resources are limited, the price is decreased performance. In other words, Windows can slow your operations down considerably.

Hardware for Windows

Seeing as how you probably already have Windows installed on your system, it might be a little late to talk about what kind of hardware you need to run Windows. Oh well, better late than never.

So, what exactly is the perfect Windows computer? First, you need a fast microprocessor. I recommend no less than an 80386 machine, and prefer operation with an 80486 chip. Next, it needs to run at a decent speed. While Windows will supposedly run on a 12 MHz computer, you're better off if your system runs at least 25 MHz.

Now you need to load up on memory. Really. As much as you can afford. You'll need at least 2M of RAM just to get Windows to load, although to get it running at any speed at all you'll need at least 4M—and Windows has far fewer problems if you upgrade your memory to 8M or more. If your computer is a little short in the memory department, don't hesitate to have your local computer store add a few more megabytes. After all, what's a little RAM between friends?

As to hard disk space, again, the more the merrier. Windows applications tend to take up a lot of disk space, and as you install a spreadsheet and a word processor and a database and a presentation program and a communications program and some games and some utilities and then you add all your document files—well, you see where I'm going. In my personal systems, I've progressed from a 20M hard disk (totally inadequate) to a 40M hard disk (barely adequate) to a 100M hard disk (it surprised me how fast that one filled up...) to my current 200M hard disk (which is already over half full!). Get as big a disk as you can afford—trust me, you'll need all the space you can get.

When you're choosing a monitor and video card, remember that Windows is most definitely a *graphical user interface*. To wit, you need a monitor that displays graphics fairly well. Invest in at least a VGA monitor/board combination, and go SuperVGA if you can afford it.

Finally, you'll need a mouse. No two ways around it.

Launching and Exiting Windows

You start Windows while you're still in DOS. From the DOS prompt, change to the WINDOWS directory by typing the following command:

CD\WINDOWS

Then, again from the DOS prompt, type:

WIN

Once you're in Windows, it's easy to exit. Simply double-click on the Control menu button (in the upper left corner of the window). Voila! Windows is closed and you're back at the DOS prompt.

Identifying Windows Parts

Windows and windows

Don't get confused by the terms Windows and windows. The term Windows (with a capital "W") always refers to Microsoft Windows itself, the entire operating environment. The term windows (with a lowercase "w") always refers to the individual window objects within Windows. In other words, you have windows in Windows.

The key to Windows is its use of *objects*. Objects are pieces and parts that perform specific tasks. Windows includes the following important objects:

* *Windows* are individual areas, enclosed in frames, that hold information or applications.

* *Icons* are little pictures that represent other objects, including applications.

* The *pointer* (also called the cursor) represents a specific screen location.

* *Dialog boxes* are special kinds of windows that let you enter data, make specific choices, or read Windows-related messages.

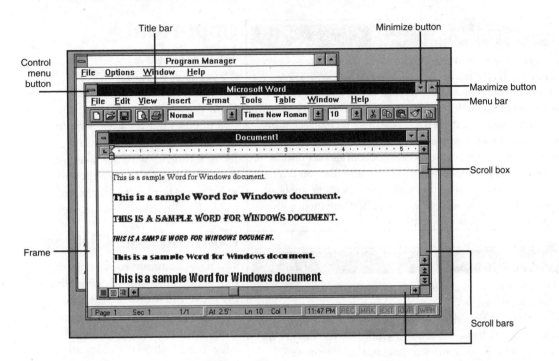

There are standard elements you'll find in almost every Windows window, including:

- The *title bar* displays the name of the current application or document.

- The *minimize button* reduces the current window to an icon.

- The *maximize button* makes the current window fill the entire screen.

- The *scroll box* enables you to manually move to another part of the window by clicking and dragging the box to a new location.

- *Scroll bars* let you to scroll through a space larger than the current window by clicking on the appropriate arrow buttons.

- The *frame* is the bar that surrounds the window itself; clicking and dragging the frame resizes the window.

- The *menu bar* displays various pull-down menus, each of which contains additional commands.

- The *Control menu button*, when clicked, pulls down the Windows Control menu. (This is a useful menu, since it contains commands that let you move, size, and close the current window.)

Windows in windows

Not to get you confused, but certain windows (lowercase "w") can contain other windows (also lowercase "w"). You see, each application is contained within its own window. Certain applications place individual documents in their own windows, and can display multiple documents at one time. So in Excel, for example, Excel itself occupies the main application window, while individual Excel spreadsheets appear in smaller document windows within the application window. Note that you can't move document windows outside the corresponding application window, even though you can move and size them within the application window. Got that? Good!

Left is right

For the purposes of discussion, I'll assume that you're right-handed, and therefore using the left mouse button as your main mouse button and the right mouse button as your secondary mouse button. If, however, you're a southpaw, you can use the Control Panel to reconfigure Windows so that your mouse operates backwards—that is, so the right mouse button is your main mouse button and the left mouse button is your secondary mouse button. So if you're left-handed, when I refer to the right mouse button, you need to transpose that to mean the left mouse button, and vice versa. Right?

Right is right

Some Windows applications use the right mouse button in addition to the left mouse button. For example, in Excel, Word, and Ami Pro, clicking on the right mouse button displays a pop-up menu with commands that directly relate to the selected object. Refer to your individual programs to see if and how they use the right mouse button.

Important Windows Operations

Now, to use Windows efficiently you need to master a few simple operations. I'll assume you're using Windows with a mouse. (If not, your life is a living hell, and you should spring the bucks for the little white thing immediately.)

Pointing and Clicking

The most common mouse operation is *pointing and clicking*. Simply move the mouse so that the pointer is pointing to the object you want to select, then click the left mouse button once. Pointing and clicking is an effective way to select menu items, directories, and files.

Double-Clicking

Sometimes you'll need to *double-click* on an item to activate an operation. This involves pointing at something on-screen with the pointer, then clicking the left mouse button twice in rapid succession. For example, to open program groups or launch individual programs, simply double-click on a specific icon.

Dragging and Dropping

Dragging is a variation of clicking. To drag an object, point at it with the pointer, then press and hold down the left mouse button. Move the mouse without releasing the mouse button, and drag the object to a new location. When you're done moving the object, release the mouse button to drop it onto the new location.

Moving and Sizing Windows

You can manipulate any open window in a variety of ways. For example, if you want to move a window around the screen, simply move the pointer to the title bar of the window, click and hold down the left mouse button, and then drag the window to another position. When you've dropped it in place, release the mouse button.

You can change the size of a window by moving the pointer to the window frame. When you click and hold the left mouse button, you can drag the frame, which resizes the window. When you release the mouse button, the window assumes the new size.

Finally, clicking on the maximize button in the upper right corner of the window causes the window to assume full-screen size. When you click on the minimize button, the window is shrunk to an icon. When you double-click on an iconized window, the window assumes its previous size. Simple, eh?

Launching Applications

The easiest way to launch an application is to double-click on its icon. There are several other ways you can start a program, however.

If you know the path and name of the program you want to launch, you can pull down the File menu and select the Run option. When the Run dialog box appears, type the program path and name into the Command dialog box and hit the OK button; the program launches automatically.

If you don't know the name of the program, you can still launch it via the File Manager. Simply open the File Manager, scroll through the directory listing until you find the directory you want, then scroll through the file listing until you find the right file. Then double-click on the file name, and the program launches. It's as simple as that.

Even More Stuff in Windows!

As a complete operating environment, Windows features several *accessories* or *applets* (kind of like "mini-applications") that enable you to perform common computing tasks. The main Windows interface is called the *Program Manager*. The Program Manager holds many separate *program groups*, which are analogous to file folders (and appear as such on-screen). Each program group, when opened, contains a number of individual programs. The Main program group, for example, contains all the main Windows applets, such as its File Manager or Print Manager. The Windows program group contains all your primary Windows applications programs, such as Excel or Word for Windows. To open a program group, simply point to it with your mouse pointer and double-click the main (left) mouse button. The group expands on-screen from an icon to a *window* (a mini-screen within the screen) to display its contents.

Grand Opening

To open a program group, simply double-click on the appropriate icon. Once a program group window is open, you can launch any program within the group by double-clicking on its icon.

Many Windows applets are vital to your everyday use of Windows. Perhaps the most important is the *File Manager*, which is where you manipulate your files. Be sure that you learn how to use the File Manager; you'll use it frequently.

Windows Pains

Windows is an incredibly complex environment and, as such, the cause of many a PC user's headaches. Not only can you inflict countless problems on yourself through user error (as with DOS), but Windows often seems to go screwy all on its own. Because the program uses so much system memory, Windows occasionally creates or exacerbates memory conflicts among various programs. If your system operates slowly to begin with, or has insufficient memory to run Windows efficiently, be prepared for long waits when you attempt to execute operation—and expect plenty of system errors. (A distinct inverse correlation exists between the amount of memory your system possesses and the number of system errors you experience when running Windows.)

Sometimes, too, it seems that Windows locks up for no apparent reason. An error message may appear (most of the time at least), but then Windows simply shuts down your current

> ### How To Make Windows Less Pane-ful
>
> The best way to ensure a pleasing Windows experience is to have a beefy computer system. That means you need at least 4M RAM, a 200M hard disk, a VGA monitor, and a mouse. Without all this, you probably ought to stick to DOS.

program or refuses to go on—period. I hate to be the bearer of bad news, but some of these problems you just have to live with if you want to run Windows on your system. You can take certain measures to entice Windows to run cleaner (such as expanding your computer's memory and watching the number of programs you run at a time), but like nearly everything else, Windows is not—and probably never will be—perfect.

A Final Word on Windows

Well, that concludes our somewhat brief guided tour of Windows. As you can tell, it's impossible to tell you everything you need to know about Windows in a few short pages. So if you want to learn more about Windows basics (or even advanced features like DDE and OLE), head back to your local retailer and pick up a more comprehensive Que Windows book. A good book to start with is *Easy Windows 3.1,* although if you want a really comprehensive guide, *Using Windows, 3.11 Edition, Special Edition* covers nearly everything you would ever want to know about Windows.

In any case, from here on I'll assume you have a basic working knowledge of Windows, or at least have another Que book you can refer to if you don't understand a particular concept or operation. Now you can move on to the next chapter, where we discuss a few things you can do to keep your system in tip-top shape!

Staying Alive: How to Keep Your System in Tip-Top Shape

One of my goals in writing this book is not only to help you recover from problems, but also to help you *prevent* problems. After all, wouldn't it be nice if you didn't have to read anything else in this book? (And don't worry—I won't take your answer personally!)

So if you want to avoid saying *OOPS!*, turn the page and check out some preventive maintenance tips from ol' Mike!

Why You Need to *Prevent* Problems...Before They *Become* Problems

Even though this book is about *solving* problems, I think it's better to *pre-vent* problems before they occur, if possible. Let's face it—even if you can fix problems when they do occur, you save yourself a lot of grief if you can avoid these problems completely. It's worth a little time spent on preventive maintenance now if it saves you hours of problem-solving and disaster re-covery at some later date.

That said, let's look at some simple, easy things you can do to reduce your chances of contracting computer problems.

Soothing the Soul of Your System Unit

Your system unit has a lot of stuff inside—everything from memory chips to disk drives to power supplies. Check out these maintenance tips to keep your system unit from flaking out on you:

- Keep your system unit in a clean, dust-free environment. Keep it away from direct sunlight and strong magnetic fields.

- Hook your system unit up to a surge suppressor to avoid deadly power spikes.

- Avoid turning your system unit on and off too often; it's better to leave it on all the time than incur frequent "power on" stress to all those delicate components. However...

- Turn off your system unit if you're going to be away for an extended period—anything longer than a day or two.

- Check all your cable connections periodically. Make sure all the con-nectors are firmly connected, and all the screws properly screwed.

- If you're really adventurous, open up the system case periodically and vacuum or wipe the dust from the inside. (Just make sure the system unit is unplugged at the time!) You should also "dust" the inside of your CD-ROM drive, and even use a swab or commercial cleaner to clean the laser lens.

- Defragment your hard disk on a periodic basis. (You can use a defragmenter utility, such as DOS 6's DEFRAG, which is explained in chapter 17.)

- Backup your hard disk regularly, as recommended in chapter 7.

- Run a disk-diagnostic program from time to time. At the very least, run the DOS CHKDSK /F command—and if you have DOS 6, run the SCANDISK utility. Even better: Run a third-party diagnostic utility, like Norton Disk Doctor.

- *Always* run anti-virus software, like DOS 6's Microsoft Anti-Virus utility.

Keeping Your Keyboard Klicking

Even something as simple as your keyboard requires a little preventive maintenance from time to time. Check out these tips:

- Keep your keyboard away from your kids and your pets! They can get dirt and hair and Silly Putty™ all over the place, and have a tendency to put way too much pressure on the keys.

- Keep your keyboard away from dust, dirt, smoke, direct sunlight, and other harmful environmental stuff.

- Use a small vacuum cleaner to periodically sweep the dirt from your keyboard. (Alternately, you can used compressed air to *blow* the dirt away.) Use a cotton swab or soft cloth to clean between the keys. If necessary, remove the keycaps to clean the switches underneath.

- If you spill something on your keyboard, disconnect it immediately and wipe up the spill. Use a soft cloth to get between the keys; if necessary, remove the keycaps and wipe up any seepage underneath. Let the keyboard dry thoroughly before trying to use it again.

Making Sure Your Mouse Keeps Rollin' Along

If you're a Windows user, you probably put over 10,000 miles a year on your mouse. Just like a car tire, anything turning over that often needs a little tender loving care. Check out these mouse maintenance tips:

- Periodically open up the bottom of your mouse and remove the roller ball. Wash the ball with water (or perhaps a mild detergent). Use a soft cloth to dry the ball before reinserting it.

- While your mouse ball is removed, use compressed air or a cotton swab to clean dust and dirt from the inside of your mouse.

- Always use a mouse pad—they really do help keep things rolling smoothly, plus they give you real good traction when you're working on those fast documents! (And while you're at it, don't forget to clean your mouse pad—it can get dirty, too!)

Monitoring Your Monitor

If you think of your monitor as a little television set, you're on the right track. Just treat your monitor as you do your TV and you'll be okay. That said, look at these preventive maintenance tips:

- As with all other important system components, keep your monitor away from direct sunlight, dust, and smoke. Make sure it has plenty of ventilation, especially around the back.

- Don't place any strong magnets in close proximity to your monitor. (This includes external speakers!)

- *With your monitor turned off*, periodically clean the monitor screen. Spray standard glass cleaner on a soft cloth (anti-static type, if possible), then wipe the screen clean.

- Don't forget to adjust the brightness and contrast controls on your monitor every now and then. Any controls can get out of whack—plus, your monitor's performance will change as it ages, and simple adjustments can often keep it looking as good as new.

Putting Your Printer in Its Place

Your printer is a complex device with a lot of moving parts. Follow these tips to keep your printouts in good shape:

- Use a soft cloth, mini-vacuum cleaner, and/or compressed air to clean the inside and outside of your printer on a periodic basis. In particular, make sure you clean the paper path of all paper shavings and dust.

- If you have a dot-matrix printer, use a soft cloth or swab to periodically clean the print head pins. Also, replace the ribbon as needed. (And *don't* reuse old ribbons—they'll just gunk up the works!)

- If you have an ink-jet printer, periodically clean the printhead jets. Use a small pin to make sure they don't get clogged.

- If you have a laser printer, replace the toner cartridge as needed. When you replace the cartridge, remember to clean the printer cleaning bar and other related parts.

- *Don't* use alcohol or other solvents to clean any rubber or plastic parts—you'll do more harm than good!

Minimizing Modem Madness

Modems don't generally give you too much trouble. There are a few things to watch out for, however:

- If you're using an external modem, make sure its power cord is plugged into a surge suppressor.

- If you know a big electrical storm is coming, unplug both the power cord and the phone line from the back of your modem. Otherwise, you risk possible damage from power surges and lightning strikes (which are just as apt to happen via the phone line as they are via the power cable!).

- When you download files from BBSs or the Internet, make sure you're running a good anti-virus program to protect your system from computer viruses.

A Final Word on Preventive Maintenance

Everything recommended in this chapter is easy to do, and can save you all sorts of headaches down the line.

That's good.

But even if you follow all my advice, you can still run into computer problems.

That's bad.

So turn to the next chapter, and I'll tell you why bad things sometimes happen to good computer users—in spite of all your precautions.

Why Bad Things Happen to Good Computer Users

I'm sure you think you're a good person. (And I believe you. Really, I do.) So why should you be the victim of computer problems? Don't you deserve better than this?

Of course you do! But the reality is that computer problems can befall *anyone*. And no matter how careful you are, the chances are good that at some time in your computing career *something* will go wrong. Your goal, then, is to ensure that nothing major goes wrong, and that you're thoroughly prepared just in case something nasty does happen, however minor.

What Causes Most Problems

Most computer problems are easy to solve, because they're really not major problems. Oh, they may *appear* to be major—especially since any problem that happens to *you* is major! But in reality, most problems result from causes that are easily fixed. So, take a look here at some of the most common sources of computer problems and how you can avoid them.

Garbage In, Garbage Out

It's a Load of Garbage!

The phrase *garbage in, garbage out* refers to a phenomenon not necessarily unique to computing. When you put garbage into the system (that is, when you make a mistake), the computer is too stupid (actually, too literal) to interpret what you meant to do, and outputs exactly what you input—mistakes and all. So, if you put garbage in, you get garbage out. After all, computers can't read your mind…yet.

I hate to be the one to break this to you, but computers very rarely make mistakes. You can't always blame your problems on the computer. That's because the most common cause of computer problems is *you*!

You see, most problems result when the user (yes, that's *you*!) does something wrong. You may not *know* you're doing something wrong—and, most certainly, you don't have evil intentions—but you do it anyway.

You know and I know that no one makes mistakes on purpose. When you make an error at your computer, you almost always do so accidentally, and you usually remain unaware of your blunder—at least until something goes terribly and unmistakably wrong with your work. The key to correcting the problem, then, is to remain calm and retrace your steps to figure out exactly what you did wrong.

Bad Typing

Because you're communicating with your computer via a keyboard, the most common errors inevitably occur when you type something wrong. If you're like me, your fingers occasionally fly across the keyboard faster than you're actually able to type—and they usually do so while you're looking at anything but the screen. Sometimes, for example, I try to type the DIR command, but my fingers inadvertently key in the following:

DIT

DOS has no idea what **DIT** means (DOS is *very* literal) and so it displays the following error message:

```
Bad command or filename
```

Now, no harm has been done, but I certainly didn't get the directory listing that I wanted—and it's my fault. I must retype the command—correctly, this time—to see my directory listing appear on-screen.

If you mistype the name of a file, on the other hand, you get a different DOS error message:

```
File not found
```

When this message appears, try retyping the file name correctly. Unless you make another typing error, the desired file should appear. (But wait! What if you check your entry on-screen and discover that you did type the file name correctly the first time? One possibility is that the file you wanted really *isn't* there. But this is another problem, discussed in Chapter 20, "What To Do When...Your Files Are Funky," and isn't dealt with here.)

If you often encounter these or similar DOS error messages or find yourself regularly retyping commands, you may want to try typing a little more slowly in the future. Sometimes s-l-o-w-e-r is more appropriate than faster. (Remember the tortoise and the

---

How To Type Better and Faster

There are actually software programs that help you type better on your computer. These programs help you improve the speed and accuracy of your typing (or keyboarding, which is not to be confused with surfboarding). The program I recommend is one sold by Que Software, called *Typing Tutor*. Ask for it by name wherever you shop for software.

---

hare?) If you find that you have trouble typing accurately even at slower speeds, perhaps consider taking a typing course or buying a typing-instruction program for your computer. You'd be surprised how much these can help increase both your typing speed and your accuracy.

But why be so concerned about mistyping a few commands? All you lose is the time you take to retype the command, right? After all, you can't do anything *really* dangerous simply by mistyping a command...can you? Unfortunately, you can. Many DOS commands have catastrophic results if used incorrectly.

For example, you never, *never* want to reformat your hard disk. (Do so, and you lose all the data residing on the disk—usually all your programs and all your documents!) But how could a simple typing error cause you to reformat your hard disk? Easy. Suppose that you're formatting floppy disks with the following command:

FORMAT A:

Now suppose that you accidentally type a C instead of an A—well, you've just reformatted your hard disk! (No, wait! Relax! You haven't pressed the Enter key yet. Your hard disk is safe. Whew!) This example isn't meant to scare you, however, but is designed to help you think twice before you go blindly typing away and pressing Enter without first looking at what you just keyed in on-screen! Just exercise a little caution, and you'll be okay.

Bad Syntax

Mistyping commands isn't the only possible input error you can inflict on your computer; you can also use *incorrect syntax* when issuing commands. (*Syntax* is, very simply, the correct wording necessary to implement a command.)

Many commands require the use of *parameters*, or operating guidelines, to function. The COPY command, for example, requires you to type both the name of the file you want to copy and the location where you want it copied—say, to a floppy disk or a different directory on your hard disk. If you forget to type one of these parameters (file name or destination), your system can't execute the command, and DOS displays the following error message:

```
Required parameter missing
```

DOS displays this message to remind you that you forgot to type something. If you're not sure what parameters to use for a given command, simply type the command and append a /? to it, as in the following example:

COPY /?

DOS then displays a list of parameters for that command, along with a guide to its proper syntax.

Dealing with computers is no different than dealing with anything else remotely complicated: you need to know what you're doing *before* you try to do it! If you're still uncertain about the correct syntax to use for a command, by all means look it up in a book first. DOS is not a subject to try to learn by trial and error.

The bottom line? If your computer doesn't seem to do what you tell it, make sure that you're telling it to do the right thing. When you input error, you get error in return. (That's the whole idea behind "garbage in, garbage out.")

Those Pesky Plugs!

> ### DOS Isn't Always So Helpful
>
> The /? switch for DOS commands only works with version 5 or later of DOS. If you're using an older version of DOS, there's no way to look up the proper syntax—which means that you probably need to invest in a high-quality, really useful Que DOS book, such as *Using MS-DOS 6.2*, Special Edition. If you have DOS 6, you can also get some very detailed help at the DOS prompt by typing HELP, followed by the command you want help with. To get help on the COPY command, for example, type HELP COPY. (You also can get a list of DOS commands by just typing HELP.)

After you eliminate user error as the source of your computer problem, check for the second most common cause of computer malfunctions: improper hookup. Hooking up a handful of cables may sound simple, but it's easy to do wrong. If you plug a cable into the wrong connector, whatever is connected to that cable won't work. If the connection isn't solid—if the plug is loose—operation can be intermittent. If the cable is old, frayed, or sharply bent, the wires inside the cable may not transmit data effectively, again causing intermittent operation. And, of course, if you forget to turn the power on—well, nothing happens at all!

If a *peripheral* (such as a printer, a monitor, or a modem) isn't working, the problem most likely lies in the connection. Make sure that all cables are solidly connected and, if necessary, securely screwed into their ports. Make certain that the printer cable actually is connected to the printer port, the keyboard cable to the keyboard port, and so on; it's easy to plug the right cable into the wrong connector. Finally, check that *both ends* of the cable are connected; a cable can work its way loose from the back of the monitor just as easily as it can from the back of the system unit.

If your entire system refuses to start, a faulty connection probably is to blame here, too. In this case, however, you need to examine the power cable. Make sure that the power cable is securely connected to your system unit and firmly plugged into a power outlet. Then make certain that the power outlet actually is *turned on*. You can't imagine how many "major problems" can be caused by a wall switch in the off position. And while you're at it, make sure that all your peripherals are also turned on; it doesn't do you any good to have a functioning system unit with a monitor that's switched off.

Of course, you're positive that all *your* cables are connected correctly. After all, you're a good computer user—and besides, everything worked fine the last time you used your system! Forget it, pal. Cables come loose. Trust me. No matter how conscientious you are, *cables come loose.* So if you're experiencing difficulties with your hardware, swallow your pride—and check the wall switch and start wiggling your cables. Nine times out of 10, you'll find your hardware problem right there.

It's a Setup!

Okay, so your entire system is hooked up and turned on—and you've *still* got hardware problems. Then again, maybe not. In some cases, your "hardware problems" actually turn out to be *software problems*.

Living in a Changing World

If you change any aspect of your computer system—for example, if you upgrade to a better monitor/video card, or add a new printer—you have to go back through all your software programs and change their settings to reflect your new hardware. If you don't, your computer won't know you've changed something, and will keep on acting the same old way—which may not be the best way to work with your new equipment.

Most software programs must be configured to work with the equipment in your system. Too many problems result when users fail to set up their software correctly. If a LaserJet printer is hooked up to your system, for example, but your word processor is configured for a dot-matrix printer, your printed output is going to look…well, messed up. If you own a 2400-baud modem but your telecommunications package is designed for a 9600-baud modem, your communications are likely to go awry. And if your monitor is a monochrome EGA model but your spreadsheet setting requires a VGA color display, consider yourself lucky if you can see anything at all on-screen.

Fortunately, most software programs configure themselves when first installed on your system. But occasionally, an installation program doesn't work quite right. Then again, sometimes you find it necessary to configure certain programs yourself, and you may select incorrect settings for it.

The solution to this problem is simple: If, for any reason, you discover that your settings are incorrect, *change them*! Most programs enable you to edit their settings after installation, either by using menu options or a separate setup program. You can't transmogrify an EGA monitor into a VGA monitor by rubbing a magic microchip and wishing it into being. If you experience really strange operational problems, check (and change) your software settings.

Bugs in the Machine

After you check for human error, make certain that everything is hooked up and turned on, and ensure that your software is configured correctly for your hardware, what do you do if you still have problems? Well, the possibility exists—however slight—that your system actually is infested with software or hardware bugs.

A Legendary Tale...of Bugs!

One of the legends in the computing biz concerns the origins of the term "bug." Legend has it that the cause of several problems in an early mainframe computer was traced to a moth fluttering about inside the machine—thus, all computer problems are now called "bugs."

Yes, I'm afraid it's true: Not every software program gets programmed perfectly, and not every piece of hardware comes from the factory totally free of mechanical inconsistencies. It's entirely possible that your software program truly doesn't do what you instruct it to do or that some component really has broken down inside your system unit or a peripheral. Can you believe it? Some problems actually are caused by *computer* error!

But how can you tell whether your software has bugs? First, read the README file included on your software floppy disks. This file (variously labeled README, README.TXT, or READ.ME) contains last-minute instructions, changes, and additions that were developed too late to include in the standard software documentation. If certain features of a program malfunction, the README file probably discusses those problems.

Two other potential sources of information about any glitches in your software include your dealer and other users of the program. The latter especially might be aware of bugs in the program that could be causing your problem. As a last resort—if README, your dealer, or other users can't help—call

Finding a Reliable Repairman (or Repairwoman)

Make sure that you take your computer to a repair shop you can trust. Call your computer's manufacturer and have it recommend a repair center in your area. (It may also have quick factory service via Federal Express or overnight mail.) You should also ask your friends (or the office techno-nerd) where they get their computers repaired. It's worth your peace of mind (and your PC's ongoing health) to do a little legwork before you entrust your computer to a stranger.

the software publisher's technical support line. The call might cost you a few pennies, but the publisher's technical support staff often can warn you of bugs in their company's programs and sometimes even help you exterminate your own particular pest.

If your software seems okay, how do you determine whether a bug in your hardware is causing the problem? The simplest thing to do—although not always the most convenient—is to replace the offending peripheral with one from a friend's computer system. If you think your printer is acting up, for example, try hooking up a friend's printer to your system. If your friend's printer works, your printer is probably at fault. (An alternative is to hook up your printer to your friend's system to see whether your device works there. If it doesn't, you definitely have problems with your printer. If it *does*…turn to "The Great Troubleshooting Road Map"—in Chapter 30— to help track down the real cause of your problem!)

You may not be able to identify every hardware problem you experience yourself; that's why so many people train to be computer repair technicians. When all else fails, never be afraid to call a repair tech; often, these specialists can fix your machine in less time than it takes you to determine if you even have a problem and, if so, where the problem originates.

Catching a Virus

One final major category of computer problems remains for discussion. Unfortunately, it is one that is growing in seriousness almost daily—the dreaded computer virus.

Chapter 9, "Germ Warfare—Protecting Your Computer from Viruses," explains about viruses in greater detail. Basically, a *virus* is a program designed to deliberately cause other programs and data to malfunction. Viruses can infiltrate regular programs and inflict extensive damage to these and other programs and data on your hard disk. Viruses are truly evil and can be enormously destructive.

How do you catch a computer virus? Like other computer data, viruses transmit through exchange of infected floppy disks or by downloading infected programs from computer bulletin boards and on-line services. Whenever you allow new programs from an outside source into your system, the chance exists—however slight—that within that data may lurk a hidden computer virus.

So, how exactly can you tell whether your computer has a virus? If your old reliable programs suddenly start acting funny, they may be infected. If you experience sudden data loss, your system may have contracted a virus. If your computer suddenly shuts down and displays a weird message on its screen, it's almost certainly suffering from a virus infection. In short, any sudden, unusual, unexplained computer behavior could be a sign that your system is infected.

How do you avoid viruses?
The only foolproof way is to
avoid all contact and communication with other computers and with disks used in
other computers. However,

such extreme measures are often impractical. Fortunately, you can take any
of several more practical precautions, including the installation of special
anti-virus software. See Chapter 9 for more information on how to practice
safe, virus-free computing.

How To Be a Better Computer User

Now that you know why *even you* can be plagued by computer problems,
what can you do about it? How can you become an even better computer
user than you already are? The next few sections provide you with some
helpful suggestions.

Careful, Careful, Careful

First, always take extra care to prevent making mistakes whenever you use
your computer. If you type a command, be sure to type it correctly. (It helps
if you actually look at the screen while you're typing, especially before you
press the Enter key to execute a command!) If you issue a complex command, make certain that you use the correct syntax and include all the right
parameters. In other words, look before you execute. It will save you *a lot*
of headaches.

Second, be very cautious when you communicate with other computers.
Whether you trade disks with another user or download programs from a
bulletin board, always be aware that *any* new files you introduce into your
system could contain a hidden computer virus. The rules of safe computing
are much like those of safe sex—know your partners and take reasonable
precautions. If you don't know where the data has been and what it might
contain, don't copy it onto your system.

Third, connect the various parts of your system together *very* carefully.
(And be extremely careful to disconnect your system from all power outlets
before connecting any of its parts; if you don't, your computer may not be
all that you short out.) Make sure that you hook up everything correctly and
that all the connections are solid. And don't forget to turn the power to
your system back on when you're done, preferably through a surge
protector.

Finally, make sure that your software is configured correctly for all the components of your system. Don't simply assume that the installation program worked—check out all the program's setup information yourself to be certain it's correct.

It's an old saying but a true one: You can never be too careful. When things go wrong—no, even *before* things go wrong—double-check anything and everything involved with your system that could possibly cause problems. Someday, you'll be glad you did.

Copy, Copy, Copy

When something is important to you, *always* keep an extra copy in case you lose the original. Whether we're talking about personal papers or computer files, anything can be damaged or misplaced. If a copy exists, you're protected should even the worst happen.

When protecting your computer files is the goal, your first priority is to copy your software programs themselves. As Chapter 7, "Preparing a PC Survival Kit," exhorts in greater detail, always make copies of all your software before you install the programs on your system! Put these copies away in a safe place—preferably somewhere well away from your computer. That way, your software remains safe even if your computer melts down in a fire or gets stolen by a cat burglar.

When a Copy Is Better Than the Original

You should use the copies you make of your software disk to install the program, rather than using the original disk. That way, if your system eats a disk, or otherwise destroys the data on the disk, you've only lost a copy, not an original.

Next, make backup copies of all your important data files as you work on them. Copy your data *frequently*. Whenever you work on an important file, save your work at least every five minutes and make copies *every half hour* (or even more frequently!) on a separate floppy disk. This ensures that you always retain a relatively up-to-date copy of your work, even if your system experiences a severe data loss.

It boils down to this: If a file is truly important to you, always make a copy of it, and keep the copy in a safe place.

Back Up, Back Up, Back Up

Making a complete and regular backup of *all* your data is every bit as important as keeping copies of individual files. If your hard disk suffers damage, a virus invades your system, you accidentally delete several files, or you inadvertently reformat your hard disk, you can recover the lost data from your backup disks. Be sure, however, to back up your hard disk on a regular basis—at least once a week and perhaps even daily. See Chapter 7 for detailed information on exactly how to back up your important data.

A Last Word on Avoiding Bad Things

Using your computer should be easy and fun—when you do everything right. Just as in any other activity—swimming, driving a car, or making a videotape recording, for example—if you do something wrong, you pay for it. The main thing to keep firmly in mind when using your computer is—all together now—*be careful*! Follow this advice faithfully, and you can prevent most problems from occurring long before you need to worry about fixing them.

Speaking of prevention, the next chapter, "Preparing a PC Survival Kit," gives you nearly everything you need to know to prepare yourself for any potential PC disaster. Make sure you read it *before* something bad happens to you!

Preparing a PC Survival Kit

You know, the Boy Scouts had it right. "Be Prepared" is a *great* motto, especially when you're dealing with personal computers!

If you're reading this book, you know the value in preparing for potential disaster. If you're prepared, the odds of recovering your valuable data are much higher than if you're not prepared. Just think of it as a way of "buying" insurance for your computer: you invest a little time today to protect yourself should the unthinkable happen to your PC and its data tomorrow.

Chewing the FAT

As explained back in Chapter 2, your disk contains a File Allocation Table (FAT) that keeps track of all the data on your disk. When you delete a file from your disk, the file itself isn't deleted; its FAT entry is simply changed to hide it from view and allow DOS to overwrite its space with new data. So if you can catch things before the old data is overwritten with new data, it's possible to restore the FAT entry and "undelete" the deleted data.

Preparing for Accidents

Some computer users simply aren't aware that they can take precautions to minimize data loss if their systems ever crash. But you *can* make such preparations, most of which require slight effort on your part. With only a little know-how, you can be ready when the worst happens.

One of the most common computer accidents occurs when you inadvertently delete files or reformat disks that contain data. Fortunately, if you have DOS 5 or DOS 6, there are ways to undelete deleted files and unformat reformatted hard and floppy disks.

As you'll learn in Chapter 20, DOS 5 and 6 include commands and utilities that allow this undelete procedure. To ensure complete undelete protection, however, you may need to activate some additional DOS protection.

Undeleting in Windows

Windows without DOS 6

If you're running Windows under an older version of DOS, you may be out of luck. I suggest either upgrading to the most recent version of DOS 6 (which, at this writing, is version 6.22), or investing in a third-party utility program (such as Norton Desktop for Windows or PC Tools for Windows) that includes an undelete utility.

If you're running Windows with DOS 6, Microsoft includes a neat little Windows-based UNDELETE utility. Just open up the Microsoft Tools program group and launch the Microsoft Undelete for Windows applet (by double-clicking on the little trashcan icon). Switch to the directory that holds your deleted file, and then click on the deleted file name. When this file is highlighted, click on the Undelete button. When the Enter First Character dialog box appears, replace the "?" with the real first character of the deleted file's name. When you then click OK, your deleted file will be automatically undeleted.

Undeleting in DOS 6

DOS 6 (and 6.2 and 6.21 and 6.22...) includes an UNDELETE command which lets you undelete recently deleted files. The degree to which UNDELETE is successful, however, depends on which level of protection you choose to implement.

Standard Protection

With Standard Protection, you don't have to do anything beforehand. When you use the UNDELETE command, it simply hunts for recently deleted files and restores their FAT entries. The degree of success depends on whether the deleted data has been overwritten with new data. If so, you're out of luck; if not, UNDELETE can be pretty successful. In addition, it's possible that DOS won't be able to locate the deleted files; after all, their FAT entries have been altered, so it's really a hunt to find recently deleted files.

Delete Tracker

Delete Tracker is a memory-resident utility that stores the location of deleted files in a hidden file called PCTRACKER.DEL. This is preferable to Standard Protection in which the location of deleted files is lost when the FAT entries are changed; with Delete Tracker, DOS always can locate deleted files.

You activate Delete Tracker by adding the following line to your AUTOEXEC.BAT file:

> **UNDELETE /TX**

Note that *X* is the drive you want to monitor. If you want to activate Delete Tracker for drive C, for example, type the following:

> **UNDELETE /TC**

The advantage to Delete Tracker is its added level of protection over Standard Protection. The disadvantages include its use of system memory and its inability to undelete files that have been overwritten with new data.

Delete Sentry

Delete Sentry provides an even greater level of protection than does Delete Tracker. Like Delete Tracker, Delete Sentry is a memory-resident program that loads via your AUTOEXEC.BAT file. Delete Sentry, however, actually creates a *copy* of each deleted file in a hidden directory called SENTRY. This means, in essence, that you really don't delete the file; it just moves into the SENTRY directory.

Delete Sentry flushes the SENTRY directory after it begins to fill up to a certain level. (After SENTRY grows to about 7% of your total hard disk space, Delete Sentry starts to automatically delete files, oldest first.)

To activate Delete Sentry, add the following line to your AUTOEXEC.BAT file:

UNDELETE /S

Which Should You Use?

While Delete Tracker and Delete Sentry may sound like better protection, Standard Protection works just fine 90% of the time—and you don't have to waste valuable memory or disk space waiting to make a delete mistake.

The advantage to Delete Sentry is that you can undelete files even if the original has been completely overwritten with new data. The disadvantages include the use of system memory, the use of large amounts of disk space, and the fact that large files will fill up the SENTRY directory quickly, which could reduce the undeletability of files.

Undeleting in DOS 5

DOS 5 also has an UNDELETE command, although it works a little different from the DOS 6 version. If you don't do anything (the Standard Protection level), UNDELETE simply restores the FAT entries for recently deleted files. DOS 5, however, doesn't have the explicit protection provided by Delete Tracker or Delete Sentry; instead, DOS 5 has a utility called MIRROR. MIRROR is a memory-resident program that keeps track of all files you delete so that they can be reconstructed later if you change your mind about removing them. MIRROR also keeps a spare map of your hard disk's contents so that the disk's structure can be restored in the event of an accidental reformat.

MIRROR Is Only for DOS 5 Users!

Remember, you should only load MIRROR (and you only *have* MIRROR) if you have DOS 5. If you have DOS 4 or before, you don't have any undelete protection, so tough luck. If you have DOS 6, you can use either the Standard Protection, Delete Tracker, or Delete Sentry. So unless you have DOS 5, you can skip this whole bit about MIRROR!

For the best results, you want MIRROR to load into memory every time you start your computer. The easiest way to ensure this is to add to your AUTOEXEC.BAT file a line that loads MIRROR, creates the file MIRROR.FIL for your system's hard disk(s), and initiates delete-tracking for your hard disk(s). If your hard disk is drive C, add the following line to your AUTOEXEC.BAT file:

MIRROR C: /TC

If your system has both a drive C and a drive D containing hard disks, add the following line to your AUTOEXEC.BAT file:

MIRROR C: D: /TC /TD

Now every time you turn on your PC, MIRROR loads and goes about its business, your silent insurance against accidental deleting and reformatting.

Backing Up Your Data

Sometimes, however, all heck breaks loose and your entire hard disk goes kaplooey. To protect yourself from this potential disaster, you need to back up all the files on your hard disk. If you have DOS 6 installed on your machine, you should use the new Microsoft Backup utility—available in

> ### Third-Party Backup Programs
>
> There are several high-quality backup programs available for use with either DOS or Windows. These include Norton Backup (also included in Norton Desktop), Central Point Backup, and FastBack. All these programs are available in either full-blown Windows versions or regular old DOS versions, and they let you perform backups with even more sophistication than Microsoft Backup allows.

both DOS and Windows versions. If you have DOS 5 or earlier, you should use the DOS-based BACKUP command. And, in any case, you have the option of using a third-party backup program.

Backing Up with Microsoft Backup

DOS 6 includes versions of Microsoft Backup for both DOS and Windows. Microsoft Backup is a utility that lets you back up all or selected files from your hard disk to floppy disks. It copies selected data on your hard disk to a series of backup disks. To fit this data on as few disks as possible (and speed up the backup process as well), Microsoft Backup stores the backup data in a special *compressed format*. When you want to transfer the data from the floppies back to your hard disk, you must decompress the backed-up data by using the restore options of Microsoft Backup, as described in Chapter 6.

Just like Norton

Microsoft Backup is actually a program that Microsoft licensed from Symantec, the publisher of Norton Backup. In fact, Microsoft Backup is simply a subset of Norton Backup. If Microsoft Backup does everything you need it to do—great! If you long for more versatility and/or complexity, go out and buy Norton Backup, for either Windows or DOS. They both work pretty much the same.

Launching Microsoft Backup—for DOS and Windows

To launch Microsoft Backup for DOS, type the following at the DOS prompt:

MSBACKUP

To launch the Windows version of Backup, simply open the Microsoft Tools program group and double-click on the Microsoft Backup for Windows icon.

Microsoft Backup Is Different from the BACKUP Command

Backups created with Microsoft Backup use a different backup format than those created with the DOS RESTORE command, so you can't use RESTORE to restore backups created with Microsoft Backup.

Different Types of Backups

Once Microsoft Backup is launched, you see the main Backup screen, which looks more or less the same in DOS or Windows. (The Windows screen is pictured here.) From here you can determine what kind of backup you want to make, as well as where you want to back up.

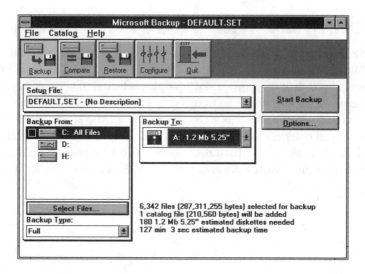

There are three types of backup available with Microsoft Backup. These are:

- *Full*, where all selected files are backed up.

- *Incremental*, where only those files created or changed from the last full or incremental backup are backed up.

- *Differential*, where only those files created or changed from the last full backup are backed up.

For our purposes, we focus on the full and differential backups. You need to perform a full backup at least once a week, to protect all the data on your hard disk. You should also perform a differential backup daily, to protect those files you created or changed since your last weekly full backup.

Backing Up Your Data

To use Microsoft Backup to create a full backup, follow these simple steps:

> ### Partially Backing Up
>
> Microsoft Backup lets you back up only selected files, if you so wish. For creating a PC Survival Kit, however, you definitely want to back up all the files on your hard disk, so we'll just ignore that Select Files button, okay?

1. Click on the Backup button.

2. Make sure that DEFAULT.SET is selected in the Setup File box.

3. Select the drive to back up from the Backup From list.

4. In the Backup Type box, select Full.

5. Use the Backup To box to select which drive you're backing up.

6. Click the Start Backup button to begin the backup.

To create a differential backup, follow all the preceding steps except step 4. In Step 4, select Differential from the Backup Type box.

Once Microsoft Backup starts the backup operation, you'll be prompted to insert blank disks in the selected disk drive. When the backup is complete, you see an on-screen message to that effect; you can then close Microsoft Backup and put your disks away for safe keeping.

Backing Up from the DOS Prompt

If you're using a version of DOS prior to DOS 6 (and you're not using a third-party Windows backup program, such as Norton Backup or FastBack), you'll need to use the standard DOS BACKUP command. It's not as fancy as DOS 6's Microsoft Backup, but it gets the job done.

At the DOS prompt, invoke the BACKUP command to initiate the backup operation. Like Microsoft Backup, BACKUP copies selected data on your hard disk to a series of disks. BACKUP, however, uses a different type of compression than Microsoft Backup, so you can't use Microsoft Backup to restore files backed up with BACKUP. When you want to transfer the data from the floppies back to your hard disk, you must decompress the backed-up data by using another DOS command called RESTORE, which is discussed in Chapter 6.

The BACKUP command, like most DOS commands, lets you add *switches* to the main command that varies its operation. These switches are simply letters preceded by a backslash, and are entered on the same line as the main command. So to back up all the files on your hard disk (drive C) to floppy disks in drive A, type the following command at the DOS prompt:

BACKUP C: A: /S

To back up your files to drive B instead of drive A, issue this command at the DOS prompt:

BACKUP C: B: /S

To create a differential backup, you need to add a few more switches to the main command. So to make a differential backup from drive C to drive A, issue this command at the DOS prompt:

BACKUP C: A: /S /M /A

This type of differential backup adds newly backed-up files to existing backup disks. It's recommended that you use one set of disks for full-disk backups and another set for all your differential backups.

Miller's Recommended Backup Procedure

I recommend that you initiate a backup schedule that involves a full-disk backup once a week, and differential backups on the remaining days. The procedure is simple:

1. On day one, perform a full-disk backup.

2. On days two through seven, perform only differential backups of any files that have been modified or added that day, using the same set of differential backup disks each day.

3. On day eight, start the process over again with another full-disk backup.

This procedure offers you the benefit of a full-disk backup on a weekly basis, while protecting modified or new files daily. If you follow this procedure, you'll never lose more than a day's worth of data in the event of a hard disk disaster.

Making a PC Survival Kit

Every smart computer user keeps a PC Survival Kit close at hand, just in case a computer emergency does develop. The contents of such a kit often are indispensable if you are to recover your data after a complete or partial hard disk crash. Thus, I consider these items to be required accessories for every PC user. You probably already have most of these components, and I'm going to show you how to complete your kit.

PC Survival Kit

- Original software disks and documentation
- Copies of software disks
- Set of data backup disks
- Disk utility software
- Bootable Emergency Disks

The most important ingredient in your PC Survival Kit is your set of original software disks and their duplicates. Always keep all your original software, along with the original documentation. And always make copies of your original disks. These copies serve in place of the originals if the latter are damaged or lost. Store both the originals and the copies in a safe place, along with the rest of your PC Survival Kit.

Copying your original software disks is easy: DOS includes a special DISKCOPY command that copies entire disks at once. To use DISKCOPY, type the following command at the DOS prompt:

DISKCOPY A: A:

Accept No Substitutes!

You can use the DISKCOPY command only with disks of exactly the same size and density. You cannot use DISKCOPY to copy data from 3 1/2-inch disks to 5 1/4-inch disks, for example, or to copy data from low-density to high-density disks.

(This particular syntax applies, of course, only if you place your software disks in drive A; if you use drive B, type B instead of A in the command.)

After you type the DISKCOPY command with its correct syntax, DOS prompts you to insert the source disk (your original software disk) into drive A. A few minutes later, DOS prompts you to insert the target disk into drive A. When this message appears, remove the original disk and insert a blank, formatted disk into drive A.

Chunky Style

DOS requires you to insert and reinsert the source and target disks when using DISKCOPY because only part of the original disk's data can be stored in system memory at one time. DOS essentially copies your disk in "chunks"; the more memory your PC has, the larger the chunks—and the less frequently you have to swap disks.

Your machine then whirrs and clicks for a while and, at last, DOS requests the source disk again. Remove the (formerly) blank disk from drive A and reinsert your original software disk. After more whirring and clicking, DOS again requests that the target disk be placed into drive A.

Continue to follow DOS's prompts; this insertion-removal-reinsertion process goes on until all the data on the source disk is copied to the target disk. After the procedure is complete, remove the target disk and label it as Copy #1 of your software disk.

Backup Disks

The next most important part of your PC Survival Kit—after your original program disks and copies—is your set of weekly backup disks. This includes (per Miller's Recommended Backup Procedure) both the full weekly backups and the incremental daily backups.

Useful Disk Utilities

Now, if you really want to play it safe, include in your survival kit at least one third-party disk utility program. These programs—such as Norton Utilities and PC Tools Deluxe—contain utilities that enable you to repair most of the damage your hard disk may incur. My own favorite utility is the Norton Disk Doctor, which comes with Norton Utilities. This useful little program analyzes your hard disk for any damage and even repairs the damage it discovers. I consider the Disk Doctor an excellent addition to anyone's PC Survival Kit.

The Bootable Emergency Disk

The final component of your PC Survival Kit is a Bootable Emergency Disk. You can use such a disk to boot your computer in the event of total hard disk failure. Include on your emergency disk all those essential DOS utilities necessary to get your system up and running after any hard disk catastrophe.

How DOS Gets Started

To create your Bootable Emergency Diskette, you must format a disk so that it can "boot" your computer. (Booting is just a fancy name for starting your system.) To understand how booting works, you must understand what happens when you first turn on your computer.

After you turn on your computer, the system immediately tries to read from drive A. If a disk is in drive A, DOS tries to boot from this disk. If a normal disk (that is, a nonbootable one) is in the drive, DOS finds no system files on the disk, and the following error message appears:

```
Non-System disk or disk error
Replace and press any key when ready
```

If you receive this message on start-up, remove the nonbootable disk from drive A and press any key to restart the system.

If drive A is empty, DOS proceeds to your hard disk, drive C, and searches for the system files it needs to start itself. After DOS locates these files, it executes the commands contained within the CONFIG.SYS file and the AUTOEXEC.BAT file.

If your hard disk is inaccessible (due to some sort of hard disk error or failure) and drive A is empty, your system doesn't start at all. And, if your computer won't start, all your valuable data is suddenly inaccessible. This nonevent is known as "the big one," and it is not a pleasant experience— unless you have a Bootable Emergency Disk ready.

Creating the Bootable Emergency Disk

What makes a disk bootable? The presence of two hidden DOS system files. You can add these hidden files to your drive A disk during the formatting procedure.

To do so, insert a blank disk of the correct density into drive A. If you're using Windows, launch the File Manager, pull down the **D**isk menu, and select **Format Disk**. When the Format Disk dialog box appears, select the proper drive and capacity, and make sure you check the **Make System Disk** option. When you click OK, Windows will create a formatted bootable diskette.

If you don't have Windows, you can create this disk by typing the following command at the DOS prompt:

FORMAT A:/S

The /S switch places the hidden DOS system files onto the disk during formatting so that it can boot your system from drive A.

What To Place on the Bootable Emergency Disk

Unfortunately, simply making a disk bootable doesn't help if you can't access the DOS files and utilities on drive C. Therefore, you must copy several important DOS files onto your Bootable Emergency Disk.

The following files, located in your DOS directory, are necessary for emergency DOS operation:

CHKDSK.EXE	Provides vital information about your hard disk.
COMMAND.COM	The DOS command interpreter, necessary for any DOS operation.
FDISK.EXE	Used before a hard disk is formatted to prepare it to accept DOS.
FORMAT.COM	Reformats a bad hard disk.
MSBACKUP.EXE	The Microsoft Backup program (only available with DOS 6).
RESTORE.EXE	Restores backed-up data to a hard disk.
SYS.COM	Places system files on a formatted hard disk.
UNDELETE.EXE	Undeletes accidentally deleted files.
UNFORMAT.COM	Unformats an accidental hard disk format.

To place these files on your Bootable Emergency Diskette from Windows, launch the File Manager, highlight the files in the file window, pull down the **File** menu, and select **Copy**. When the Copy dialog box appears, type **A:** in the **To** edit box, and then click OK.

If you don't have Windows, issue the following commands from the DOS prompt (if necessary, replacing A with B, for drive B):

COPY C: \DOS\CHKDSK.EXE A:

COPY C: \DOS\COMMAND.COM A:

COPY C: \DOS\FDISK.EXE A:

COPY C: \DOS\FORMAT.COM A:

COPY C: \DOS\MSBACKUP.EXE A:

COPY C: \DOS\RESTORE.EXE A:

COPY C: \DOS\SYS.COM A:

COPY C: \DOS\UNDELETE.EXE A:

COPY C: \DOS\UNFORMAT.COM A:

After you finish copying these programs to your Bootable Emergency Diskette, your PC Survival Kit has a floppy that can actually get your system back up and running if "the big one" ever hits your system. Remove the disk from your computer and label it, and then put it in a safe (but handy!) place in case you ever need it.

> **Protect Your Disk!**
>
> For an added level of protection, you should write-protect your Bootable Emergency Disk. If you have a 5 1/4-inch disk, use a little patch of tape to cover up the notch on the top right edge of the disk. If you have a 3 1/2-inch disk, slide the little plastic tab on the lower left corner of the disk down, making a new opening. These procedures make your disk read-only, meaning that you can't accidentally erase your valuable files!

The Last Word on Your PC Survival Kit

Okay. You now have your PC Survival Kit, complete with original program disk (and copies), weekly and daily backup disk, your favorite disk utilities, and your Bootable Emergency Disk. So how exactly do you use this kit to save your system if "the big one" hits? To find out, read the next chapter, "Recovering When 'The Big One' Hits."

Recovering When "The Big One" Hits

When I talk about "the big one," I'm not talking about President Clinton, Elvis, or the Pope; I'm talking about that rarest of situations—when your hard disk completely and irrevocably shuts down.

Dead.

Kaput.

Deceased.

Not working at all.

As you can guess, this isn't a desirable situation. So what do you do? Well, begin by turning the page, and I'll tell you what to do when you have a "late" computer.

Don't Panic!

The first thing to remember when your hard disk dies is—*don't panic!* If you followed the precautions advised in Chapter 7, you have every reason to believe that you can at least partially, if not completely, recover your important data. (Of course, if you *didn't* follow these precautions, then my advice is—*panic!*)

But how exactly do you know that you're facing "the big one" and not another, lesser catastrophe? Check for one of the following symptoms; either is a dead giveaway—and I *do* mean *dead!*

Bad Disk Symptoms

When Death Is Near

In some instances, you may get warning signs that your hard disk is about to go south. If your hard disk begins to run slower and slower, for example, or starts sending you too many error messages, or no longer copies data the way it used to, the poor thing is probably on its deathbed. If you think your hard disk may be about to give up the ghost, back up all your data and then put in an emergency call to your local repair center.

If your computer doesn't boot correctly—if, in fact, it can't even access your hard disk—you'll notice one of two symptoms. Symptom One is that nothing happens—nothing at all. You have a blank screen, no lights and no noises, and your system just sits there like Monty Python's proverbial dead Norwegian Blue parrot, with its claws nailed to the perch. (Not a pleasant thought, eh?)

Symptom Two is that your system tries to start but then displays one of the following error messages:

```
Bad or Missing Command Interpreter

Cannot load COMMAND, system halted

Cannot read file allocation table

Disk boot failure

Error loading operating system

File allocation table bad, drive C

Abort, Retry, Fail?
```

```
Invalid COMMAND.COM, system halted

Missing operating system

No system on default drive

Non-System disk or disk error

Replace and strike any key when ready
```

If you receive one of these error messages, take a look at ten actions you can try to get your system up and running again. (And if you want more information on DOS error messages, see Chapter 28, "DOS Error Messages…What They Mean and How To Deal with Them.")

10 Actions To Try

Any number of problems can cause your system not to boot. Fortunately, a set of procedures exists that you can undertake either to resurrect your system or at least to help you diagnose the exact nature of your problem. In order, then, try the following:

1. *Make sure that everything is plugged in and turned on.* Possibly, your system is actually booting, but your monitor isn't working. Trust me, I've seen it happen.

2. *Try booting again.* That's right. Turn your system off and then back on again. Don't ask why, but sometimes this fixes things.

3. *Make sure that a nonbootable disk is not in drive A.* If you have this problem, remove the disk and reboot your system by pressing **Ctrl+Alt+Del**.

4. *Make sure that the bootable disk in drive A is inserted correctly and the disk drive latch is closed.* Fix the problem and reboot your system by pressing **Ctrl+Alt+Del**.

5. *If your hard disk still doesn't boot, insert your Bootable Emergency Disk (explained in Chapter 5) into drive A and restart your system.* Once your system boots from this disk, type the following command to copy a fresh version of the command interpreter to your hard disk:

    COPY A:\COMMAND.COMC:\DOS\COMMAND.COM

Some systems have COMMAND.COM in the root directory. If the preceding command does not work, type

COPY A:\COMMAND.COM C:\COMMAND.COM.

If your system reboots, you could be home safe. Remove the disk from drive A and reboot your system by pressing **Ctrl+Alt+Del.**

6. *If an error message tells you that you can't copy COMMAND.COM to your hard disk, or if suggestion 5 doesn't get you up and running, you may have a completely trashed hard disk.* Try using the DIR command to see what, if anything, is left on drive C. From the Bootable Emergency Disk, type

DIR C:

If you get an error message, you probably have a damaged hard disk. If you don't get an error message, but no files are listed, something has erased the files from your hard disk.

7. *If your hard disk is undamaged but empty, you may have accidentally formatted the hard disk.* Try using the UNFORMAT command from the Bootable Emergency Disk by typing

UNFORMAT C:

If your disk was accidentally formatted, this command unformats it. Just follow the directions on-screen to complete the procedure.

8. *If your hard disk was not accidentally formatted, something else wiped the disk clean.* (This something could be a computer virus, a vengeful ex-employee, or some other fiend out to destroy your data.) To get your hard disk back to normal, you first need to add the DOS system files to your hard disk. From the Bootable Emergency Disk, type

SYS C:

You then need to restore the backed-up files to your hard disk, as described in "Restoring Backup Data," later in this chapter.

9. *If your disk is actually damaged, try to reformat the disk and restore your data files.* This procedure is described later in this chapter.

10. *If you can't reformat your disk, or if you continue to encounter problems after reformatting, you probably have more serious hard disk problems.* You may need to consult a computer repair technician.

Recovering from Disaster

All right, if you have tried some or all of the 10 Actions To Try, and you've come to the conclusion that your hard disk is toast, stay calm. Before you call in the pros, you can try rebuilding your disk yourself.

Sounds Easy—Not!

Okay, so rebuilding a hard disk really doesn't sound that easy. If you're not comfortable doing it yourself, that's okay too. Besides, you should only try rebuilding your hard disk if you're extremely confident of your skills and if you have a complete set of recent backup disks. If you don't want to do it yourself—or if you don't have backup disks—you should take your entire system to a qualified computer technician, who may be able to salvage most or all of your data through professional means. Remember, if you try to do it yourself and screw up, there's a very good chance that not even the best technician in the world can recover any of your data without the use of backup disks!

Rebuilding Your Hard Disk

The procedure of rebuilding a damaged hard disk includes two required steps and one optional step. The required steps can be accomplished by anyone familiar with DOS commands. The optional step, which I'll discuss first, requires the use of a third-party disk utility.

Using Third-Party Utilities

Before you rebuild your disk, you may want to check the disk itself for physical damage and fix that damage, if possible. Unfortunately, DOS can't do either. You need a third-party utility package, such as Norton Disk Doctor (included with Norton Utilities). Running a program

Do It By the Book

All this partitioning and formatting business can get kind of complicated, especially with any version of DOS prior to DOS 4. (If you have one of these older versions, save yourself some hassles and upgrade to the latest version of DOS—version 6.22.) If you're really intent on using FDISK yourself (rather than letting a pro do it), check out Que's *Using MS-DOS 6.2,* Special Edition, for more detailed instructions and information.

such as Norton Disk Doctor locates and fixes (if possible) any physical damage to your hard disk. If you don't have access to a copy of Norton Disk Doctor, or you feel uncomfortable with this level of complexity, the time to call a professional technician has arrived.

Preparing Your Disk with FDISK

If you have DOS 4 or above, you can prepare your hard disk by typing the following command from your Bootable Emergency Disk to partition your hard disk:

FDISK

If you have an older version of DOS, you need to divide it into partitions. I'm not going to go into all that, however, because **YOU OUGHT TO HAVE A NEWER VERSION OF DOS!** (Okay?)

Formatting Your Hard Disk

After your hard disk has been partitioned with FDISK, you're ready to format it. The command is straightforward, and you use the /S switch to add DOS system files to the disk. Just type

FORMAT C: /S

You'll be prompted that all data on the drive will be lost, and you'll answer Y to proceed with the format. When the format is complete, DOS displays the following message:

Wipe Out!

Don't type the FORMAT /S command if your hard disk is functioning normally and contains data. This command wipes out any data present on the disk and should be used only in an emergency.

```
Format complete
```

Then the system files are transferred to the hard disk, and DOS displays this message:

```
System Transferred
```

Next, you are prompted to supply a name for your disk by the following message:

```
Volume label (11 characters, ENTER for none)?
```

If you don't want to name your disk, just press Enter. If you do want to assign a name to your disk, type a name of no more than 11 characters and then press Enter.

Finally, DOS displays a report showing the disk space formatted, the bytes used by the system files, any defective sectors, and the number of bytes available on the disk.

> **When Bad Sectors Are Okay**
>
> Don't get upset if DOS reports that your disk has defective sectors. Almost all disks do, and during formatting, DOS marks these sectors as unusable and avoids them in future operations, so they're no threat to the operation of your system.

After your hard disk is formatted, you can restore your backed-up data with Microsoft Backup or the RESTORE command, as discussed next.

Restoring Backup Data

You don't need to reformat your hard disk in order to restore backed-up data. You can restore files from your backup disks at any time, for any reason. (In fact, you don't even have to restore your entire hard disk—you can restore data one file at a time if you want to!)

Whether you used Microsoft Backup or the RESTORE command, your backup files are in a compressed format that is unreadable and unusable by DOS and your software programs. In order to use these files, you must restore them to their native format.

Using Microsoft Backup for DOS

Whether you backed up your data with Microsoft Backup for Windows or Microsoft Windows for DOS (both included with DOS 6), you need to restore the data using Microsoft Backup for DOS. (Naturally, if you can't access your hard disk, you can't start Windows, which means you can't use Microsoft Backup for Windows.) If you followed my recommendations back in Chapter 7, you have a copy of Microsoft Backup for DOS on your Emergency Backup Disk.

To start Microsoft Backup for DOS, issue the following command at the DOS prompt:

    MSBACKUP

When the main Microsoft Backup screen appears, select the Restore option. This displays the Restore screen, which you use to restore your backed-up files.

If you followed Miller's Recommended Backup Procedure in Chapter 7, you have both a full weekly backup set and a differential daily backup set. You need to use both sets to restore data to your hard disk.

Begin with the full weekly backup set. Insert the first disk from this set, and then set the Restore From setting to the proper disk drive, and the Restore To setting for Original Locations. You also need to select a Backup Set Catalog (essentially the name of the backup set); if you can't remember or find the right name, just select the DEFAULT.CAT option. Now you can select the Start Restore option, and Microsoft Backup begins the restoration procedure. The program prompts you to insert each backup disk, in order. Microsoft Backup also displays the progress of the restore operation and notifies you when it's done.

Next, you'll want to restore the files on your differential backup disks. Simply follow the above procedure, but use the differential backup disks. When you're finished, your entire hard disk is back in the same condition it was in right before your last backup.

Using the RESTORE Command

If you backed up your data with the BACKUP command (from the DOS prompt), you need to use the RESTORE command to restore the data. (You can't use Microsoft Backup for DOS—or Windows—to restore backups made with the BACKUP command.)

Begin with your full weekly backup set. Insert the first disk from the set, and type

RESTORE A: C: /S /N

When this operation is completed, you can restore the files from your differential backup set. Just insert the first disk from your differential backup set, and type

RESTORE A: C: /M /S

It's a Switch!

DOS commands can often perform variations of their basic functions. These variations are turned on and off by switches, which appear after the command—but on the same line—and are preceded by the backslash (/) character. So if you look at the two RESTORE operations described above, you'll see different switches used in each operation, because restoring a differential backup is slightly different from restoring a full backup, at least as far as DOS is concerned.

Turning to Professional Help

When all else fails, don't be embarrassed about turning to a pro for help if need be. A qualified computer technician often stands a better chance of fixing your system and restoring your data after a major disk disaster than you do.

If you try and try and try again and still can't bring your hard disk back from the dead, then by all means call someone who gets paid to do the dirty work.

Recovering from "The Big One"

As you can see, some actions you can take when your hard disk crashes are easy, and others require somewhat more expertise. The main point to remember is not to attempt anything you're uncomfortable with. You can always take your backup disks and your system to a qualified computer technician to do the work for you. And if you take the precautions advised back in Chapter 7, there's every reason to believe you can recover—even from "the big one."

Okay, this chapter covered the computer mega-disaster. Time now to turn to a multitude of micro-menaces. The next chapter, then, gives you some clues on how to immunize your computer system against the threat of those nasty little germs we call computer viruses.

Germ Warfare— Protecting Your Computer from Viruses

It's dirty work down in the trenches—the trenches of computer germ warfare. You have to engage in hand-to-hand combat to eliminate the dangers of a computer virus.

These viruses are nasty opponents. They may sound benign, with names like Michelangelo, Stoned, Joshi, and Jerusalem-B. But they can stop your system dead in its tracks, and you can get them anywhere you get regular computer programs.

Computer viruses are not the figment of some computer geek's imagination. They're all too real, and they can cause real damage to your computer system. You must protect your system from the danger they pose—or run the risk of catastrophic system failure and data loss.

What Is a Computer Virus?

A *computer virus* actually is similar in many ways to a biological virus. A biological virus invades your body's system and replicates itself; likewise, a computer virus invades your computer's system and also replicates itself. Computer viruses can be destructive (like the AIDS virus) or simply annoying (like any of several viruses that cause the common cold). Just as you try to protect your own body from biological viruses and find a cure when you become infected, you want to protect your computer from computer viruses and find a cure if its system ever becomes infected.

Unlike biological viruses, a computer virus is not alive (although it may seem like it if one of the pesky things manages to infest your computer). A virus is actually a rogue computer program that injects copies of itself into other programs on your computer system. Most viruses do not infect mere data files (such as word processing documents and spreadsheets). Instead, they invade executable program and system files—the very heart of your computer system. Some viruses merely display an annoying message on your screen; other more deadly viruses actually destroy your software programs or system information. The worst of this loathsome bunch are difficult both to detect and dislodge because they craftily conceal themselves from observation and doggedly defend against removal.

How Viruses Work

A computer virus is actually nothing more than a computer program that places copies of itself in other programs on your system. Most viruses infect program files; data files are rarely infected. Literally thousands of different viruses have been detected to date, and most fall into one of two categories: *file-infecting viruses* and *boot-infecting viruses*.

File-Infecting Viruses

A *file-infecting virus* infects executable program files (those with EXE, COM, SYS, OVL, and DRV extensions). Some viruses damage these files permanently by overwriting sections of the program's code. Other more insidious viruses actually attach themselves to the program's code, allowing the program itself to continue functioning while the virus itself courses its destructive way through other files by using the system's memory as its pipeline.

Fortunately, most file-infecting viruses can be removed without causing irreparable damage to your original program files. In addition, few file-infecting viruses cause damage to your disk's system areas.

Boot-Infecting Viruses

The second type of virus is much more dangerous than the file-infecting variety. The *boot-infecting virus* damages or even replaces the system files that your computer uses to boot up when you first turn it on. These viruses can actually prevent your system from starting up—or at the very least keep you from accessing information on your hard disk.

These viruses are not easily removed from your system. While some anti-virus utilities (including the Microsoft Anti-Virus utility that comes with DOS 6) can remove some boot-infecting viruses, there are instances where the only way to rid your system of the virus is to completely reformat your hard disk—losing at least some of your data in the process.

Common Virus Symptoms

How do you know whether your computer system has been infected with a virus? You may notice one or more of the following symptoms:

- Strange messages appear on your monitor screen, such as

  `You've been stoned.`

- Strange graphics appear on your monitor screen, such as bouncing balls or a simulation of your screen "melting."

- Strange noises ("beeps," "boops," "squeals," "phffts," and so on) emanate from your computer speaker.

- Normally well-behaved programs start operating erratically or crash intermittently.

- Files you know you haven't erased turn up missing.

- Common program files appear to have grown in size since your last analysis.

- Your system begins to act sluggish.

- Your system fails to boot.

If your computer exhibits one or more of these symptoms—and if you have recently engaged in behavior conducive to contracting a virus (see the next section)—the prognosis is not good: it may very well be infected.

How To Catch a Virus

Home Alone

If by chance you do operate a completely isolated computer, never sharing disks or using modems, you're probably pretty safe from viruses. So if I were you, I wouldn't get overly concerned about all the warnings and advice in this chapter—unless, of course, you change your computing habits.

Whenever you share data with another computer or computer user, you risk exposing your computer to potential viruses. When you use a disk given to you by another user, you take the chance that the disk harbors a virus. If you use a modem to download programs from a BBS, an on-line service, or from the Internet, you're tacitly accepting the risk that this data could transmit a virus to your computer. In fact, even when you load a brand-new, shrink-wrapped piece of software onto your computer system (after removing the shrink wrap, of course), you should be aware that it's possible—if unlikely—for even this new, direct-from-the-factory software to carry a virus! Egads! Is *nothing* safe?

Practicing Safe Computing

Is It Safe?

Is it possible to completely protect your system against computer viruses? Unfortunately, the answer is no—unless you never add another piece of software (even new software) to your system, never accept disks from strangers, and never communicate via modem with other computer users. The reality is that computer viruses are created by evil people with destruction on their minds, and—just like real-world terrorism—it is impossible to completely guard against these random acts of computing terrorism. That doesn't mean you have to live the rest of your computing life in fear, but it does mean you should take whatever precautions are prudent to reduce your risk factors.

If you live in the real world, you can't be 100 percent safe from the threat of computer viruses. You can, however, take three steps to reduce the risk associated with these havoc-inducing programs.

1. *Share disks only with users you know and trust.* If you don't know where a disk comes from, don't stick it in your disk drive.

2. *Download programs only from reliable sources.* If you're connecting for the first time to an anonymous BBS run out of some guy's basement, avoid the temptation to download files until you're comfortable you're dealing with a reputable service. Otherwise,

use reliable on-line services (such as CompuServe or America OnLine) or established sites on the Internet.

3. *Use anti-virus software.* If you have DOS 6, use Microsoft Anti-Virus. If you have a previous version of DOS, buy a third-party package like Norton Anti-Virus or Central Point Anti-Virus. And once you buy them, install them and *use them.*

These three precautions, taken together, should provide good insurance against the threat of computer viruses.

A Shot of Protection

Anti-virus software programs are capable of detecting known viruses and protecting your system against new, unknown viruses. DOS 6 includes a new utility—Microsoft Anti-Virus—that comes in both DOS and Windows versions to protect your system against viruses.

About Microsoft Anti-Virus

Microsoft Anti-Virus is a new utility included with DOS 6. In essence, a subset of the Central Point Anti-Virus commercial program, Microsoft Anti-Virus can detect and remove 1,000 different file- and boot-infecting computer viruses from your system. The program also allows you to view a list of the viruses it protects against and update the list to include newly discovered viruses.

To launch Microsoft Anti-Virus for Windows, simply double-click on the Anti-Virus icon in the Microsoft Tools program group.

To launch Microsoft Anti-Virus for DOS, type the following command at the DOS prompt:

> **DOS or Windows?**
>
> Which version of Microsoft Anti-Virus should you use—DOS or Windows? Well, if you have Windows, use the Windows version; if you don't have Windows, use the DOS version. They both operate pretty much the same, although the Windows version is prettier.

MSAV

Working with the Virus List

Key to the operation of Microsoft Anti-Virus is the virus list. This list is sorted by virus name and tells you other names the virus may be known by, the type of virus, the size of the virus code itself, and the number of known variants of the virus.

Updating the Virus List

You can update the virus list by obtaining new virus list files directly from Central Point Software. You can obtain these files from Central Point's BBS (503-690-2660), or from the Central Point forum on CompuServe.

To examine the virus list, pull down the Scan menu and select the Virus List option. When the Virus List window appears, you can scroll through the list of viruses to find the virus you're interested in. To see more detailed information on any specific virus, select the virus name in the virus list and then click the Info button. This displays the Information About Virus window, which informs you about how the selected virus works and what side effects it creates.

Scanning and Removing Viruses

It's pretty much a one-button operation to use Microsoft Anti-Virus to scan your system for viruses and eliminate any found viruses. From the main Anti-Virus window, just click on the drive or drives you wish to scan, and then click on the Detect and Clean button. Microsoft Anti-Virus then scans every directory and file on your hard disk, comparing its findings with its list of known viruses.

If a virus is found, Microsoft Anti-Virus displays a dialog box that asks if you want to clean the infected file. You then can elect to clean the virus from the file, ignore the infected file, stop the scan, or delete the infected file from your system. In the instance where a virus has actually destroyed a file, Microsoft Anti-Virus displays a message to that effect, as well. When the scanning is finished, a screen is displayed that informs you of your system's viral status.

It's as simple as that—click a button and check your system for viruses. If you engage in any behavior that may expose your computer to viruses, it's worth a minute or two to check your system with Microsoft Anti-Virus.

Background Protection with VSafe

There is an additional utility included with DOS 6 that monitors your system for any activity that may indicate a virus infection. VSafe is a DOS-based program that

When Files Are Damaged

If a virus has actually damaged a file, you need to delete the damaged file from your disk and then restore a copy of that file—either from your backup disks or the original program disks.

loads into memory to detect any suspicious program behavior. If suspicious behavior is detected, VSafe displays a warning message.

It's a bit of a hassle to load VSafe since both a DOS and Windows component must be loaded (if you're running Windows). So, follow these steps carefully to get it right the first time.

No StartUp Group?

If you're using a version of Windows prior to version 3.1, you don't have the StartUp group option. Instead, you need to add the following line to the beginning of your WIN.INI file:

    LOAD=MWAVTSR.EXE

First, edit your AUTOEXEC.BAT file to add the following line:

VSAFE

Next, if you're running Windows, add the VSafe Manager icon (found in the Microsoft Tools program group) to the

When Anti-Virus Software Doesn't Work

There are some viruses that even VSafe and Microsoft Anti-Virus can't protect you against. These insidious infectors destroy the boot sector of your hard disk, making it impossible for your system to start and, in essence, erasing your entire hard disk. If you're unfortunate enough to be hit by one of these monsters, your only option is to reformat your hard disk and restore all data from your backup diskettes.

StartUp program group. (Any icon included in the StartUp group automatically loads any time Windows is started.)

After these changes have been made, reboot your computer. Now every time you start your computer, your system will be protected from any new viruses not listed in Microsoft Anti-Virus' virus list.

The Final Word on Computer Viruses

If you're a serious computer user, you must use some type of anti-virus software, whether that be Microsoft Anti-Virus or some third-party program. Otherwise, if you share any data at all with other users, it's dead certain that your system will become infected at some point in time. Don't take that risk—protect your computer from this all-too-real electronic menace.

Well, that about does it for the "preventive medicine" part of this book. I hope you picked up a few tips that will help you avoid some problems in the future. The next section helps you get started figuring out how to fix a variety of Windows problems. Good luck!

Figuring Out What Went Wrong

Your System Won't Start

You're all ready to start computing. Your desk is clean, your chair is positioned *just right*, your mouse is all warmed up, you've just loaded some cool tunes in your CD player, you turn that big power switch *on*, and then...

Nothing.

Nothing at all.

Your computer is dead, dead, dead. It just sits there, like a big, beige, beached whale, refusing to start.

Well, before you panic and do something stupid (like throw your PC out the window!), turn the page and let me tell you how to get your system up and running.

What Happens When You Turn On Your Computer

So what happens when you first turn on your computer? What complex chain of events is initiated when you flip your power switch to the "on" position?

Getting the Boot

Computer buffs never can use simple, understandable names for common procedures. For example, computer buffs never "turn on" their computers; they "boot" their computers. The term *boot* comes from the old expression "pulling yourself up by your own bootstraps." (I don't know why, but it does.)

The first thing that happens is that power is sent through the PC's power supply to the boards in the system unit. This initial power surge (called a *power-on reset*) resets your system's memory, microprocessor, and other electronics. Then your system, using instructions stored in a special battery-powered memory called CMOS RAM, does a power-on self-test. During this test, you see some messages scroll down your screen, letting you know how much RAM is available and that the system checks out as expected.

DoubleSpace Makes It More Complicated

If you're using DOS 6.0 or 6.2's DoubleSpace (or DOS 6.22's DriveSpace) disk compression (not available with DOS 6.21!), DOS looks for a third system file, labeled DBLSPACE.BIN. This file controls the hidden file that functions as your compressed drive; if this file isn't found, your computer thinks the compressed drive no longer exists.

After the self-test, your computer tries to access drive A, looking for a bootable disk. A bootable disk, as explained in Chapter 7, contains two important system files necessary for your system to operate. (These files, IO.SYS and MSDOS.SYS, are hidden files, which aren't displayed in a normal directory listing.) If a bootable disk is in drive A, your system proceeds; if not, it defaults to drive C to look for the system files.

What's a Device Driver?

Device drivers are small files that are loaded into memory so your system can operate system peripherals and devices. For example, to manage your system's high memory area (HMA), you need to load the HIMEM.SYS driver. Device drivers are loaded through either the CONFIG.SYS or AUTOEXEC.BAT files.

When your computer accesses drive C, its system reads into memory the contents of the disk's *boot sector*, which tells the system how to load the operating system. The system loads the operating system (DOS) and looks for the CONFIG.SYS file, which should be located in the disk's root, or home, directory.

If CONFIG.SYS is present, your system loads the file and carries out any instructions specified by it. CONFIG.SYS is one of two start-up files (the other being AUTOEXEC.BAT) which typically contain several lines of commands that load device drivers into system memory and set various system configuration options. The CONFIG.SYS file is executed one line at a time, and if you look closely and don't blink, you'll see each line flash across your screen as it executes.

A typical CONFIG.SYS file might look something like this:

```
DEVICE=C:\WINDOWS\HIMEM.SYS
FILES=60
BUFFERS=20
LASTDRIVE=E
SHELL=C:\DOS\COMMAND.COM C:\DOS\ /E:256 /p
STACKS=9,256
```

After loading CONFIG.SYS, your system locates the COMMAND.COM file and loads it into memory. COMMAND.COM is the DOS *command interpreter*, and takes control of your system as soon as COMMAND.COM is loaded.

The command interpreter then locates and runs the AUTOEXEC.BAT file, which should also be in the disk's root directory. AUTOEXEC.BAT is similar to CONFIG.SYS in that it contains several lines of commands that load devices, start programs, and set system parameters. AUTOEXEC.BAT, like CONFIG.SYS, is executed one line at a time, and as each line is executed, it flashes across the screen. A typical AUTOEXEC.BAT file might look like this:

```
PATH C:\;C:\DOS;C:\WINDOWS;C:\BATCH;C:\UTILITY
PROMPT $P$G
C:\WINDOWS\MOUSE.COM /Y /S
SET DIRCMD=/P /O:EN
CD\
CLS
```

Taking Command

Don't even ask what all these commands mean; that's not what this book is about. If you're really curious, check out Que's *Using MS-DOS 6.2*, Special Edition, for more detailed information.

Adding to the Batch

You can add commands to your AUTOEXEC.BAT file that cause other programs to load at startup, thus bypassing the DOS prompt. For example, if you add the command DOSSHELL as the last line in AUTOEXEC.BAT, the DOS Shell is started automatically. (Assuming, of course, that you're using a version of DOS that includes the DOS Shell!) If you don't see the DOS prompt on start-up and get launched into a specific program, you have one of these lines in your AUTOEXEC.BAT file.

After AUTOEXEC.BAT is done executing, your start-up is complete and you are presented with the DOS prompt. This prompt indicates that COMMAND.COM is loaded into memory, ready and willing to receive your next command.

All this activity during start-up is accompanied by beeps and whirrs and clicks and flashing lights, which just indicate that your system is doing its job. If you don't hear all the beeps and whirrs and clicks and see the flashing lights, and if your system doesn't load the boot program, the system files, the command interpreter, and the start-up files, you have a problem.

What You Need To Get Booted

You would think that booting your system is a snap—after all, all you have to do is flip a switch, right? Well, there's more to it than that, as you'll soon find out.

What exactly is necessary for you to boot your system? Check the items on the following list:

- *Power.* Make sure that the power cable is plugged into a power outlet (or into a surge suppressor that is plugged into a power outlet) and that the power outlet is switched on. Also make sure that the power cable is firmly connected to the back of your system unit.

- *A bootable disk.* If your system has a hard disk, make sure that DOS has been installed on the disk and that the two system files (IO.SYS and MSDOS.SYS) are in the root directory. You can verify this fact by typing the following command at the DOS prompt:

    ```
    DIR /AS
    ```

(This special version of the DIR command lists the two hidden system files. If the two files are present, they'll be listed. If not, well, you probably couldn't run your system—or the command—anyway.)

- *The command interpreter*. The other file you need to get going is COMMAND.COM, which is found either in your root directory or (more likely) in your DOS directory. Verify this file's presence by typing this command at the DOS prompt:

    DIR COMMAND.COM /S

    (This special version of the DIR command lists any occurrence of the COMMAND.COM file anywhere on your hard disk. If COMMAND.COM isn't on your hard disk, you need to copy it there from your original DOS disks or your Bootable Emergency Disk.)

- *CONFIG.SYS file*. This file is not required for your system to boot but is necessary to set up the system correctly. Read one of Que's DOS books for detailed information on setting up your CONFIG.SYS file.

- *AUTOEXEC.BAT file*. Like CONFIG.SYS, this file is not required for your computer to boot but is necessary to set up its system correctly. Again, read one of Que's many well-written DOS books for information.

- *Well-connected peripherals*. The monitor should be plugged in and turned on, and the keyboard should be plugged in before you turn on your system. Your computer may boot without these peripherals present (then again, it may not), but you won't be able to get much done without a functioning monitor and keyboard. (If you have a mouse, external disk drive, external modem, or other important peripherals, make sure that they're plugged in, too.)

Be sure to go through this checklist when you first hook up your system. If you're missing any of these items—well, your system just can't do what it's supposed to do.

10 Do's and Don'ts When Starting Your System

1. *Do* plug your system's power cable into a surge suppressor for added protection against power-line surges.

2. *Don't* leave a nonbootable disk in drive A. (Unless, of course, you're trying to boot from drive A—then make sure that it's a *bootable disk*!)

3. *Do* configure your CONFIG.SYS and AUTOEXEC.BAT files to maximize your system resources, such as memory. (And *DO* consult a more technical Que book—such as Que's *Using MS-DOS 6.2,* Special Edition—for additional configuration information.)

4. *Don't* turn on your system unit and *then* turn on your monitor or plug in your keyboard; these items must be up and running before your machine starts its boot procedure.

5. *Do* make sure that all your DOS files match the same version of DOS; you can't use a COMMAND.COM from DOS 4 with utilities from DOS 6, for example.

6. *Don't* try to jump-start your computer by hooking up jumper cables from the battery of your Land Rover.

7. *Do* press the Esc key or the Ctrl+C keys if your booting procedure hangs up for some reason; if these keys don't do the job, restart the computer by pressing Ctrl+Alt+Del.

8. *Don't* delete your COMMAND.COM file from your hard disk.

9. *Do* have patience; the booting procedure might take a minute or two on some machines.

10. *Don't* boot a portable computer on an airplane during takeoff or landing; you'll make the flight attendant *really* mad!

What To Do When You Can't Turn On Your Computer

There can be many possible reasons for your computer not starting. In fact, a computer might not start in several different ways. Read on for some analysis.

Problem 1:
Your computer doesn't start—you hear no noises and see no lights

First things first—*don't panic*!

Now, very calmly, look at the back of your system unit. Is the power cable plugged into the right connector? Now follow the power cord to the other end. Is it firmly connected to a power outlet? Now check the wall switch. Is it turned on? Now walk to your fuse or circuit-breaker box. Is the fuse good or the circuit breaker set? Now go back to your computer. If it still isn't working, unplug the computer from the power outlet and plug in something that you know works (a lamp or a radio, perhaps). If the appliance doesn't work, you have a bad power outlet. If the appliance *does* work, you really do have computer problems.

If you're positive that your computer is getting power and that you're turning it on correctly, you probably have a hardware problem. The most likely suspect is the power supply in the system unit. To determine the culprit and fix the problem, however, you'll need to call in professional help at this point. Take your system to a certified repair center and let its technicians get to work.

Problem 2:
Your computer doesn't start, but it makes the normal start-up noises

Well, at least you know your system is getting power. The most common causes of this particular problem are poorly connected cables or a non-functioning monitor. Begin by checking your monitor. Is it turned on? Is it plugged into a power outlet? Is the power outlet turned on? Is the monitor connected to the correct port on your system unit? Is the connection solid? Is the connection solid in the back of the monitor? Are the brightness and contrast controls turned up so that you can actually see a picture?

If all this checks out, you might have monitor problems. Is the monitor's power light on? If not, your monitor may have power supply problems that need attention from a professional. If your monitor's little green light is on but nothing shows on-screen, the video card in your system unit may be loose or set up incorrectly. Turn off your system, open the computer case, and check the video card to make sure it's installed, seated, and connected properly.

It's also possible that your keyboard isn't plugged in properly, or that you have some other internal problem that causes your system to halt during start-up. See Problem #5 for more suggestions.

Problem 3:
Your computer doesn't start, and it generates a series of beeps

No, aliens aren't trying to contact you via Morse code. This strange audio communication is supposed to alert you to a wrong video card setting on the motherboard. (Some engineer had the bright idea that if your video wasn't working you couldn't see an error message, so the error message would have to be transmitted audibly.)

If you've recently changed video cards, you may need to change some switches on your motherboard to accommodate your new card. This process gets pretty technical, so I recommend either reinstalling your old card for the time being or taking your computer into the repair shop to have switches set. If you're brave, you can dig through all your instruction manuals (for your system unit *and* your new video card) and try to set the switches yourself.

Turn Off the Power!

Remember always to turn off the power and unplug your system unit before you open the case to do any work.

The beeping can also occur if your video card is not firmly seated in its slot. Open the system unit and make sure that the card is plugged snugly into position; then close the case and reboot. If the problem persists, you may have a defective video card or a problem on the motherboard, both of which require professional attention.

Another cause of these beeps could be the video settings in the CMOS setup. Your CMOS RAM chip stores certain system settings in battery-operated memory; if the CMOS battery is weak or dead, these settings may be corrupted. Have your local repair person replace your CMOS battery and reset your system settings.

Problem 4:
Your computer starts, but the monitor displays an error message

Your system uses error messages to communicate with you when it encounters certain problems. (Turn to Chapter 28 for a listing of DOS error messages.) Here are some of the most common error messages you may encounter on start-up, their causes, and how to fix the problem.

```
Non-system disk or disk error
```

```
Replace and press any key when ready
```

You see this message when you have a nonbootable disk in drive A. Check the disk drive and remove the disk, and then press any key to restart the boot procedure using the hard disk drive.

If you intended to boot from drive A, you still could have a nonbootable disk in the drive. (If so, replace the current disk with a bootable one.) You also could have a bootable disk that is inserted incorrectly (upside down, sideways, not pushed in all the way) or inserted without the drive latch in the closed position. Take the disk out and reinsert it; then press any key to restart the boot procedure.

```
Bad or missing command interpreter
```

```
Invalid COMMAND.COM, system not loaded
```

```
Cannot load COMMAND.COM, system halted
```

You receive one of these messages when you boot from a disk that does not include the COMMAND.COM file. If you're booting from your hard disk, something has erased COMMAND.COM. Reboot from your Bootable Emergency Disk, and then copy COMMAND.COM from the disk to the root directory (C:\) on your hard disk.

If you're booting from a floppy disk, the message means that the disk does not include the COMMAND.COM file. Remove this disk and reboot from another disk that does include COMMAND.COM, such as your Bootable Emergency Disk.

It's also possible that you have COMMAND.COM on your disk, but it's from the wrong version of DOS. In this case, recopy COMMAND.COM to your hard disk from your original DOS disks.

```
Keyboard error, press F2 to continue
```

It sounds kind of silly to ask you to use your keyboard to confirm that your keyboard isn't working, doesn't it? (But that's DOS for you.) This message is generated when the rest of your system works but the PC can't find the keyboard. If you receive this message, your keyboard probably is disconnected or has a loose connection. Check the connecting cable (at both ends) and reboot. If you still receive this message, you have a keyboard problem. Verify this fact by plugging in a keyboard from a friend's machine. If you do have a keyboard problem, it's probably cheaper to buy a new keyboard than to get your old one fixed.

```
File allocation table bad, drive x:
```

This message is not good. Something has messed up your FAT (File Allocation Table), which DOS must have to operate. One of the most common causes of this problem is a computer virus. Another cause is some sort of physical damage to your hard disk, caused by contaminants or plain old wear and tear. If you have actual physical damage to your disk, you may need to use a third-party utility program, such as Norton Disk Doctor, to repair the damage.

You have two options when you receive this dreaded message. You can take your computer into the shop and let a professional help you. Or you can reformat your hard disk and restore your backed-up data files to the disk, as described in Chapter 8.

```
General failure reading drive x
```

```
General failure writing drive x
```

This is another very bad message, regardless of which version you receive. It essentially means something is wrong with your computer, and it has no idea what the trouble is. Try shutting down your system for a few minutes and then rebooting; sometimes this message is generated when the system gets a little cranky. More than likely, however, you have something seriously wrong somewhere, which means it's time to hop in the car and drop your PC off at your local computer repair center. The pros there have diagnostic software and equipment that can pinpoint problems much more easily than you or I can.

```
Bad or missing filename.SYS
```

```
Error in CONFIG.SYS line XX
```

While your computer was booting, the CONFIG.SYS file tried to load a driver that did not exist. Usually, DOS generates this message (obviously not loading the missing driver) and then continues with the rest of the boot. You probably mistyped the given line in the CONFIG.SYS file, or the line does not include the complete directory path for the file. It's also possible that the referenced driver has been deleted from your hard disk. You need to examine your CONFIG.SYS file and edit the specified line to correct any mistakes or erase the line if the driver no longer exists. Then you can reboot your system and start again.

```
Incorrect DOS version
```

This message is displayed when you have one or more DOS files that are from different versions of DOS. Try recopying the COMMAND.COM file to your hard disk from your original DOS disks. If this doesn't work, you might have to reinstall DOS from your original disks. (See your original DOS manuals for information on how to perform the reinstallation procedure.)

```
System halted
```

This message, typically generated while DOS is trying to execute the CONFIG.SYS file, is caused by an invalid, incompatible, or corrupted device driver. If you're using DOS 6, you should reboot your system but quickly press the F5 key during startup—this bypasses your startup files; you can then check your CONFIG.SYS file for any bad drivers. (If you have an earlier version of DOS, you should reboot from your Bootable Emergency Disk— which bypasses the execution of CONFIG.SYS—and then check your CONFIG.SYS file.) You may also need to reinstall any drivers in question from your original DOS disks.

```
Invalid drive specification
```

```
Drive not ready
```

Either of these error messages indicates that you're having problems with the drive you're trying to boot from. If you're booting from a floppy disk drive, your bootable disk may be bad. Try using another bootable disk.

If the problem persists, or if you're booting from a hard disk drive, the problem may reside in the drive mechanism itself. Sometimes an older drive can operate too slowly to always boot properly; try rebooting your system. If the problem persists, have a professional check out your system. The drive in question may need to be replaced.

```
CMOS RAM error
```

This message appears when something is bad in the setup held in memory by your system's CMOS RAM chip. (This chip holds important system information in permanent, battery-powered memory.) When you see this or any similar message, you are given the opportunity to press the F1 key to continue. Do this, and adjust your CMOS setup accordingly. (See your system's documentation for information on how to do the latter.) If this message persists, you may have a dead CMOS battery; see your repair center to replace the battery.

```
Memory size error

Memory size mismatch

Not enough memory

Insufficient memory

Parity check xxx

Parity error x
```

Any of these messages indicates that something is wrong with your computer's memory. Your CMOS setup may be incorrect, or you could have some bad or improperly seated memory chips. It's also possible that you recently added extra memory to your system and it isn't configured correctly. You probably want to consult a computer professional about this problem.

Problem 5:
Your computer starts but then suddenly halts during start-up

This problem happens most often when DOS is trying to execute the CONFIG.SYS file. The difficulty is caused by an invalid, incompatible, or corrupted device driver. To get going again, you should do a clean reboot of your computer by pressing F5 during startup, and then check your CONFIG.SYS file for any bad drivers. (This only works with DOS 6; if you have an earlier version of DOS, you should reboot from your Bootable Emergency Disk—which bypasses the execution of CONFIG.SYS—and then check your CONFIG.SYS file.) You may also need to reinstall any drivers in question from your original DOS disks.

Your system can also halt if you accidentally press Esc or Ctrl+C or Ctrl+Break during the start-up procedure. If you do this, reboot your system by pressing **Ctrl+Alt+Del**.

Another cause of start-up halts is when a cable accidentally becomes disconnected, which often occurs with the keyboard cable. Check your connections and reboot.

Problem 6:
Your computer starts but doesn't act normally

First, are you booting from your usual disk? If you normally boot from your hard disk, have you accidentally booted from a bootable disk in drive A? If so, you've bypassed your regular CONFIG.SYS and AUTOEXEC.BAT files, so your system isn't set up the same way it generally is. Remove the disk from drive A and reboot using your hard drive.

If you're still booting from your normal drive, it's possible your CONFIG.SYS or AUTOEXEC.BAT files have been changed, damaged, or deleted. First, verify that the files are in your root directory by typing the following two commands:

DIR C:\AUTOEXEC.BAT

DIR C:\CONFIG.SYS

If the files aren't there, you need to make new ones or restore your old ones from your backup disks. If you need to start from scratch, see one of Que's DOS books for more information. To restore these files from backup disks, start Microsoft Backup (in DOS 6) or use the DOS RESTORE command to restore the individual files.

If the files *are* there, you need to check to see whether they have been accidentally edited. Start the DOS Editor (included with DOS 5 and 6) by typing the following:

EDIT C:\AUTOEXEC.BAT

or

EDIT C:\CONFIG.SYS

When the Editor appears (with the specified file open), check for any recent changes and make any edits required. Press **Alt+F**, **S** to save the file, and **Alt+F**, **X** to exit from the Editor.

Alternatively, you can restore old versions of these files to replace the current, possibly erroneous, versions; use Microsoft Backup (in DOS 6) or the DOS RESTORE command to transfer files from your backup disks to your hard disk.

It's also possible that the CMOS RAM chip in your system has lost its memory. If the CMOS chip's battery has gone bad, you may experience a loss of date, time, memory, disk, or system information; you may even receive an error message on start-up. The solution is simple—replace the battery. Because this involves working inside the computer case, it's best to take your unit into a repair center to have this done.

The Last Word on Starting Your System

Words cannot describe the terror felt when you flick the power switch and your PC doesn't respond. I know; it's happened to me on more than one occasion.

However, if you keep calm and track down the problem logically, you can often get things up and running in a matter of minutes. Of course, there is always the possibility that your computer does have a serious problem that requires immediate professional attention. But don't let that scare you. If you took the precautions outlined in Chapter 7, the most you'll lose is some time without your computer. Let this chapter serve as yet another reminder to back up your important data—and do it frequently.

What To Do When...

Your Computer Freezes Up

CHAPTER ELEVEN

It's happened to everyone. You're computing along, everything is going fine, no problems, when all of a sudden you realize that...

Your computer has frozen.

Stopped working.

Given up the ghost.

Just like that. No warning, no nothing.

What can you do when this happens to you? Simple...just turn the page for some comfort and advice!

How To Keep Your System Up and Running

Don't panic!

That's the best advice when your computer freezes up. You see, whatever harm could be done *has* been done, and there's not much you can do about it at this point. Not very comforting, I know, but true.

In any event, about the only thing you can do (assuming the problem isn't something simple, like a loose connection) is reboot your computer. The good news in this situation is that—should rebooting be your only recourse—you probably won't damage any of your software programs. (A pretty weak consolation prize, eh?) The bad news is, of course, if you reboot your computer, you lose all the data you've entered since you last issued the Save command.

Sorry.

Why Your Computer Quits

What makes a computer simply stop in its tracks? Several common causes come readily to mind, among them are the following:

- *Something came loose.* Yes, it's the old loose connector trick again. One likely culprit is your keyboard cable, although on occasion your monitor cable can cause you fits, too. Sometimes you can just reconnect the cable and pick up where you left off. Other times, you must reboot after you reconnect the cable.

- *You typed too fast.* I know this probably still sounds strange, but at times you might type too fast for your computer. Some keyboards and systems can accept only so much data in a given period. In other words, you can actually out-type your keyboard! Sometimes, when this happens, you just have to sit back and let your keyboard catch up to you; other times, you might even have to reboot your system.

- *You did something wrong.* I know, I know. You never do anything wrong. But sometimes typing a command incorrectly, inserting the wrong disk, or even just pressing the wrong key can make your computer freeze up. If you suspect this to be the case (be honest, now!), then retrace your steps, try to figure out exactly what you did wrong, and either correct it or reboot your system.

- *Your memory is full.* No, not *your* memory, your *computer's* memory! Occasionally a program can use too much memory and provoke what DOS calls a *memory allocation error*. This doesn't happen often, but when it does, you probably must reboot your system to correct the problem. If it happens too often, however, you may find it necessary to increase the number of FILES and BUFFERS in your CONFIG.SYS file.

- *Your programs are in conflict.* The world has become a pretty dismal place when not even your own software programs can live together peacefully. Unfortunately, some programs just don't get along with other programs—they want to use the same memory space, or they try to access the disk at the same time, or they just plain don't like each other. You probably have no choice but to reboot if two (or more) warring programs lock up your system. After you have your machine up and running again, however, experiment with your programs to determine which ones are in conflict. If you normally load one program before the other, for example, load them in reverse order this time to see if that does the trick. (This affects which program gets what memory when and can resolve some conflicts.) If not, well, you may be forced to admit defeat and forevermore avoid running the two rival programs at the same time. Let that be your personal contribution to (computer) world peace.

- *A virus has attacked your computer system.* Oh no! Not that! Anything but that! (Oh, calm down, will you?) Refer back to Chapter 9 for information about fighting those nasty viruses.

- *Somebody turned off the power.* It sounds stupid, but make sure that you didn't accidentally flip off your PC's power switch, turn off the juice at the wall switch, or trip over the cord and unplug it from the wall. (If all the lights in your house went off at the same time, it's also possible your entire circuit has gone dead—or your metropolitan area is experiencing a blackout!)

- *Your computer broke.* Well, it happens. Maybe your microprocessor stopped processing, or a transistor ceased transmitting, or your power supply lost power. If the entire system goes down (no lights, no beeps, nothing), you may indeed have serious hardware problems.

- *The stars are not in alignment today.* If you can't ferret out any other reasons for your system stalling, and it reboots okay, then the only possible answer must be that your biorhythms and your horoscope are in conflict, the moon is in the seventh house, the tide is high, and gravity is especially strong today. In other words, some things you never figure out—so don't lose any sleep over it. Just reboot and get on with your life.

What To Do When Your PC's System Quits

Is It Really Dead?

Before you reboot, make sure that your system is really and truly locked up. Don't mistake a long wait time during a complex operation for a complete system freeze. Look for signs that your computer is still working, such as noises from your disk drive or blinking lights on your system unit. The last thing you want to do is reboot—and lose your current data—when you don't have to.

When the system freezes, more often than not, you must reboot to get your computer working again. Rebooting loses whatever you typed since you last saved the file you were in when the machine froze, but the process really doesn't hurt either your computer or your software programs. Try first to reboot from the keyboard by pressing the **Ctrl+Alt+Del** key combination. If that doesn't work, use the Reset button or the main power switch on your system unit.

Naturally, your computer's system can stall for any number of reasons. Some of the most common causes of this annoyance, along with their solutions, are described in the following sections.

10 Do's and Don'ts To Keep Your PC Running

1. *Do* check all your cables, especially your keyboard cable; if your keyboard isn't connected, the system freezes up.

2. *Don't* press **Ctrl+Alt+Del** unless you're really, *really* sure that the system is irreparably locked up; you may lose data if you reboot in the middle of an important document.

3. *Do* feel free to scream and yell and curse; it really doesn't hurt anything, and it might relieve your frustration.

4. *Don't* unplug your computer from the wall while it's locked; not only do you lose all work in progress, but you might even damage parts of the system and/or your program files in the bargain. If necessary, press **Ctrl+Alt+Del** instead, or use the computer's on/off switch.

5. *Do* try pressing the **Esc** and **Ctrl+C** and **Ctrl+Break** and **Ctrl+X** keys, in case you're merely stuck in a slow program or an endless batch-file loop.

6. *Don't* hit the keyboard with a hammer; as tempting as this may be, it only makes matters worse.

7. *Do* remember that if a Windows application freezes, all may not be lost. Pressing **Ctrl+Alt+Del** will often let you close *that particular program* without affecting all of Windows and your other open Windows applications.

8. *Don't* engage the services of a professional magician; you won't be able to talk to your dead computer, even during a seance!

9. *Do* call your friendly neighborhood computer repair person if you're accessing a really important file and don't want to lose your work; it's just possible he or she can help.

10. *Don't* sell your computer just yet; whatever is wrong is probably fixable.

Problem 1:
Your system halts—nothing remains on-screen, and all power is off

This is a scary one. Two probable causes exist for this problem. First, you (or someone for whom you will soon have an intense dislike) accidentally cut the power to your system by turning off the system unit, turning off the wall switch, tripping over the power cord and yanking it from the socket, or tapping the off switch on your surge suppresser. Second, a major calamity has just struck your system's power supply. (This is a heavy-duty device inside your computer that "transforms" AC electrical current to a different type of current used by your system's electrical components.) If you discover the cause of its inaction to be the former problem, simply turn your machine back on by whatever means necessary. If you decide that it must be the latter—well, it's time to take your electronic buddy to the shop.

Problem 2:
Your system halts—your system unit has power, but your keyboard isn't working

If no error messages appear on-screen, you probably face a simple problem: Your keyboard is unplugged. So plug it back in.

Of course, the solution might not be quite that simple. One of the many causes of system freeze-up discussed earlier may actually have reared its troublesome head. If replugging your keyboard doesn't work, reboot. If you still experience difficulties after rebooting, you may actually be the not-so-proud possessor of a bad keyboard. Try plugging another keyboard into your PC, or your keyboard into another PC, to determine whether keyboard failure is at the root of your problem.

This predicament can also be caused by two software programs interfering with each other. Maybe the culprits attempted to access the same peripheral at the same time, or to use the same memory area simultaneously. If so, you probably must reboot to get your keyboard functioning again. If you continue to experience such difficulties when using the same two programs together, you almost certainly are caught in the crossfire of a serious program conflict. Try reversing the order in which you normally load these programs, as described in the section "Why Your Computer Quits—Your programs are in conflict" earlier in this chapter. If that doesn't work, and all else fails, well, just don't use those two programs together, okay?

If, on the other hand, your keyboard freezes *and* an error message appears, turn immediately to either Problem #3 or Problem #5 for instructions.

> **Getting Loaded**
>
> Some systems are set up to load programs automatically when your system starts. This is done by placing command lines in your AUTOEXEC.BAT file, which is located in your hard disk's root directory. To load programs in a different order, simply change the order of the command lines in the AUTOEXEC.BAT file.

Problem 3:
Your system halts while running Windows—an error message appears

Windows can sometimes exhibit perplexing behavior. (Computer people refer to this type of behavior as "unstable." I prefer to call it "screwy.") When Windows freezes up, it normally displays one of the following error messages (in a pretty-looking little Windows dialog box, of course):

```
General Protection Fault
```

or

```
Unrecoverable Application Error
```

These messages are just nice ways to say that something (who knows what) has bombed. More often than not, it's just your current program that has frozen, and not all of Windows. That being the case—assuming you have Windows 3.1—you can simply close the current program, and get back to using the rest of Windows. (Although it may be best to close Windows, reboot your computer, and then start over when you have a program freeze.)

If you get the GPF (General Protection Fault) message and you're running Windows 3.1, you see a message that lets you either close the current program or ignore the problem and continue. Well, you can try ignoring it if you want, but the chances weigh heavily against your doing so successfully. The problem almost certainly will reoccur, and you'll just have to close the program, anyway. My recommendation—close the offending program and start over.

If you get a UAE (Unrecoverable Application Error) message, you're running Windows 3.0 or earlier. Your only choice in this case is to reboot your entire system (by pressing **Ctrl+Alt+Del**). Sorry.

If you get these messages frequently, you probably don't have enough memory in your system to run Windows comfortably. If you get these messages infrequently—great! Don't worry about it! Worse things have happened.

Problem 4:
Your system halts while running Windows—no error message appears

Sometimes Windows freezes without displaying an error message. One of two things has happened: (1) Windows itself has locked up, or (2) Your current Windows application has locked up.

In either case, the solution is the same: Press **Ctrl+Alt+Del**.

If Windows itself has frozen, either nothing will happen (in which case you'll need to press **Ctrl+Alt+Del** to fully reboot, or you may have to press the reset button on your system unit); or you'll be shown a screen saying Windows has frozen and you need to press **Ctrl+Alt+Del** again (which you should do). In other words, if Windows freezes, you need to reboot!

When Windows Freezes—Reboot!

Whenever Windows freezes, even if you can recover by closing a program and keeping Windows running, you should always close Windows, reboot your computer, then restart Windows before continuing. This is because a bombed program can sometimes scramble Windows memory, and the only way to ensure against another problem, in short order, is to clear things up by a close and reboot.

If, on the other hand, it's an errant program that freezes up, a screen saying your current application has locked up will appear, and you can either (1) Press Enter to return to the frozen program (and why would you want to do that?) or (2) Press **Ctrl+Alt+Del** again to close the application.

Do number two.

Problem 5:
Your system halts—it displays a DOS error message

If your system stops short and blatantly displays a DOS error message, turn to Chapter 28, "DOS Error Messages—What They Mean and How To Deal with Them." Armed with the handy information in that chapter, you can undoubtedly decipher the message and discover its cause. For your convenience, however, several of the more common error messages that accompany this situation are listed as follows:

```
Not enough memory
```
or
```
Insufficient memory
```

If either of these two error messages appears, DOS has tried to load a program, but not enough unused memory remains on your system for that program to run. If other programs currently are running, try closing one or more to free up additional memory for the newcomer. Occasionally, however, not all your system's memory is freed when you close a program, so you might need to reboot to recover the extra memory space.

Another possibility that can evoke a memory-error message is that you might be running two copies of DOS. Now, wait! Just how could something like that happen? Well, many programs now enable you to access DOS while continuing to run the application. (Instead of closing the program to access DOS, you often simply execute a menu option labeled, appropriately enough, *DOS*.) Sometimes your system carries out this procedure by actually firing up a second copy of DOS. To exit this second DOS command interpreter and return to your original program—after you've finished dealing with DOS—you must type EXIT.

Suppose, however, that you forget you're currently running the auxiliary DOS; perhaps you've performed several lengthy DOS operations, and it's late and…well, you get the picture. Now, all thought of the program from which you originally accessed DOS has long-since evaporated from your mind. So, you attempt to start yet another program from the second DOS prompt. Wham! Up pops one of these memory-error messages. Yes, it could happen even to such a careful computer user as you. So if you ever do find yourself treated to an out-of-memory message, whether you truly believe you're in DOS 1 or realize you're actually in DOS 2, put first things first and try typing EXIT—just in case. The worst that can happen if you haven't shelled to DOS and you type EXIT is that you'll be given a DOS prompt.

```
General failure error reading drive x:
Abort, Retry, Fail?
```

This message appears when something is wrong with the disk in the selected drive. If you're trying to access a floppy disk when DOS displays this message, the warning could indicate that the disk is unformatted, that you're using the wrong type of disk (high-density when your computer only takes low-density), that it's inserted incorrectly, or that it's just plain bad. Press A to abort the operation and return to the DOS prompt. (In some cases, aborting doesn't do the trick, and you keep getting the same Abort, Retry, Fail? error message. If this happens, press F, which should finally stop the operation.)

If, on the other hand, DOS issues this message in regard to your hard drive, it might be the harbinger of major hard disk problems. Try pressing R to retry the operation; if you keep getting the message, reboot your system. If problems persist after rebooting, read Chapter 6 to figure out what to do.

Bad or missing Command Interpreter

Uh oh! Something untoward has happened to your COMMAND.COM file. Either it has been accidentally erased, or an older version of the file has overwritten a newer version. Try rebooting your computer. If the system starts and runs fine, chalk the incident up to experience and get back to computing. Should this message crop up on an initial start-up, however, you'd better plan on breaking out your Bootable Emergency Diskette (created back in Chapter 7). Use it to reboot the system, and then recopy the COMMAND.COM file from the disk to your hard drive.

Problem 6:
Your system halts—it appears to be stuck in a loop

Cooking Up a Batch File

A *batch file* is a special type of file with a BAT extension. Batch files can include multiple DOS commands, each on its own line. When a batch file is run, each line is executed, one at a time. Special batch file commands—such as the GOTO command—let you perform more complex operations from the batch file. For more batch file information, check out Que's *Using MS-DOS 6.2, Special Edition*.

This problem really *is* caused by a *loop*—an endless program loop, to be exact. Loops often result when you're running a new batch file that contains several *GOTO* statements. GOTO statements instruct your program to loop to another part of the program until a certain event takes place. A poorly thought-out program can actually loop perpetually from point to point within itself, allowing you no chance to input a loop-ending command.

If you believe your problem stems from a runaway loop, try pressing **Ctrl+C**. This often "breaks" the loop and temporarily halts the program. (The Esc key and the Ctrl+Break keys sometimes have the same effect.) Occasionally, you must reboot your system with the Ctrl+Alt+Del keys to escape the loop. If a batch file is making you jump through loops, edit the guilty file to eliminate the loop. If another commercial program is at fault— well, I'd say it's high time to ring up the software company's technical support staff, wouldn't you?

The Last Word on Keeping Your System Up and Running

You've heard it several times already, but it bears repeating: If your system halts and you can't figure out why, reboot. The rest of your computing session will probably be just fine, unless you can duplicate exactly the circumstances that led to the freeze-up. (And, if you're like me, you can never do something the same way twice.)

Of course, if you receive one of those dreaded error messages, or if your entire system goes crashing down and won't come up again, you undoubtedly have a far more serious problem to contend with—the solution to which, in most cases, rests in your local computer repair emporium. Otherwise, fortunately, you can just grin—and start over.

What To Do When...

Your Keyboard Won't Type

CHAPTER TWELVE

Since we don't yet have talking computers (a la *Star Trek*), we have to communicate with our big beige machines through other means. If you have Windows, you get to use a mouse for some communications. But Windows or not, your main means of interfacing with your computer is through your keyboard.

So what happens if your keyboard quits working?

Fortunately, keyboard problems are few and far between, and easily corrected. If you have a quirky keyboard, however, this is little consolation. So turn the page, and learn what to do when your keyboard starts acting up.

How To Keep Typing through Thick and Thin

So, just what do you need to know about your keyboard? Fortunately, not a great deal. It's one of the least complicated parts of your computer system.

All about Keyboards

A keyboard is basically just a bunch of switches that send electrical impulses to the system unit when you press a key. In fact, some of the original computer keyboards didn't even have keys; they had flat touch pads. These "Chiclet" keyboards weren't too popular with touch typists, however, because they didn't have the same "feel" as the old mechanical typewriters. So hardware manufacturers added mechanical devices to provide a stiffer action and add clicking sounds. (In fact, you'll find that the feel and sounds of keyboards vary from manufacturer to manufacturer.) Touch typists were happier, and the computer revolution was free to continue.

Two major types of keyboards are available on personal computers: the *regular keyboard* and the *enhanced keyboard.* The enhanced keyboard has a few more keys than the normal keyboard and is the type sold with most PCs marketed during the past few years.

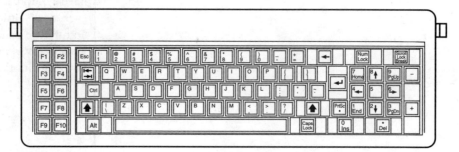

Regular Keyboard

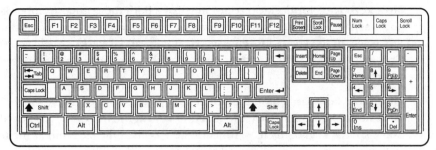

Enhanced Keyboard

Special Keys on Your Keyboard

All PC keyboards include a few keys you won't find on normal typewriters. You'll find keys that move the cursor around the screen (the arrow—or *cursor control*—keys); keys that let you page through entire screens in a single keystroke (the Page Down, Page Up, Home, and End keys); and function keys, which perform special functions for specific software programs (F1, F2, and so on). Pressing F1, for example, accesses the Help system in many programs.

All PC keyboards also have a Caps Lock key, which shifts the keyboard to type all capital letters; a Num Lock key, which shifts the numeric keypad keys to type numbers instead of serving as directional keys; and a Scroll Lock key, which keeps the screen

Don't Drink and Type!

About the worst thing you can do to your keyboard is to spill something on it. When you spill the contents of your glass onto your keyboard, several things might happen:

- *Nothing.* You're lucky. You should still turn off your computer, unplug your keyboard, and let it dry out for a day or so before using it again, just to make sure that none of the electronics are damaged.

- *It shorts out.* Liquids and electronics don't mix. Spilling water or any other liquid onto your keyboard could cause the circuitry to short-circuit. If this happens, take it into the shop or buy a new one. Whatever you do, don't use the keyboard again until it dries out or you get it fixed!

- *It gets gummed up.* The sugar in most soft drinks can get down into the switches under the keys on your keyboard. This can cause them to malfunction or stick. If this happens, take your keyboard to a repair center where they can clean out all the sticky gunk and get things clicking back to normal. (Some techies recommend trying to *wash* the keyboard, but this can often cause more problems than you had to begin with!)

Whichever happens, make sure that you turn off your PC before you unplug your keyboard or even worse stuff could happen!

from scrolling in some programs. There are also keys that enable you to print the screen contents (Print Screen), insert new characters (Insert), and delete old characters (Delete).

Most keyboards for desktop computers have both the regular number keys and a separate numeric keypad for quick entry of numbers; some portable PCs leave off the keypad to save space. Finally, all PC keyboards have Esc, Ctrl, and Alt keys, which—when pressed with other keys—access special program operations.

Most older keyboards have the function keys at the left of the keyboard. Most newer keyboards have the function keys at the top of the keyboard. Some special keyboards have function keys both at the side and at the top, so you can use whichever you're most comfortable with. Some of these keyboards even let you *reprogram* some of the keys. This way, you can have the Ctrl key do what the F12 key normally does, if you really want to.

Why Good Keyboards Go Bad

Keeping Your Keyboard Kleen!

It's good to perform some periodic maintenance on your keyboard. Use a mini-vacuum or small brush to blow or wipe dust from between the keys. If necessary, *carefully* pull individual keys off to clean underneath. (And do all of this *with your computer turned off!*)

What can go wrong with your computer keyboard? It can get unplugged. The keys can start sticking. (This is exacerbated when you pour soda or coffee on the keyboard; try to avoid doing this.) The key mechanisms can simply go off and not transmit the proper electrical impulses. Some of the other electronic parts in the keyboard can go bad. You can type so fast that your system can't keep up with you. (Keyboard signals are stored in a kind of temporary memory called a *buffer* until your system can get around to processing them; you can actually fill up the buffer if you type quickly enough, causing a "buffer overflow" effect.) And, finally, you can set up parts of your system incorrectly so that your keyboard seems to be messed up.

10 Do's and Don'ts To Keep Your Keyboard Clicking Away

1. *Do* try typing an entry again, but slower this time and with feeling.

2. *Don't* press the Caps Lock key accidentally.

3. *Do* check to make sure that your keyboard is plugged in properly.

4. *Don't* pour 10W40 onto your keyboard, in the hopes that "oiling it up" will make it go faster.

5. *Do* reprogram your keyboard to put your keys where you want them, if your keyboard allows you to do this.

6. *Don't* leave your Num Lock key on unless you have a separate numeric keypad.

7. *Do* buy a typing instruction software program if you're a really poor typist; *Typing Tutor* from Que Software is a good one.

8. *Don't* change your keyboard's COUNTRY or KEYB setups unless you really want to use a foreign keyboard layout.

9. *Do* clean your keyboard periodically with appropriate kits available at office supply stores.

10. *Don't* line up a bass player and drummer to accompany you on the "keys"; it's not *that* kind of keyboard!

If your keyboard does happen to go bad, you probably should just throw it away. Most new keyboards cost less than $100, and you'll probably pay that much to get your old one fixed. It's actually cheaper to buy a new one.

What To Do When Your Keyboard Won't Work

Fortunately, only a few things can go wrong with your keyboard, and here they are, along with some suggestions on how to correct them:

Problem 1:
Your keyboard won't type—no characters appear on-screen

First, check to make sure that the keyboard is firmly connected to the system unit. If need be, reboot so that DOS realizes that the keyboard is actually there.

Plugging Away

Not all keyboards use the same types of plugs. It may be impossible, for example, to plug a normal keyboard into the back of a computer that has connectors for an enhanced keyboard. So if you want or need to replace your keyboard, be sure to replace it with one that actually can plug into your system unit. Be certain, too, that you're connecting the plug correctly, because most keyboard plugs can go in only one way, with the flat spot or slot

---

If that doesn't solve your problem, you probably have a bad keyboard. Try hooking another keyboard to your computer. If the new keyboard works and your own keyboard doesn't, you have a bad keyboard.

If another keyboard doesn't work on your system either, you have some weird problem in your system unit—maybe a bad connector. Call the repair shop, and take it in for repairs.

Problem 2:
Your keyboard freezes up while you're using Windows

This problem is most often caused by an incorrect keyboard driver within Windows. (Windows uses device drivers to operate various devices, including your keyboard.) Run the Windows Setup program (type **SETUP** at the DOS prompt), and select a different keyboard driver from the supplied list.

Of course, it's also possible that your keyboard became disconnected while you were using Windows. Check the keyboard cable—at both ends—to make sure that all connections are solid. (If your keyboard was disconnected, you may need to reboot your system to get it back to normal.)

And don't dismiss the blatantly obvious—you may have a bad keyboard. If all else fails, try using a keyboard from another PC; if it works, you really do have a bad keyboard.

Problem 3:
You spill some liquid on the keyboard

OOPS! What a clumsy goof you are! Fortunately, all may not be lost.

The first thing to do is turn off your computer and unplug your keyboard. Then use a soft cloth to wipe up the spill as much as possible. You can then pull off individual keycaps, taking care not to damage the switches underneath, and clean up any excess liquid there.

It's a good idea to let the keyboard dry overnight before testing it again. After drying, plug it back in and fire up your PC; if you're lucky, everything will work fine.

The worst that can happen is that you spill a liquid with a high sugar content (like a cola or other soft drink), and the residue gunks up your keyboard switches. If this happens, you can take the keyboard in for a professional cleaning, or just spring for a new keyboard.

Problem 4:
Your keyboard won't type—every time you press a key, you hear a beep

Your keyboard is probably connected, but maybe not correctly. Make sure that the connectors are firmly plugged into one another. If that isn't it, something funny has happened while you were typing—maybe you typed too fast and filled the keyboard buffer. Try rebooting. (If your keyboard is really dead, you can't reboot by pressing **Ctrl+Alt+Del**, so you have to turn the system on and off from the reset button or the main power switch.)

> **Type What You're Supposed To!**
>
> If your keyboard doesn't respond to what you type, maybe you're not typing the right thing! If you're in a program that expects a certain kind of input, and you type something entirely different from what it expects, your system probably won't accept it. So if your keyboard beeps at you, always check first to make sure that you're actually typing what you're supposed to type!

It's also possible that you have the wrong keyboard hooked up to your computer. Regular keyboards usually can't be interchanged with enhanced keyboards, for example. Some keyboards actually have a switch underneath that makes them look (to your system) like other types of keyboards. Look for this switch, and click it into the other position.

If, after rebooting, you still have keyboard problems, try hooking up another keyboard to your PC; if it works, you need to buy a new keyboard. Fortunately, keyboards aren't that expensive to replace.

Problem 5:
Your keyboard quits working after you install a new peripheral or run MemMaker

I've warned you before—you add something new to your system (or change some parameters in your startup files with MemMaker) and it can screw up anything you'd previously had running right. What do you do?

Making Amends with MemMaker

MemMaker, discussed in Chapter 3, is a new utility in DOS 6 that automatically reconfigures your startup files to maximize memory use. Unfortunately, it can sometimes be *too* efficient, and map two devices to the same memory area! You'll know you've run MemMaker if you look at your CONFIG.SYS or AUTOEXEC.BAT files and see lines that include things like "I=B000-B7FF" or "/L:2,36256." These are instructions to DOS to load certain files and devices into specific areas of memory. Unfortunately, these areas may sometimes conflict with where other devices (like your keyboard) load. The answer is to change or eliminate these specific memory area instructions.

The most probable cause of a frozen keyboard after a major system change is a memory conflict. Your new device (or an old device, moved around in memory by MemMaker) is now trying to share the same memory space needed by your keyboard. You need to fix this.

The most likely conflict involves the EMM386 extended memory driver. In your CONFIG.SYS file, look for the line that looks something like:

DEVICE=C:\DOS\EMM386.EXE NOEMS HIGHSCAN I=*XXXX-XXXX*

To remove this driver from the specific memory location (the bit with the I=), simply edit the line to remove the I=*XXXX-XXXX* section.

If, when you reboot your machine, you still have problems, you need to look for other potential memory conflicts. In particular, look for lines in your AUTOEXEC.BAT file that include sections that look like:

LH /L: *X,XXXX*

One by one, remove these LH sections from the lines in question, rebooting your PC each time. When your mouse starts working again, you've found the line causing the problems.

As always, if this seems too technical for you, don't feel bad about asking your neighborhood or office computer guru to search out the memory conflict for you. (If you're in over your head, you could probably screw up your startup files by editing the wrong things!)

Problem 6:
You type a lowercase letter, but an uppercase letter appears on-screen

You have the Caps Lock key on. Press **Caps Lock** again to turn it off. (The Caps Lock light should reflect the position of the key; if the light is on, the key is on.)

Sometimes your system can get confused and think that Caps Lock is on when it really isn't supposed to be. I don't know what causes this, but I've noticed the problem when using various third-party keyboards with some off-brand computers. (I'm told that some types of memory-management software, if not set up correctly, also can be at fault in this.) If it happens, you may have to reboot to reset the system.

Problem 7:
You type a number, but the on-screen cursor moves instead

You have the Num Lock key on. Press **Num Lock** again to turn it off. (The Num Lock light should reflect the position of the key; if the light is on, the key is on.)

As noted in Problem #6, sometimes your system can get confused and think that Num Lock is on when it really isn't supposed to be. If this happens, you might have to reboot to reset the system.

Problem 8:
Your Num Lock or Caps Lock light doesn't reflect the true position of the key

As noted in Problems #6 and #7, sometimes your system gets confused and thinks Caps Lock and Num Lock are on when they're supposed to be off. Exit your current program, and reboot your computer to reset this configuration.

Problem 9:
You type one key, and a different character appears on-screen

The following can cause this problem:

- You really didn't type what you thought you did. Look at your fingers. Now look at the screen. Now look at your fingers again. Is everything the way it should be? Good!

- You or someone else may have used the COUNTRY or KEYB command to reset your keyboard to emulate a foreign-language keyboard. Check your CONFIG.SYS file to make sure that it doesn't include a line that starts COUNTRY=xxx; if it does include this line, remove it. Also try typing the following command at the DOS prompt to reset the country code back to a United States keyboard:

    KEYB/US

- If you have a programmable keyboard, you or someone else may have reprogrammed the keys so that they don't do what they normally do. Refer to the keyboard manual for instructions about how to reprogram the keys.

- If you're in a specific software program, some programs let you reprogram the keyboard from within the program. When you exit the program, your keyboard should be back to normal.

- It's possible your keyboard is broken. Try hooking up another keyboard to your system and see how it works.

Problem 10:
A keyboard-related error message appears on-screen

Several error messages relate to keyboards. These include:

```
Invalid keyboard
```

```
Keyboard not found
```

```
Interface/Keyboard error
```

One of these messages might appear when DOS cannot find the keyboard. This could be because your keyboard is disconnected; if so, reconnect the keyboard. (You also may need to reboot the system with the keyboard plugged in, so that DOS can recognize that the keyboard is back.) The message can also indicate that you have a bad keyboard. If nothing else seems to work, replace your keyboard.

```
Bad or Missing Keyboard definition table
```

This message is displayed when the KEYBOARD.SYS file is missing or damaged. Recopy this file from your original DOS disks back to the DOS directory on your hard disk.

```
Invalid keyboard code specified
```

```
Current keyboard does not support this code page
```

These messages appear when you try to set a different keyboard code (for foreign-language keyboards) with the KEYB command and you enter an incorrect code for your keyboard. Consult your DOS manual for a list of the correct codes.

Keyboard and other error messages are discussed more fully in Chapter 28, "DOS Error Messages…What They Mean and How To Deal with Them."

A Final Word on Keyboards

The keyboard is your main connection to your PC. Treat it right. Don't eat when you're at the keyboard, because you might spill something on it. (And be careful drinking around the keyboard—if you spill something on it, it may be a goner!) Don't hit the keyboard or pound it on the table. Don't stretch the cable so far that you could break the internal wiring. And above all, don't drop the keyboard on the floor. The thing's fragile, for heaven's sake, and you have to treat it with care. If you don't, it breaks. It's as simple as that.

What To Do When...

Your Mouse Won't Point

Next to your keyboard (both metaphorically and physically), your mouse is the part of your system you use most often. If you're using Windows, your mouse is constantly in your right hand (unless you're left-handed, of course), rolling along your mouse pad as you point your cursor at one or another part of Windows.

So what do you do if it quits working?

Well, you *could* learn how to use Windows without a mouse (which is possible, but darned difficult). Or you could turn the page and get some more of Miller's advice on coping with recalcitrant rodents.

How a Mouse Works

Alternate Rodents

If you don't like a mouse, there are other options. First, you can get a trackball, which is kind of like an upside-down mouse. If you're a games junkie, you could try using a joystick in place of a mouse. If you're a graphics wizard, you can always use a tablet pointer as a mouse. And, if you're on the bleeding edge of technology, you can use a pen-based computer that uses a stylus to point at the screen in lieu of a mouse. All in all, I recommend you stay with the rodent you know—your friendly Microsoft-compatible mouse.

A mouse is nothing more than a little roller ball in a case with a couple of buttons on top. The mouse connects to your PC through one of the ports on the back of the system unit.

For a mouse to operate, a mouse driver must be loaded into the system's memory. (*Drivers* are memory-resident files that tell the system how to use specific devices.) If the mouse driver has a COM extension, such as MOUSE.COM, it can be loaded into memory from the AUTOEXEC.BAT file. If the mouse driver has a SYS extension, such as MOUSE.SYS, it has to be loaded from the CONFIG.SYS file. Refer to the documentation for your mouse for detailed instructions on loading the driver.

Keeping Your Rodent Clean

Mouse maintenance is important. Most manufacturers let you open up the bottom of your mouse to clean the roller ball mechanism, which you can do with a small brush or mini-vacuum. You should do this once a month or so, or if your mouse starts acting erratically.

When the mouse is correctly hooked up, you can use it to move an on-screen cursor, or pointer. When you point to something on-screen and click one of the mouse buttons, a program-dependent operation is initiated. The mouse is most often used in programs that make heavy use of graphics, including the graphical user interface of Microsoft Windows.

Some mouse drivers come with special control panel software. This software (like the CPANEL.COM program that comes with the Microsoft mouse) lets you adjust various mouse settings, such as sensitivity and speed. Because each type of mouse works differently, refer to your mouse documentation for instructions.

10 Do's and Don'ts for Keeping Your Mouse Running

1. *Do* install your mouse driver in either your CONFIG.SYS or AUTOEXEC.BAT file.

2. *Don't* swing your mouse by the tail and use it to swat flies.

3. *Do* clean your mouse by removing the roller ball and cleaning out any dirt and debris.

4. *Don't* roll your mouse over your computer screen—the proper signals are transmitted by the cable, thank you.

5. *Do* adjust your mouse settings from the control panel software, if available.

6. *Don't* pick up your mouse and talk into the bottom of it, saying things like "Beam me up, Scotty."

7. *Do* use a mouse pad; it gives you better traction.

8. *Don't* try to use your keyboard arrow keys instead of a mouse; they just don't work as well, no matter how hard you try.

9. *Do* set up your software (especially your Windows software) for the specific mouse hooked up to your system.

10. *Don't* connect another peripheral to the same port as that used by your mouse (or a conflicting port).

What To Do When Your Mouse Doesn't Work

A mouse is relatively easy to set up and relatively easy to use. It needs little maintenance, and few things can go wrong with it. But given the right circumstances, something will go wrong. Look at this list to determine what problems your mouse might be causing you.

Problem 1:
Your mouse doesn't work at all

Tweaking the Microsoft Mouse in Windows

The Microsoft Mouse includes a utility that lets you tweak the operation of your mouse in Windows. Just open Control Panel and double-click the Mouse icon. When you do, the Microsoft Mouse dialog box appears. From here, you can adjust lots of mouse options—for example, you can change the acceleration of the mouse, the speed of an acceptable double-click, and the sensitivity of the pointer movement.

When you click on the Buttons button (I've always wanted to say that…), you can reverse the order of the left and right mouse buttons. (Great if you're a southpaw!) When you click on the Pointer button, you open a Pointer Options dialog box that actually lets you change the size and color of the pointer itself, as well as set the growth characteristics of a large pointer and activate the ability of your pointer to leave a trail behind it on-screen. (And, no, these are not called "mouse droppings"!)

The list of options you see depends on the version number of the Microsoft Mouse driver you're using—the newer your mouse (and mouse driver), the more options you'll have!

First, make sure that your mouse is connected correctly to the back of the system unit. You may have the mouse connected to the wrong port on your machine.

Next, check to see whether the mouse driver is loaded. Look for a line in your CONFIG.SYS file such as the following:

```
DEVICE=C:\MOUSE\MOUSE.SYS
```

Or look for a line in your AUTOEXEC.BAT file such as this:

```
C:\MOUSE\MOUSE.COM
```

Finally, the mouse driver may conflict with some other device on the system. Your mouse is probably installed on the port named COM1. This is fine and dandy, but if another device in the system (like a modem) is using the port named COM3, conflicts may develop between the two devices. (Don't ask me why, but it all gets pretty technical and has to do with IRQ lines and interrupts and other stuff regular people don't understand.) If you can reconfigure your mouse to use port COM2, or your other device to use port COM4, you might solve the problem. Each type of device has its own methods for changing ports, so you'll need to check the instructions for your specific mouse and other devices. If this adjustment is beyond you, call in a computer pro, who can do it faster than you can microwave a hot dog.

Problem 2:
Your mouse doesn't work right in Windows

If your mouse just plain doesn't work in Windows, check out all the potential causes in Problem #1. If you still have problems, make sure that you have the right mouse driver selected in the Windows Setup program. (If in doubt, select Microsoft Mouse; nearly every mouse is Microsoft-compatible.) Then make sure that you have the latest driver for your mouse—an older driver might cause erratic or nonexistent operation. If this doesn't fix things, your mouse driver is probably in conflict with some other device on your system (as explained in Problem #1).

If you can't see your mouse pointer when you start Windows, Windows can't correctly detect the kind of mouse you're using. During Setup, Windows attempted to determine which mouse was connected to your system and loaded the appropriate mouse driver. However, sometimes Windows gets it wrong. (Surprise!) If this is the case, you'll need to run the Setup utility and select a different mouse.

If your mouse just quits working in the middle of a Windows session, you probably have a port conflict (COM1/COM3 or COM2/COM4), often after the conflicting device is used (say, after you use your modem or printer). The solution is the same as outlined in Problem #1—you need to reassign your ports.

Problem 3:
You spilled something on your mouse

Just like a keyboard, your mouse doesn't like liquids (or even solids) entering its innards. (Which means: don't spill stuff on your mouse!)

If you do create a wet or dirty mouse, all hope is not lost. First, if possible, take your mouse apart and remove the roller ball. Carefully wash the ball, and use a soft cloth to soak up any excess liquid on the outside and inside of the mouse. Dry the mouse (and all mouse parts) overnight, and then reassemble your mouse. If you plug it in and all works fine, good job! If not... well, fortunately a new mouse only costs $100 or so.

Problem 4:
Your mouse doesn't work with all DOS programs

Some DOS programs automatically load their own mouse drivers when they start. If you get multiple rogue mouse drivers floating around in system memory, some conflicts are bound to occur. Some mouse drivers might cancel out each other and leave you without any functioning mouse drivers. If you think this is your problem, disable one or more of the proprietary mouse drivers.

Problem 5:
Your mouse doesn't work in DOS programs running from within Windows

If your mouse works in Windows but not in a DOS program running within Windows, there could be several causes. First, you have to have a separate mouse driver loaded for your DOS program—that is, just loading a Windows mouse driver won't make your mouse work in a DOS program. Make sure you load a DOS mouse driver before you launch Windows. Normally, this is done by including a line in your AUTOEXEC.BAT file such as:

C:\MOUSE\MOUSE.COM

Note that, depending on your system, you'll load either MOUSE.COM or MOUSE.SYS. If you have a choice, use MOUSE.COM; it works better from within Windows.

One more thing to try: Edit your SYSTEM.INI file and find the [NonWindowsApp] section. If it doesn't already exist, add the following line:

MouseInDOSBox=1

When you restart Windows, this will turn on the ability to use a mouse in a DOS window.

If you do have a DOS mouse driver loaded and the right line in your SYSTEM.INI file, you could have other problems. Try running your DOS program full-screen instead of in a window; this will work sometimes. Also, your DOS mouse won't work in Windows if it's hooked up to COM2 and there's no COM1 active on your system. You may need to reassign your mouse to COM1 to get things moving.

Finally, if you have Windows 3.0 or earlier, you simply can't use your mouse with DOS windows. Upgrade to Windows 3.1 to get mouseability within your DOS windows.

Problem 6:
Your pointer appears, but your mouse doesn't move it

If your mouse pointer appears frozen on-screen, there are two probable reasons why. First, your mouse may not be hooked up properly to your PC. Check your mouse cable to make sure it's firmly connected to the correct port on the back of your system unit.

If that's not the problem, your mouse driver is incorrectly installed—or you have the wrong mouse driver installed. If you're in Windows, run the Windows Setup program and confirm all your mouse settings—make sure that you have the right mouse selected, as well as the right port (if that's an option). If you're in a DOS program, check that you have the right loading line or lines in your CONFIG.SYS or AUTOEXEC.BAT files.

Problem 7:
Using other peripherals causes your mouse to act up

If your mouse quits working after you initiate a print job or use your modem, chances are you have this peripheral on a conflicting interrupt with your mouse. (It's the old COM1/COM3 problem again.) You'll need to change the port assignment of either your mouse or your other peripheral to resolve this conflict.

Problem 8:
Your mouse moves erratically

If you find your mouse jumping around of its own accord (Hah! A mouse with a mind of its own!) or just not holding its position correctly while you're moving it around, chances are you have a bad or incorrect mouse driver loaded on your hard drive. Check with your mouse manufacturer to make sure you have the latest version of the right driver for your mouse. It's also possible that your mouse is dirty or broken; try taking the mouse apart and cleaning it, as discussed earlier in this chapter. Finally, the old interrupt conflict (COM1 vs. COM3) also can cause this problem. Make sure that you have your mouse hooked up to a port that doesn't conflict with other accessories in your system.

It's possible, too, that you need to adjust the settings in your mouse control panel program. Different programs work differently; read the instructions that came with your mouse to determine how to run the control panel program.

Problem 9:
Your mouse moves too fast (or too slow)

This is a matter of taste, of course. Nearly every mouse has some sort of control panel that lets you change its various settings; you'll want to access this utility and make the appropriate adjustments. For example, if you're in Windows, open the Mouse icon in Control Panel and then change the Acceleration setting. (While you're at it, you may want to change the Double Click Speed and Sensitivity settings, which are somewhat related to mouse speed.)

Problem 10:
You can't find your mouse pointer on-screen

Many displays—especially those on portable computers—have trouble tracking fast motion (like that of your mouse), making it look like the pointer disappears when you're moving the mouse. Normally, the pointer reappears when you're finished moving your mouse. There are several solutions to this problem, all enabled by tweaking settings in your mouse control software.

The first thing to do is to change the size of the mouse pointer. You also may be able to change the color of the pointer, and to leave a "mouse trail" behind the cursor. (This puts a trail of pointer images on-screen behind the movement of your mouse pointer.)

There are also third-party solutions to the disappearing pointer problem. Check with your software dealer for utility programs that let you change the shape and size of your mouse pointer.

Problem 11:
You receive an error message about your mouse

Try Before You Buy!

You may want to try swapping your (apparently) dead mouse with a friend's still living rodent. If your friend's mouse works and yours doesn't, that means you really do have a dead mouse. If your friend's mouse *doesn't* work, that means you have problems inside your system unit—or with some system settings!

If you receive an error message saying that the mouse driver could not find the mouse, the mouse was not connected correctly when you booted your computer. Reconnect your mouse and reboot. If you still receive this message, you could have a dead mouse. Buy a new one.

A Final Word on the Mouse

Throughout this chapter, I've successfully avoided using the term "mouses" as the plural of the term "mouse." (This is equivalent to saying "Supermans" instead of "Supermen" when referring to the plural of "Superman.") Some users prefer the term "mice," and others revert to their cartoon-watching youth and use the term "meeces." In the end, it really doesn't matter.

What does matter is that you treat your mouse with respect, because it is one of the two major lifelines to your computer. Use it with care, keep it properly cleaned, and you'll have years of happy mousing with your PC.

What To Do When...

Your Display Looks Funny

CHAPTER FOURTEEN

It's a complicated procedure to put a picture on your computer monitor. First, your PC (or operating system or program) has to generate the instructions to display a character or image. Next, a video card has to interpret this command and then generate the electronic impulses that create the image. Finally, these impulses have to be transmitted (via cable) to your display monitor, which fires up a series of phosphor dots in such a way that a picture is displayed.

Okay, you're saying, so why do I care about all this?

Simple. Any one of these things can go bad, causing you to have display problems.

And fixing problems is what this book is about, so turn the page and learn all about finding and fixing problems with your computer display!

How Your Monitor Works

Most computer systems come out of the box with the video card and monitor already set up and ready to run. That doesn't mean that you can't change cards and monitors, however. Before I proceed with the trouble-shooting part of this chapter, look at how the words and pictures get put on the monitor screen.

A monitor really does work like a TV set. It receives a video signal from the system unit through a standard video cable. This cable is different from the kind used on your home TV set, however, because PC video is different from TV video. It's impossible to view normal TV on a PC monitor without a special adapter card installed in the system unit.

It's the Frequency That Counts

What's the Frequency?

Video signals—such as radio and television signals—are transmitted electronically, at specific frequencies. In the case of PC video, the higher the frequency transmitted, the higher the resolution of the picture. Therefore, a VGA card transmits at a higher frequency than an EGA card and delivers a higher-resolution picture to boot.

For the monitor to work at all, you need a PC video card installed in the system unit. This card generates video images at a specified *resolution*, the measurement of how detailed your picture is (the higher the resolution, the sharper the picture). These video images then are displayed on the monitor. The resolution of the card must match the resolution of the monitor, or you get gibberish on-screen. The resolution is actually a by-product of the *video frequency* generated by the card.

Many newer monitors are called *multifrequency* monitors because they can reproduce images at a variety of frequencies and resolutions. With a multi-frequency monitor, you can change video cards or even change resolution on the same video card, without having to buy a new monitor.

More Colors, Slower Speed

When you choose a more complex video driver—such as one with higher resolution or more colors—you run a good chance of slowing down the performance of your system. The more complex the video images, the more slowly your monitor runs. Unless you have a video card with lots of onboard video memory, you may want to use a standard 16-color VGA driver to maximize your system's performance.

As explained in Chapter 2, there are several display standards for personal computers. The most common displays today have VGA resolution, which displays 640 x 480 pixels. Some newer cards and monitors are capable of Super VGA resolution, which pushes the display to 800 x 600 resolution or higher. The more pixels in the display, the more detailed the information you can display on-screen.

Note, however, that although the system may be capable of displaying a higher resolution, you may prefer a lower-resolution display. With a higher-resolution display, more information is displayed on-screen, but the information itself (whether the number of characters or Windows) is smaller. Many users will compromise the amount of information they can display in order to have that information displayed at a size they can view comfortably.

Getting in the Driver's Seat

Your system must be told what resolution the card uses. This is done by loading a *driver* for the video display into the system's memory. You don't need to load a driver for normal DOS operation. To display more lines on

> ### Getting Pixelated
>
> A *pixel* is one dot of information on your screen. The more dots your monitor can display, the higher the resolution of your video image. Different video standards display different amounts of pixels; for example, VGA cards and monitors display a picture that's 640 pixels wide by 480 pixels tall.

your screen or more characters per line, however, you need to load the video driver into memory (normally through a command in the CONFIG.SYS or AUTOEXEC.BAT file) and configure the driver to the mode you want to display. See your video card's documentation for more detailed information.

Some programs, like Microsoft Windows, often require specific drivers to be loaded to take advantage of their various graphical modes. Many of these programs load the drivers automatically when the programs start, and then you have the capability to select the video mode from a setup menu within your program. Make sure that your programs are set up correctly for your video card.

The card must also be set up for the monitor and the system. Most cards use a software program for this purpose, although some cards require you to set switches on the card itself to make these changes. Because each card has its own switch layout, consult the card's documentation for instructions on how to set the switches for your system. In addition, the *motherboard* may have a switch or two that sometimes require adjusting for various types of video cards. Check your system documentation for more details.

What Can Give You Bad Video

All this video card and monitor business sounds fairly complicated to set up, but should run fine after setup, right? Sure, and I have some swamp land in Florida to sell you, too. No, as with any other part of your computer system, things can go wrong with your video setup. Let me count the ways....

- *Your cables may be disconnected.* If the cable from the card to the monitor isn't firmly connected, all sorts of strange images can show up on-screen—or absolutely nothing at all shows up. *Always* check the connections, including the power cable. And while you're at it, make sure that you don't have any bent pins on your cable plugs.

- *Your monitor may need adjusting.* Most monitors have the same type of picture controls as your TV set—contrast, brightness, and even vertical and horizontal hold on some models. Some monitors let you adjust the size and position of the display image itself. If your display doesn't look right, adjust it.

- *You may have a bad monitor-card combination.* Believe it or not, some cards don't work with some monitors. In particular, you can't use a higher-resolution card with a lower-resolution monitor. Check with your dealer to make sure that you have the right monitor-card combination.

- *Your video card may be inserted wrong.* The video card is just like any other card in your computer. If the video card isn't seated in its slot correctly, it won't work right.

- *Your video card may be set up incorrectly.* Most video cards use either software programs or switches on the card itself to adapt them to a particular monitor and system. If the card's switches are set wrong, the display might not work at all. Check your card's switch settings against those recommended in the card's documentation.

- *Your drivers may be set up incorrectly.* If you've loaded the wrong video driver for your card or monitor, you could get gibberish on your screen. Always check the driver setup.

- *You may need a new video driver.* Check with the manufacturer of your video card to make sure that you have the latest version of its video driver. Older drivers may not work with newer versions of your programs.

- *You may have the wrong driver for your particular system.* Some video cards come with drivers for several different resolutions. Remember, you can't use a high-resolution driver with a low-resolution monitor, no matter which video card is installed in your system.

- *You may have the wrong video driver installed in Windows.* This is probably the most common Windows video problem. Run the Windows Setup program and make sure that you selected the right driver for your video card.

- *Your programs may be set up incorrectly.* If the video setup in a specific program is incorrect, you could get gibberish on your screen. Check all your programs to make sure that they're set up for your video card.

- *You may have an upper-memory conflict.* That's right, your video card may be in conflict with something else in system memory. If so, you'll have to modify your SYSTEM.INI file or consult a pro to provide a fix.

- *Your monitor may be on the fritz.* If your TV can go on the fritz, your PC monitor can go on the fritz, too. If you get lots of lines on-screen, or smoke out the back of the monitor, or if nothing at all happens, suspect the worst.

- *Your video card may be bad.* Enough said.

10 Do's and Don'ts for Your System Video

1. *Do* buy the best monitor and video card you can afford, and run the monitor at the highest resolution you can.

2. *Don't* set up your programs with a different display driver from the one that matches your video card. (See your system or video card documentation to determine what driver you are using.)

3. *Do* use a screen-saver program to prevent phosphor burn-in. This prevents "ghost" images from appearing on your monitor if a static image is left on-screen too long.

4. *Don't* install more than one video card in your PC.

5. *Do* adjust the contrast and brightness to obtain the best picture.

6. *Don't* get upset if you measure your monitor and find that it comes up smaller than what was advertised. For some reason, PC manufacturers measure the size of your monitor's picture tube before it's inserted into its case, so that the supposedly 14-inch diagonal monitor you bought only has 13 inches of diagonal viewing space.

7. *Do* make sure that your monitor is actually plugged in, turned on, and correctly hooked up to your PC.

8. *Don't* use an outdated video driver for your system.

9. *Do* clean your monitor screen to prevent dirt and dust buildup.

10. *Don't* expect to hook your monitor up to cable to watch *Mystery Science Theater 3000*—PC monitors can't display normal television or cable signals without a special adapter card.

What To Do When Your Display Goes Bad

Now I get down to the juicy part—figuring out what's causing what. Here's a look at some of the most common display problems you may encounter.

Problem 1:
Your monitor is dead—the power light is not on

Check all the cables. Is the power cable for the monitor plugged into a power source? Is the power source turned on? Is the monitor turned on?

If the cables are okay and the monitor is turned on and has power, you have a problem with your monitor, probably in the power supply. See your local repair center.

Problem 2:
Your monitor is dead—the power light is on

If the power light for the monitor is on, all the power cables are okay. The cable from the monitor to the system unit, however, may have a bad connection. You should also check your video card to make sure that it is installed and set up properly. In addition, check your monitor's contrast and brightness controls to make sure that they're turned up enough to display a picture.

If you still don't have a picture, try connecting another monitor to the system. If that monitor displays, you have a hardware problem with your monitor. If the second monitor doesn't work either, the problem is probably with your video card. Try installing a new card or having your existing setup examined by a professional.

Problem 3:
Your monitor does not display—the system unit issues a series of beeps

Your computer system uses beeps to communicate with you when something is wrong with the video setup. Check the settings on your video card to make sure that they're correct for your system. Also check any switches on the motherboard to make sure that they're set up correctly for your type of video card. (You should consult your system's instruction manual for details on this procedure.) Check to make sure that your video card is seated properly in its slots. If none of these suggestions works, try a new video card, or have your system examined by a professional.

The Big Switch

When your video card is installed and set up properly, you probably will never need to change its switch settings—unless, of course, you hook up a higher-resolution monitor and you set up your card to send higher-resolution signals. About the only time you have to worry about these switches is when you first install the card; if everything works okay then, you'll never have to touch your switches.

If you have two video cards installed in a system, they can interfere with each other and cause neither to work properly. Make sure that you remove your old card when you install a new card.

Problem 4:
Your monitor does not display—it makes a high-pitched whine

This whine indicates that your monitor, for some reason, is operating at the wrong frequency. Turn it off *immediately*—this problem could seriously damage your monitor! Now check the settings on your video card. Chances are that it's set to a higher resolution than your monitor is capable of displaying. If this isn't the problem, your video card itself could be defective. If your video card is okay, your monitor may be defective.

Problem 5:
Your Windows video looks like garbage

If you're having trouble with your video from within Windows, there are several common causes:

- *You're using the wrong video display driver.* Run the Windows Setup program from the DOS prompt and check the driver you have installed.

- *You're using an outdated video driver.* Check with your video card's manufacturer to obtain the latest version of the video driver.

- *You're using a screen saver that Windows doesn't like.* Some screen savers leave garbage on-screen when you close them. Try disabling your screen saver and see if that rectifies your problem.

- *Windows isn't configured properly for your system.* It's possible that you may have the wrong screen grabber installed on your hard disk or selected in your SYSTEM.INI file. Try reinstalling Windows to get the right grabber on your disk—or see a Windows pro if you don't know what a screen grabber is.

- *You have a loose connection or a bad cable.* Check all your connections and cables. Make it a rule to be certain that all the parts of your system are hooked up and set up properly.

Problem 6:
Your monitor displays nonsense characters

First, check the cables. A bad connection or a damaged cable can cause garbage to be sent to the monitor.

The most likely cause for this problem, however, is an incorrect video driver setup. Check the video setup (if any) in your AUTOEXEC.BAT or CONFIG.SYS file, as well as the video setup in all your software programs. Make sure that the right driver for your video card is selected. Remember, you can't make a low-resolution card and monitor into high resolution just by selecting a different driver. The driver must match the video card.

It's also possible that a certain software program needs a newer version of the video driver to work correctly. Contact the manufacturer of your video card or the vendor of your software program to make sure that you have the most up-to-date driver available. (Updated drivers—actually small computer files—are usually available for free or for a nominal charge.)

Problem 7:
Your monitor pops and crackles and starts to smell

Like the rest of a computer system, monitors can get dusty. When dust builds up inside the monitor, it can generate static charges.

It's also possible that the power supply inside the monitor has become defective. If the monitor demonstrates these symptoms, turn it off immediately and take it to a repair center. The technicians can either clean your monitor or replace the power supply, if necessary.

Problem 8:
Your monitor displays characters or graphics that are larger (or smaller) than expected

As with Problem 6, this problem is caused by an incorrect video driver setup. Check your software programs and make sure that you have the right driver—and the right video mode—selected.

Note that sometimes new software programs can affect the settings on your older programs. For example, a new program may reset your system to a different video mode. Make sure that all your programs have the right video mode selected in their setup routines.

It's also possible that a particular software program needs a newer version of the video driver to work correctly. Contact the manufacturer of your video card to make sure that you have the most up-to-date driver available.

Problem 9:
Your monitor displays an error message

At least, if you see an error message, you know that video signals are getting to your monitor. Look for these common messages:

```
Bad or missing ANSI.SYS
```

Some programs need the ANSI.SYS driver loaded in order to function. (For example, if you want to display your DOS prompt in colors, you need first to load the ANSI.SYS driver.) Check your CONFIG.SYS file to make sure that it includes a line similar to the following:

```
DEVICE=C:\DOS\ANSI.SYS
```

If this line is not in your CONFIG.SYS file, add it. If this line is in your file, ANSI.SYS is in a different directory or has been erased from your hard disk. Recopy the file to your DOS directory from your original DOS disks and reboot your computer.

```
Bad or missing FILENAME
```

In this message, the FILENAME refers to your video card's device driver file. Make sure that the driver has been copied to your hard disk and that it is referenced correctly in either your CONFIG.SYS or AUTOEXEC.BAT file.

```
4xx
5xx
23xx
24xx
32xx
39xx
74xx
```

One of these messages indicates that you have a defective video card or a problem on the motherboard, or that you are trying to display in a mode that your system can't display. Check all the switch settings on your card and motherboard, and if the problem persists, see a repair technician.

Problem 10:
Your display is missing lines or text

This problem indicates that your software setup is incorrect for your current video card. You could be forcing a higher resolution on a card that can display only lower resolutions. Check your settings to make sure that they're correct.

It's also possible that the DOS MODE command has been used incorrectly. This command sets your DOS display for either 80-column monochrome display (BW), 40-column color display (CO40), or 80-column color display (CO80). Reset the mode by typing the following command:

    MODE CO80

(If necessary, replace CO80 with BW or CO40, depending on the display you select.)

Your video card may have come with a utility that allows you to set other higher-resolution text display modes. If you're using this utility, make sure that you're not pushing your card or monitor to display modes it isn't capable of.

Finally, it's possible that the monitor may be at fault. A defective multifrequency monitor might not be switching to the right modes when instructed. If all else fails, have a technician check your monitor—and the rest of your system.

Problem 11:
You can't find your mouse pointer on-screen

Many displays—especially those on laptop computers—have trouble tracking fast motion (like that of your mouse), making it look as though the pointer disappears when you're moving the mouse. Normally the pointer reappears when you're done moving your mouse.

There are several solutions to this problem, all enabled by tweaking the options available in the control software that comes with the mouse. The first thing to do is to change the size of the mouse pointer. You can also change the color of the pointer, or instruct your programs to leave a "mouse trail" behind the cursor.

There are also third-party solutions to the disappearing pointer problem. Check with your software dealer for utility programs that let you change the shape and size of your mouse pointer.

This situation can also happen with some programs that allow you to change the shape or color of the on-screen pointer. Make sure that you haven't accidentally created a cursor you can't see (such as a blue cursor on a blue background).

Problem 12:
The display on your portable computer is dim

This problem can happen with an LCD display subjected to temperature extremes. If the screen is too hot or too cold, the liquid crystals may not react properly to the electrical impulses used to generate the display images. If this is your problem, turn off your laptop and let it adjust to normal room temperature before you use it again.

Another cause of this problem is that your computer's battery may be getting weak. It's also possible that your LCD display is going bad or that your contrast or brightness controls are not adjusted correctly. If the problem persists under normal conditions, go to a repair center.

Problem 13:
Your screen display flickers

Some high resolution displays (1024 × 768) use what is called *interlaced display technology*. An interlaced display lets you run higher resolutions on lower-cost hardware, but sometimes results in a very annoying screen flicker. Your options are to buy a video card/monitor combination that can run in *noninterlaced* mode, or to select a lower video resolution, such as 800 x 600 or normal VGA (640 × 480).

Problem 14:
Your fonts don't display properly

It's possible that you may have the wrong fonts installed in one or more of your programs (or within the Windows environment). Check to make sure that you have the right fonts installed for your system. (You might try uninstalling all your fonts, and then *reinstalling* them one at a time.)

If you're in Windows and trying to view TrueType fonts at a very small type size, you may be disappointed. True-Type is not optimized for small type sizes, so Windows substitutes the generic MS Sans Serif font for whatever TrueType font you selected below a specific size.

Also note that most fonts displayed at very large sizes will look somewhat jagged

---

In Search of Missing Fonts

A common problem with certain Windows applications, including Word for Windows and Ami Pro, occurs when you have a font installed, yet you can't access the font from your application. You check your font setup and verify that the font is really installed, but it still doesn't show up in your application. What's the deal? You have to have a *printer* selected in your application before the application will display all your available fonts. That's right, if you don't have a printer selected, Word for Windows and other applications won't let you use all your pretty screen fonts. So use Control Panel to select a printer, and all your fonts will show up in your application's font selection list.

---

on-screen. This is just a function of how most programs handle fonts, and won't affect how the fonts are actually printed on paper.

A Final Word on Looking at Your Computer

Some people claim that working at a computer for an extended period can be bad for your eyesight. To minimize any eye strain, make sure that you have the brightness and contrast of your monitor adjusted to a comfortable level and that you're using a screen resolution that doesn't make you squint to see small characters. Also, make sure that your room lighting is adjusted for proper PC use. You might want to turn down the room lights a bit, and make sure that no lights are shining directly on your screen or into your eyes. When you create a more comfortable workspace, the hours spent at your computer are much more satisfying—and productive.

What To Do When...

Your Printer Won't Print

CHAPTER FIFTEEN

The nice thing about a printer problem is that it really doesn't throw all your plans into jeopardy. Even if your printer isn't printing, you can always copy the files you want to print to a disk and take that disk to another PC to print.

However, if your printer isn't printing, sooner or later you do want to fix the problem. After all, the old "sneaker net" just isn't high-tech enough (or convenient enough!) if you really can get your printer back in tip-top shape—without *too* much fuss and muss!

How Printers Print

In the early days of personal computing, you needed to be a technical wizard to get your printer set up and printing. You had to worry about DIP switches and serial ports and device names and control codes. It almost made you want to forget the printer entirely and just take Polaroids of your computer screen.

These days, most of the technical stuff is taken care of by the operating system and software programs, making your life a whole lot easier. All you have to do is plug in the printer, hook it up to your computer, and tell your software programs what kind of printer you're using. In a matter of minutes, you're printing, and you can use your Polaroid camera for better things.

Printers print when they receive data transmitted from your computer system. In almost all instances, the data is generated by a software program, formatted for your type of printer, translated into a form your printer can understand, and transmitted through ports and cables to the printer. There the information is fed into the printer's memory (yes, even printers have small amounts of memory) and printed on sheets or rolls of paper. Different printers print in different ways, however.

Impact Printers

An *impact printer* is so named because ink is put on paper by means of some sort of impact. There are two main types of impact printers—*dot-matrix* and *daisywheel*.

Dot-matrix printers are low priced, noisy, and fast, and they produce output not quite suitable for publication. They're great, however, for producing continuous numeric data, like that produced by spreadsheets. They're not so great for producing high-quality letters or desktop-published newsletters.

With a dot-matrix printer, a print head—composed of a matrix of dots, hence the name—strikes the paper through an inked ribbon. (Actually, the dots are made by metal pins on the print head.) The greater the number of pins, the more detailed the printed resolution. Most dot-matrix printers have either 9 or 24 pins, with the 24-pin models providing the sharpest output.

Dot-matrix printers typically print on tractor-fed, continuous-feed paper. (This type of paper is normally referred to as "computer paper" and is available in plain white or the stylish two-tone green-bar variety.) You need to change the printer ribbon periodically and watch for the deterioration of the print heads over time.

Daisy-wheel printers, on the other hand, used to be popular, but aren't used much in today's computing world. Essentially, they work just like an electric typewriter, with a "daisywheel" composed of specific print characters. The wheel revolves and strikes the paper through an inked ribbon. Print quality from a daisywheel printer is higher than that of a dot-matrix printer, but the printers themselves are slow and noisy and totally incapable of producing graphics.

Nonimpact Printers

Nonimpact printers are where the market's at today. Computer users want good print quality, high-quality graphics, noiseless operation, and low cost—which, today, comes from nonimpact inkjet and laserjet printers.

The lowest-priced nonimpact printer is the *inkjet printer*. Inkjet printers produce printout by spraying ink through holes in a matrix, producing output similar to that of dot-matrix printers. These printers are quieter (although slightly slower) than dot-matrix printers and are capable of producing high-quality graphics. You can also get color inkjet printers at affordable prices.

The best printers available today are *laser printers*. Popularized by Hewlett-Packard's LaserJet models, these printers use a small laser to transfer *toner* (a kind of ink in powder form) to paper. Like inkjet printers, laser printers print on single-sheet paper, with the only moving parts being in the paper-feed mechanism. Laser printer output is extremely high quality, and the process is fast and quiet.

Laser printers, like inkjet printers, use *page description languages* (PDLs). A PDL is essentially a way of printing both text and graphics through a series of mathematical descriptions sent from the software program. These languages produce text using software-defined *fonts*, as opposed to the hardware-specific fonts used by impact printers. You can add fonts to your system through add-on software packages, such as those available by Adobe or Bitstream.

The most advanced PDL is *PostScript*, developed by Adobe. PostScript printers, although more expensive than printers using HP's PDL, have a wider variety of high-quality fonts available to them. PostScript printers typically cost several hundred dollars more than HP-compatible printers, but a PostScript printer is worth the extra cost if you do professional desktop publishing.

How To Get and Keep Your Printer Printing

Even though you'll need to perform some periodic maintenance to keep your printer in perfect working shape, this extra work pays off in extended life for your printer, and less down time for you. And, speaking of extra work, you have some additional setup options to consider if you're running Windows. But, all in all, it's easy to hook up your printer—and even easier to keep it printing.

Hooking Your Printer to Your Computer

Hooking up your printer is a piece of cake. Begin by plugging it into a power source and filling it with paper. (Also make sure that you have a new ribbon or toner cartridge installed.) Then run the printer cable (normally supplied with your printer) to your computer, and plug it into the appropriate port on the back of the computer. (A *port* is what serious computer users call the connectors that stick out the back of your system unit. Each port serves a specific purpose and can be connected to a printer, a monitor, a modem, a mouse, and so on.) That's it—the hookup is complete.

Now, you still need to set up all the programs on the system to recognize your new printer. Setup operations differ from program to program, but in general, you need to tell each program the make and model of printer you've just hooked up. Each program then loads a *printer driver* specific to your printer, which it uses to create the print files it sends to the printer.

A printer driver is nothing more than a small file that contains the instructions necessary for your system to use the corresponding device. In this case, the device is the printer, which is physically attached to the back of your PC's system unit. The device driver, as with all files, is installed on your hard disk. You must have the right driver for your particular printer present on your hard disk and loaded (via an option in each of your software programs). If you use multiple printers, you use multiple printer drivers. If you add a new printer to your system, you must install a new printer driver. This is important to remember.

Printing from Windows

Windows, being a nice, unified operating environment, centralizes all printing functions into what it calls the Print Manager. From here you select which printer(s) Windows will use, and then all Windows programs use these same printers—and the same printer settings. If you want to add more printer

Selecting a Driver

If you can't find your printer's driver listed in your program's setup routine, there are some generic drivers you can use. For example, if you have a dot-matrix printer, it probably can emulate an Epson printer, so you can safely select the Epson printer driver. Most laser printers can emulate the Hewlett-Packard LaserJet, so you can select the LaserJet driver. If worse comes to worst, you can generally choose a generic or "vanilla" driver that functions adequately for most printers.

fonts to your system, you again add them globally—once Windows has them loaded, they're accessible from all Windows applications. This saves you mucho time and trouble, and works pretty well in most cases.

You add new printers to Windows by opening the Control Panel and double-clicking the Printers icon. When the Printers dialog box appears, you're presented with a listing of current Installed Printers.

Printing by Default

Even though you may have multiple printers installed on your system, only one of these can be your main, or *default*, printer at any given time. (The default printer is the printer that your applications automatically use for printing, unless instructed otherwise.) To set one of the printers listed in the Printers dialog box as the default printer, simply select the printer and then click on the Set As Default Printer button.

To add a new printer, you need to select the Add button. At that point the Printers dialog box expands to show a List of Printers. Scroll through this list and select the printer you want to install; then press the Install button. (If your printer is not listed—which is not likely—you'll need to select the Install Unlisted or Updated Printer option and follow the instructions from there.)

If you're lucky, the printer driver for the new printer is already on your hard disk, in which case Windows simply adds the new printer to the Installed Printers list. If the driver is not on your hard disk, Windows will prompt you to insert a particular installation disk into your disk drive. Windows will then copy the printer driver from this disk to your hard disk, and proceed with the installation.

Windows Printing Made Easier

If you're using an HP LaserJet printer from Windows, there's a new add-on that can speed up your printing. Microsoft (yes, *that* Microsoft!) is now selling something called the *Windows Printing System*. This kit consists of a special cartridge you plug into the front of your LaserJet, along with a special software program that you install and run from Windows. The software program replaces the Windows Print Manager, and gives you additional control over the printing process. The cartridge includes 79 different TrueType fonts. The Windows Printing System is a must for all Windows users with LaserJet printers!

After the printer is installed, you can then configure a myriad number of options within Windows that will affect the way your printer prints. When you select the Setup button in the Printers dialog box, you're presented with a dialog box full of options specific to your selected printer. You may even have additional options available to you beyond this dialog box. Because each printer driver has different options, I can't tell you exactly what you'll see. I will tell you that the default options are generally acceptable, although you may want to call in your resident PC pro to guide you through some of the more obscure features of your printer.

Using Fonts

A Font of Knowledge

A font is, technically, a specific combination of typeface and style. Each typeface has a name (such as Helvetica or Times Roman), and can be printed in specific styles (such as bold or italic). Different fonts have different impacts in your printed documents; you generally want to use serif fonts (fonts that have those little decorations on the ends of letters) for body text, and sans serif fonts (fonts without those little decorations) for headlines. You also don't want to use too many fonts in a single document; it makes the page less readable, plus it takes more time to print!

After your printer is connected and you've been using it for a while, you may start to get bored with the selection of *fonts* available to you. If you're using Windows 3.1, you have access to *TrueType* font technology, which makes it easy to add new fonts that can be printed with good results on just about any printer. If you're a DOS user, you'll need to add a font package specific to the application(s) you're using. (For example, many companies sell font packages for WordPerfect; these WordPerfect fonts generally won't work with other programs.)

To add new fonts to Windows, you must open the Control Panel and double-click the Fonts icon. The Fonts dialog box displays all Installed Fonts, along with a Sample of the currently selected font. When you want to add new fonts, select the Add button to display the Add Fonts dialog box. From the Add Fonts dialog box, you need to instruct Windows where to look for the new fonts. When you select the OK button, Windows will go through the font installation procedure, during which you'll click OK a couple of times to install your new fonts to your hard disk and to Windows. Now, when you next access your favorite Windows program, your new fonts will show up in your font listing boxes along with all your previously installed fonts.

Adding new fonts to DOS programs is not a universal experience. You need to consult the directions for your specific software program (and font package) to figure out exactly how to install fonts for your specific programs.

Some Simple Printer Maintenance

It helps to spend a little time on printer maintenance to ensure continued peak performance over the life of your printer. Yeah, it's a little time-consuming, but a lot less so than getting your printer repaired!

If you have a dot-matrix or daisywheel printer, you'll want to change the printer ribbon periodically. (You can tell when it's getting old by the deteriorating quality of the printout; characters will be lighter and fuzzier than they were when the ribbon was new.) You'll also want to clean dirt and paper shavings from the inside of the printer; use a small hand-held vacuum or even a small brush.

Laser printers require less maintenance. You will need to replace the toner cartridge periodically; most laser printers will display a message when the toner is getting low. When you replace the cartridge, you also need to wipe

> ### Take Your Printer to Alcoholics Anonymous!
>
> Here's a big no-no for printer maintenance: Don't use alcohol, solvents, or thinners to clean any of your printer's internal parts. These substances cause rubber parts to dry out and become brittle. Instead, use a soft cloth dampened with a mild detergent solution.

clean some of the internal parts. Normally, a swab is included with new cartridges for this purpose, along with cleaning instructions.

Inkjet printers also require replacement of ink cartridges, with very little additional maintenance.

In general, you should check the connections on your printer from time to time. Make sure that all cables are securely fastened to the back of the printer and to the back of your computer. Check the cables for flexibility; cables can get stiff over time and the internal wiring inside can actually snap. Also, check the paper feed on your printer, and keep it free of paper shavings and torn paper.

What Can Go Wrong When You Print

Now that you have your printer drivers installed and your fonts loaded, what possibly could go wrong with your printer? Plenty, pardner!

First, you may have the wrong printer driver installed in Windows or a specific software program. You may have either simply selected the wrong driver for your printer, or the driver selected may be out of date. While we're in this area, it's also possible that various aspects of your printer setup may be incorrect, which can cause some highly unusual problems. You should also check your font setup, because fonts themselves can cause perplexing problems if they're not installed correctly.

If you're using Windows, you may not have enough disk space or memory to print. Make sure that you have plenty of both, because Windows needs all the space it can get to complete the printing operation. Also, make sure that you're not trying to print from both a Windows and a DOS application at the same time—it just won't work.

Finally, you could have real printer hardware problems. These problems range from the mundane (you're out of paper, you forgot to turn on the printer, you have a bad connection) to the fairly serious (your printer is broken!). Check all your cables and connections—and make sure that your printer is actually turned on!

The bottom line is, there are a lot of things you need to check if you have printer problems, both hardware and software related. So if you have printing problems, hunker down and plow through the problems/solutions section after the Top 10 list.

10 Do's and Don'ts for Your Printer

1. *Do* keep your printer in a well-ventilated area, free from dust and cigarette smoke.

2. *Don't* pull out a sheet of paper while the printer is still printing. Also, don't pull out tractor-fed paper by the paper itself; use the knob on the side of the printer.

3. *Do* recycle the toner cartridges on your laser printer.

4. *Don't* turn off your printer in the middle of a print job if you can help it.

5. *Do* connect your printer to a surge suppressor.

6. *Don't* stick a chocolate candy bar into the paper feed opening; giving your printer a "sugar buzz" won't speed up the printing one iota.

7. *Do* perform periodic maintenance, such as cleaning dust from the inside of the paper path.

8. *Don't* run your printer 24 hours a day without a break; this kind of continuous use requires an industrial-grade printer, not a consumer model.

9. *Do* reuse old paper in a laser printer by reinserting it upside down in your paper tray to print on the back side.

10. *Don't* use the wrong kind of paper for your specific printer; using paper that is too thin or too thick can really gum up the works.

What To Do When Your Printer Doesn't Print

The types of problems you may encounter with your printer fall into four basic categories: The printer has no power, the printer doesn't print, the printout is garbled, or pages of the printout are missing. Read on to find out more about each problem and ways to solve it.

Problem 1:
Your printer has no power

This is the perennial problem with computer hardware. By now you know the drill:

1. Make sure that the power cord is plugged into both the power outlet and the back of the printer.

2. Make sure that the power outlet has power; check all fuses and circuit breakers, as well as surge suppressors.

3. Make sure that the printer is on-line. (This is normally accomplished by a front-panel button of some sort.)

4. Check the internal fuse in the printer itself.

If all the right parts in your system have power and your printer is on-line, your problem is more serious. The biggest potential source for this type of problem is the power supply in the printer. At this point, it's time to call the repair center and ready your checkbook.

Problem 2:
Your printer has power but doesn't print

> **Turn It Off To Make It Work**
>
> Anytime you change *any* connection between your system unit and any external device (such as your printer), you probably need to turn your computer off and then back on again for the connection change to register with your system. So if you're plugging in cables, reboot your system when you're done.

The first item to check is whether your printer is connected correctly to your computer. Check the connecting cable to make sure that the connections are tight. You also should unplug each end of the cable to ensure that none of the connecting wires are bent, making a bad connection. You might also want to change the printer cable. Cables can get old, and the wires inside can break; try a new cable and see whether this change fixes the problem.

Next, you should make sure that the printer is connected to the correct port on the back of your computer. Checking the port connection is not always as simple as it seems. Some computers come with more than one printer port, and your printer may be hooked up to the wrong one. If you have additional printer ports, try plugging your printer into the other ports.

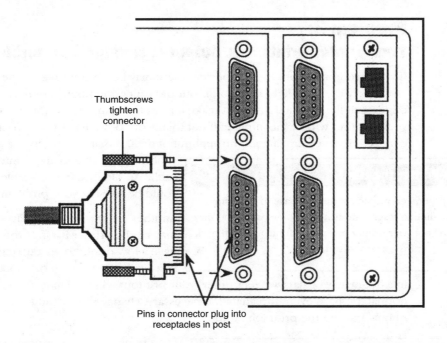

Thumbscrews
tighten
connector

Pins in connector plug into
receptacles in post

If your computer has multiple printer ports, it's also possible that your software is set up incorrectly. Make sure that you have the same printer port selected in your software that you're using with your printer. While you're at it, make sure that the rest of your printer setup in your software is correct. If you're using a dot-matrix printer but your software thinks you have a LaserJet, you're bound to have some sort of problem sooner or later.

Next, check the paper feed of your printer. If you're out of paper, your printer can't print. You also should check the paper path inside the printer to make sure that no stray pieces of paper are lodged inside. Make certain, too, that your printer is *on-line*, or set in the *on* position.

It's also possible that your printer is paused. Check your front panel buttons to make sure that your printer is on-line.

If none of these suggestions solves your problem, you're looking at a major computer or printer problem. Try hooking up another printer to your computer; if the new printer works, it's time to take your old printer into the shop. If the new printer doesn't work, you more than likely have a defective port in your computer.

Problem 3:
Your printer prints, but output is smudged or garbled

If your printout is not as you expected, there may be several causes. The most likely cause, believe it or not, is our old friend the poorly connected cable. If all the instructions don't make it from the computer to the printer, your printout will be incomplete, if not totally out of whack. Check all cable connections to ensure a good throughput of data. If that doesn't fix the problem, just change the printer cable. An old or damaged cable could be causing your problems.

Another cause of print garbage may be the printer itself. If you have a low or old toner cartridge in a laser printer or an old ribbon in a dot-matrix or daisywheel printer, your printout will be lighter than normal, perhaps even unreadable. If necessary, change the cartridge or ribbon and run the print job again.

If you're using a laser printer, you may get black streaks on your output. These are most often caused by an old toner cartridge, or by a dirty roller or printer cleaning bar. If you replace the toner cartridge and clean the suspect parts (using a cotton swab) and you *still* experience black streaks, your printer may need service.

If you're using a dot-matrix or ink-jet printer, it's possible that your print head or print jets are clogged. You'll need to clean the print head (with a commercial print-head cleaner, or just by rubbing a piece of paper across the print head) or unclog the print jet (by inserting a small pin into the jet).

Give Your Printer the Boot

If you have a paper-feed problem, you may have to put your printer back on-line to resume printing. In some cases, you may even have to reboot your printer by turning it off and then back on again to recover from a paper-feed error.

Do As I Say, Not As I Do

The day after I wrote the printing chapter for the first edition of this book, I tried to print out the chapter and received a page of garbage in response. Well, since I'm supposedly an expert in these things, I spent the next hour installing new printer drivers and changing setup configurations, all without changing the resulting output. Finally I remembered to check my cables, and—lo and behold—one of the connectors had come loose. A quick push of the plug later and my output was back to normal. So please—*please!*—learn from my experience and *check your cables first!*

It's also possible that a paper
misfeed in your printer
caused the printout to become smudged or out of
line; if this is the case,
straighten the paper feed
and start the print job again.

An incorrect software setup can also cause unusual printouts. Make sure
that your software is set up for the exact type of printer you're using. Also
make sure that you have the correct landscape (horizontal) or portrait (vertical) printing option selected.

If you're using an add-on
font program, such as Adobe
Type Manager (or using
TrueType fonts under Win-
dows 3.1), make sure that
you have the same fonts
installed and selected for on-
screen and printer use. If
you're using one font for
display and another for
printout, you may be disappointed in the results.

If none of this works, you probably have a problem somewhere in your
printer. Although a bad printer port on your PC could be the culprit, more
than likely some internal problem with your printer is causing the poor
printout. Consult your friendly repair center.

Problem 4:
Your printed page looks half finished

If you're using a laser printer and trying to print a document with a lot of
graphics, you may find that your printer doesn't have enough memory to
print the entire document. What you'll get is about half the document—and
not always a contiguous half! You can do one of several things to rectify the
problem:

1. *Add more memory to your printer.* If you do a lot of heavy graphics
   printing, you probably need at least 1M of RAM installed in your
   printer. You may be able to add the memory yourself, or you may
   want to have a qualified laser printer technician do the job for you.

2. *Instruct your program to print this document at a lower resolution.* Many programs (including the Windows environment) have options that let you lower the output resolution (often called printing in "draft" mode), which requires less memory—and gives you less finely detailed output.

3. *Simplify your document.* If you're using a lot of different fonts and graphics, take some out. It's not an ideal solution, but it may be the only way you'll get this particular document printed on time!

Problem 5:
Your printer prints, but pages are missing

If you're missing the last page of a printout, it's possible that it is still in your printer's memory, waiting for a *form feed* signal from your computer. (The fact that the printer didn't get the signal indicates that your software is probably not set up correctly.) This problem is especially common with laser printers, and the immediate solution is to press the form-feed button on your printer to eject the page.

It's also possible that the last page is stuck in your printer. Check the paper path to make sure that no pages are gumming up the works.

Sometimes, an incorrect software setup can cause bizarre printing problems. (This problem seems to be most acute with laser printers, because they have more setup options.) If, for example, you have your software set up for legal paper but your printer thinks it's printing letter-sized sheets, you'll get results that only remotely could be considered readable. Again, check your software program to make sure that the printer setup is correct.

Problem 6:
Your printer prints, but fonts aren't correct

Font problems are becoming major setbacks in today's computing environment. Many programs come with add-on fonts, such as Adobe Type Manager (ATM), TrueType, and PostScript. When you install a new font, you actually install one font for the screen display and another for printed output. It's possible that the fonts for the screen display are different from those for the printer, or that only the screen fonts were installed. If you have a font mismatch, check your font setup to make sure that you're using fonts that are actually installed for printing. If the font isn't there, or if you suspect that it was installed incorrectly, reinstall the font.

This problem often occurs with documents created on one PC and transferred to another PC. It's possible that the original PC had fonts installed that aren't installed on the second PC. In this case, you may need to edit the document to change to fonts that do exist on that system.

Problem 7:
Your printer ribbon gets damaged (or twisted, or just doesn't work right)

If your printer ribbon is not installed properly, it can get twisted as it moves back and forth across your printer's print head. A twisted ribbon might eventually tear or jam, or may deplete its ink supply—leaving you with very light (or no) printing on paper. Check your ribbon to make sure that it's inserted properly (not backwards!), with no twists, turns, or kinks in its path.

Problem 8:
Your color printer doesn't print all available colors

This could be caused by a couple of problems. First, you may not have a color ink cartridge or ribbon inserted. You can't print color from black-and-white cartridges and ribbons!

Second, your ink cartridge or ribbon may be getting old. Typically, some colors will get depleted before others, throwing off your color output. If you're seeing less blue (or red or yellow or black) than normal, chances are it's time to change your cartridge or ribbon.

Problem 9:
Paper jams in your printer

If you're using a dot-matrix or daisywheel printer, it's possible that your form-feed paper has become misaligned on your tractor feed. Remove the paper, realign the little holes on the side with the form-feed mechanism, and start over. (This problem often occurs if you're using a cheap grade of paper, or paper that is extra-thin; you might try beefing up the quality and weight of your form-feed paper.)

If you're using a laser or inkjet printer, it's possible that your printer's internal paper-feed mechanisms are getting dirty. You can try taking the printer apart yourself to clean out any pieces of scrap paper or other debris, or you may want to take it into the shop to let a pro deal with it.

You may also be getting some paper sticking to other sheets of paper in your paper tray. Try thumbing through the stack of paper before inserting it into the tray; this should loosen up the paper and make it feed easier into your printer.

Finally, as with dot-matrix and daisywheel printers, you may need to change the grade of paper you use with your laser or inkjet printer. Lightweight papers tend to jam up the works, so switch to something heavier if you experience a lot of problems.

Problem 10:
Your printer is *slo-o-o-o-w*

Well, sometimes printing *is* slow! Check these hints for speeding up your printer's performance:

- *Simplify your documents.* If you use a lot of different fonts or graphics, they all take longer to print.

- *Print in "draft" mode, if available.* Many programs let you print in a lower-resolution mode, which takes less time than the normal high-resolution mode.

- *Make sure that you have the right fonts installed in your program.* Whenever possible, use fonts that are built into your printer, or available via a print cartridge; these often print faster than software-based fonts.

- *Add memory to your printer.* Most laser printers print faster if they have more memory.

- *Use the fonts built into your printer.* Downloading scalable fonts (such as TrueType and ATM fonts) takes time and memory. If, instead, you use the fonts included with your printer, you'll speed up your printing time dramatically.

- *If you're in Windows, use TrueType fonts.* Microsoft's TrueType fonts are often faster to print than ATM fonts; use 'em!

- *Free up extra memory and disk space.* If you're printing from Windows, make sure that you have plenty of free memory and free disk space. Windows printing uses both RAM and disk space to buffer information during printing, and a lack of either can slow things down.

- *If you're using an HP LaserJet printer in Windows, use Microsoft's Windows Printing System.* This add-on kit can really speed up your Windows printing!

The Last Word on Printers

Most printer problems are easily corrected. Those that aren't often result in costly repairs. For that reason, make sure that you keep your printer clean and functioning. Treat your printer with respect, and it will give you years of dedicated service. Don't, and it can be a real pain in the neck.

What To Do When...

Your Computer Won't Communicate

CHAPTER SIXTEEN

Computer bulletin boards.

Prodigy.

America OnLine.

CompuServe.

The Internet.

The Information Superhighway.

These are all ways to communicate with other computer users, using your computer and a modem. On-line communicating is the biggest computing trend of the '90s, and it isn't as easy as it sounds. In fact, using your modem can be downright problematic, unless you turn the page and read Miller's advice on how to make on-line communications a piece of cake!

All About Communicating On-Line

When one computer speaks directly to another computer over the telephone lines, techie types call it *on-line communication*, or *telecommunication*. Other, more hip people call it "entering *cyberspace*" or "cruising the *information superhighway*" or "information surfing." Whatever you call it, however, it's a great way to talk to other computer users (via your keyboards and monitor screens) or exchange information (via computer files and programs).

You can converse screen-to-screen with other users; you can contact local *bulletin board systems (BBSs)* for information to download into your computer; and you can dial up national on-line services that enable you to exchange *electronic mail (e-mail)* messages and data files with other users. You can even access that great network of networks, the on-ramp to the international information superhighway, *the Internet*.

Interested? Well, before you join the wide, wide world of on-line communications, you need to learn some basic information.

All About Cyberspace and the Information Superhighway

"Information Superhighway" is a great phrase, because it means so many different things to so many different people. To some (such as Vice President Al Gore) it's a futuristic public works project, similar to the federal interstate highway system (but for electronic voyages). To others, it refers to just about anything accessed on-line: BBSs, commercial services, and the Internet. Whatever your definition, the "infobahn" (this is the newest and hippest catchphrase) is the future of interpersonal computing.

The on-line world of the information superhighway is commonly referred to as "cyberspace." This is because when you're on-line, you're really not anywhere physical; you're occupying some artificial place in a cyberreality.

Whatever you call all this stuff, it's pretty fun—and pretty daunting. The variety of what you can find on-line is truly awe-inspiring, whether you're cruising the local bulletin boards or surfing the Internet.

Browsing Bulletin Boards

On-line services range from operations as small as one guy with his computer hooked up to a modem, all the way to giant multinational corporations that serve thousands of users around the world with banks of mainframe computers. (That's right, you could even run your own BBS from your own PC if you really wanted to!) The bigger the service, the more options that are available to you—and the higher the cost, too, I'm afraid.

You see, running a BBS actually costs money. Even if the service amounts to just one guy with a computer in his basement, the cost for telephone lines—and the very real cost in time that's involved in managing such a system—can quickly add up. So naturally, the bigger the system, the higher are its costs to run and maintain. That's why so many BBSs require you to pay a *use fee* when you first log on. The big worldwide services charge you by the minute—and more if you access certain special services. So if you're determined to participate in the wide world of telecommunicating, be prepared to pay for the privilege.

So what exactly *do* you get for your money when you dial up one of these on-line services? Small BBSs often offer you little more than e-mail and a few files to download. Many such BBSs focus on a limited area of interest—you may find science fiction BBSs, game BBSs, even BBSs that specialize in business or adult materials. The larger on-line services, however, encompass a wide range of topics and provide individual subsections (called *forums*) to meet specialized needs.

You often have to type in a password to actually gain access to an on-line service; that's so other people can't read your private messages. After you're "in," you can upload and download messages, conference with other members on-line, and download any files from the BBS's file libraries that pique your interest. Some services may act as "gateways" to larger databases and networks, where you can access reams of specialized information (for a price, of course). Going on-line, therefore, can be a great way not only to learn more about the world but to meet some fascinating people in the process.

Cruising Commercial Services

You can think of a commercial on-line service as kind of a giant BBS. These large national and international services offer many more options than do even the most extensive local BBSs, as well as a greater number and variety of people with whom to communicate.

Use CompuServe To Talk to Que!

Que has just opened its own CompuServe forum. You can log onto the Que forum (which is part of the Macmillan Computer Publishing forum) by typing "GO QUE" or "GO MCP" at any CompuServe prompt. From there you can talk to the staff at Que (including me!), converse with Que authors, and download lots and lots of useful utilities and files from the Que library.

CompuServe is the largest and best-known of these services. It features literally hundreds of special-interest forums, such as those for aquarium lovers, science fiction fans, gamers, avid travelers, and comic book readers. You can do much of your weekly shopping through CompuServe's *On-line Mall*, and you can access several on-line travel and airline ticket booking services. CompuServe's biggest claim to fame, however, is its technical forums run by software companies. If you're having trouble with a Microsoft product, you can log onto one of the Microsoft forums and ask a pro for advice. Numerous programs are available to make your CompuServe sessions relatively painless; the two most popular are *CompuServe Information Manager* (in both DOS and Windows versions) and *CompuServe Navigator*.

America OnLine (AOL) is an up-and-coming service, with much the same user profile as CompuServe. AOL's interface is a little more user-friendly than that of CompuServe, and there is a little more commercial information and news available, as well.

Nothing Is Free

One of the things more experienced users tend to dislike about Prodigy is its incessant display of advertising. By selling on-screen ad space, Prodigy helps to lower the cost to users; however, many users just don't like the intrusion. My advice? Decide for yourself!

Prodigy is a more user-friendly service aimed at users who are less technically proficient than those who deal with CompuServe or America OnLine. Many novices find Prodigy easier to use than the other services, and Prodigy charges less for many services than do its more established rivals. Prodigy offers many of the same services as CompuServe, but it focuses more on "regular-people" stuff rather than "techno-nerd" items—although some find it too slow and commercial.

You can usually find local numbers for these services in your telephone book, or your local computer store can help you connect to the service of your choice.

Interfacing with the Internet

The mother of all on-line services really isn't a service at all. The *Internet* is like a giant network that connects you to other networks, including those at large universities and corporations worldwide. Because of its size (over 25 million users worldwide, and growing at about 1 million users per month!), the variety of information available is nothing less than overwhelming.

Believe it or not, the Internet is a "free" service. This is because no one really owns "the Net." It started 25 years ago as a collection of government networks, and before long a lot of universities in the U.S. and around the world were also hooking in. Today, the Internet culture is best described as a democratic anarchy, where it kind of runs itself with the help of proactive users.

How do you hook up to the Internet? Well, first you need an access number. If you're a student on a college campus, or an employee of the government or a large corporation, your local area network may actually be connected to the Net. Otherwise, you need to find a service provider that will let you dial in with your modem.

Accessing the Internet Through a BBS

Many local bulletin boards now include some form of access to the Internet. (Since the Net is just a "network of networks," it's fairly easy for a BBS to hook itself into the loop.) Some boards provide limited access to Internet e-mail and "newsgroups" (kind of like discussion forums); other BBSs supply more robust connections. Generally, the more robust the Internet hookup, the more likely the BBS will charge for the service.

Some Internet service providers have their own "front ends" to the Net. Others offer only a portal, to which you need to supply a front-end program (such as *Mosaic* or *Chameleon*). You can find these front ends on the Net itself (which creates a bit of a catch-22—how can you download something that you need to download itself?), or through other sources. One good source for these front ends are in the many books on the Internet available at your local reseller. Look for books like Que's *Using the Internet* or Hayden's *Internet Starter Kit* that include a disk with Internet front end software.

Once you're on the Net, a whole new world will open up for your browsing pleasure. Everything from e-mail to newsgroups to file libraries to research information is available *somewhere* on the Net. It's a real kick when you start corresponding with someone on another continent, just like they lived next door!

Learning the Lingo

Before you venture too quickly into cyberspace, you must first learn at least the more common terms that are now firmly entrenched in the special vocabulary used by on-line regulars. So put on your thinking caps, all you jargon-lovers out there, and repeat after me....

- When you talk to other users through the use of electronic mail (e-mail), you're "messaging" with them.

- When you talk to them in real time (that is, your words appear on another user's monitor as you type them on your keyboard), you're "conferencing" with them.

- When you transmit a file from your machine to a BBS, you're "uploading" the file.

- When you transmit a file from a BBS to your machine, you're "downloading" the file.

- You "log on" to the BBS when your modem connects to the service, and you "log off" when you disconnect.

- The guy or gal who runs a bulletin board is called the systems operator, or "sysop."

- A "forum" or "newsgroup" is like a big community special-interest discussion group, where you leave messages that are read by other users with similar interests.

Got all that? Good...now it's time to learn some slightly *different* lingo!

Tele-Expressing Your Emotions

When you "message" or "conference" on-line with other computer users, you sometimes want to express an emotion or attitude that may be difficult to convey just in words on a computer screen. That's why a special system of expressions has developed among on-line telecommunicators. These on-line expressions are called "emoticons" (emotion icons) or "smileys" (because they sometimes look like that little yellow smiling face, turned sideways).

When you look at an emoticon sideways (with your head turned to the left), it looks like a face in a particular expression. For example, :-) is an emoticon for happy. (See—I told you they sometimes look like little yellow smiling faces!) And :-(is an emoticon for sad. There are many different emoticons, including some that are completely off the wall. (Would you believe that =:-|> is the emoticon for a punk rocker with a goatee?) Notice, however, that plain old bracketed comments also serve as emoticons to some users; when you see a <g>, which is a shorthand for "grin," it means that the user is just kidding. Pretty cool, eh? <g>.

Of course, there are other emotions expressed in cyberspace. When you send a nasty e-mail message to another user, it's called "flaming" that user. It's not uncommon to see a lot of "flames" on the Internet and other services; it seems a lot of users forget about manners when they go on-line.

Learning about Modems

To travel down the information superhighway, you must first connect your computer to a phone line. To do that, you need to add a *modem* to your system. A modem is, in essence, a little electronic telephone. It can be installed either on a card inside your system unit or outside the unit, hooked up to a communications, or COM, port. Your modem accepts data you input via your keyboard and translates that data into bits and bytes, which the modem then transmits across the phone lines. After another computer or on-line system has received your telephoned transmission, its modem translates these bits and bytes back into readable form, and your telecommunicating begins.

Types of Modems

Modems come in a variety of types, brands, and models. Currently, the most popular modems are based on a standard that was set by the Hayes-brand modems; such modems are referred to as *Hayes-compatible*. Different modems transmit data at varying rates; the faster its transmission rate, the more

---

Put Your Money Where Your Modem Is

Yes, you *can* save money with a faster modem. Using a modem with a faster transmission speed (9,600 baud or more) results in less time spent on-line to those services that charge you by the minute. And the more data that you can transmit in the least amount of time adds up to a corresponding reduction in your on-line bills. Be aware, however, that not all BBSs can transmit over 2,400 baud—and some services charge you an increased rate if you use higher transmission speeds!

---

expensive the modem. Transmission speed is measured in *bauds*. A 2,400-baud modem, for example, is roughly twice as fast as a 1,200-baud modem. Many new modems now transmit at 9,600 or even 14,400 baud!

Communicating Via Fax Modem

As if communicating via modem weren't exciting enough, you can now buy special modems that also let you send and receive faxes from your computer. These *fax modems* communicate both in the language used by other modems and in the language used by fax machines. With special fax modem software, you can send documents from your word processor to other fax machines, and read documents faxed to you directly on-screen. Fax modems often cost a little more than traditional modems, but if you do a lot of faxing, they're worth the price.

Hooking Up a Modem

Unless it's an internal model that comes as a plug-in card, a modem must be connected to a specific communications port on your system unit. (Remember that your mouse also is hooked up to a COM port; these two devices can conflict with one another, so be careful not to set them for the same port!) When you configure your modem, make certain that it really is configured for the port that it's plugged into. See both your computer and modem instruction manuals for detailed setup instructions.

Not All Settings Are Set in Stone

Be aware that the settings listed in the accompanying table might not work on every system. These are just general settings that work for a great many setups—but don't take them as gospel. Read the instructions for your own hardware and software to determine the correct settings for your specific system.

After it's connected to your computer, your modem must be configured correctly for the particular on-line systems you intend to access. You must obtain information on several rather technical details before you can access any on-line service. You must know the *baud rate* of your modem (discussed earlier), which *terminal emulation mode* to use, the *parity* to use, the number of *data bits* and *stop bits* your modem is set up for, the downloading *protocol* you must use, the *dial commands* for your modem…the list goes on and on. Fortunately, most on-line systems employ the same settings, so most telecommunications software comes from the publisher already set up for these defaults.

This book isn't the place for a detailed discussion of such details, however, so make sure that you carefully read all the documentation that comes with both your modem and your software to ensure that your system is set up correctly. In the meantime, to give you a general idea to start with, the following table lists the most common settings for these categories.

Terminal emulation mode	ANSI (or IBM PC)
Baud rate	2,400 (1,200 if you have an older modem)
Parity	None
Data bits	8
Stop bits	None or 1
Dial command	ATD or ATDT
Download protocol	XMODEM

Using Telecommunications Software

Okay, now you own a modem and know how to configure it for both your computer and the on-line services you want to access. To actually use your modem, however, you must install telecommunications software on your system.

Operating by Remote Control

Believe it or not, certain telecommunications programs actually enable you to operate one PC from another PC at a remote location. Such programs as Carbon Copy Plus, for example, enable you to operate your work PC from your home PC—or even to troubleshoot PC problems directly from a repair shop!

These programs enable you to transmit data through your modem, because they handle all the various protocols discussed in the preceding section. So remember—you can't use a modem without telecommunications software!

The best telecommunications software—such as ProComm Plus or CrossTalk—truly automates all the dialing and log-in processes associated with on-line communications. With such a program, you can assign different settings for different services, dial specific numbers, send and retrieve messages to and from various BBSs, and delegate many tedious uploading and downloading chores entirely to your computer. You can even use these multitalented programs to conduct real-time conversations with other computer users from all around the world without first accessing a BBS.

If you're telecommunicating from within Windows, you can use either DOS-based or Windows-based telecommunications software. If you use DOS-based software from within Windows, you may want to set up the software to operate in the background, so that you can be downloading files in one window while you use other Windows applications in another window. Sometimes DOS-based telecommunications software doesn't work too well in Windows; if you have trouble with a DOS-based program, configure it so that it runs exclusively in a full screen. Naturally, a Windows-based telecommunications program, such as ProComm Plus for Windows or CrossTalk for Windows, is preferable to a DOS-based program, and will work much more reliably in the Windows environment.

Finally, many commercial services have their own front-end software that you either should or must use to access the service. In addition, there are several special front ends available to ease your access to the Internet. In almost all cases, these special front-end programs work better (because they're service-specific) than more general telecommunications software.

A Sample On-Line Session

Now you know what kind of hardware and software you need for telecommunicating—but what exactly happens when you use your modem? How do you actually go about getting on-line? The steps are simple: you start by commanding your telecommunications software to dial a number. Your system then accesses your telephone line; you hear a dial tone, followed by several beeps to signify that your computer is dialing a number.

When the system at the other end of the line (called the host system) answers, you hear a noise—similar to the sound heard when two FAX machines connect—which is actually the voices of the two systems speaking to each other. Your system and the host system exchange greetings and establish the electronic connection to enable you to access the host system. At this point, you do whatever you want to do on the service—messaging, conferencing, or downloading files. When you finish, you issue the command required to exit the host system, and your software sends a disconnect code. The host system says good-bye to you, and your system disconnects itself from your phone line. And that's it. Pretty painless, isn't it?

What Can Go Wrong with Your On-Line Communications

Okay, you're convinced. You can't wait to join the cyberspace revolution and use your computer to cruise the information superhighway. After all, what can go wrong?

First, you can hook up your modem incorrectly. Maybe you fail to seat an internal modem securely into its slot on the motherboard, or perhaps you plug an external modem into the wrong port on your system unit. It *has* been done before. Oh, and if you attempt such tasks too early in the morning, before you finish your first cup of coffee or otherwise completely wake up, I suppose you can even forget to connect the modem to a working telephone jack. (If you're reading this book, you're undoubtedly too sharp to overlook something so simple, but I mention it, just in case….)

Next, you can sabotage your setup, partially or entirely, by configuring the modem's switches or your communications software—or both—incorrectly. Given all the different settings possible for the various hardware and software packages available, such mistakes in setup aren't difficult to make. It's possible, too, to create a COM port conflict by designating your modem and your mouse for either the same COM port or a conflicting COM port (see Problem #9, later in this chapter). Configuring your software differently from the settings required to log onto your favorite BBS is another common error.

If you're telecommunicating from within Windows, Windows itself can sometimes cause you trouble—especially if your system is low on memory. If you find your modem working faster than Windows, you might need to close some other programs before you begin telecommunicating. If you're running a DOS-based communications program, the chances for trouble increase, since Windows doesn't always like to let DOS programs use the system resources necessary for proper telecommunicating.

You can also be cursed with a noisy telephone line. You'd be surprised at the amount of trouble this seemingly minor annoyance can cause. Even if you get everything else right, good ol' Ma Bell can cut you right down in your tracks. It's just not fair, is it?

Finally, the place you're connecting to (commercial service or Internet service provider) may not be operating up to par. Now that the Internet is experiencing astronomic growth, it's not uncommon to run into "traffic jams" at popular sites, and access to commercial providers (such as CompuServe) is known to slow down during the heaviest-trafficked times of the day.

So, considering all the variables involved in on-line communications, it's imperative that you concentrate on all its details and make certain that everything within your control is handled the right way (and the first time, if possible). Otherwise…well, you just won't stack up as much of a cyberspace navigator, will you?

10 Do's and Don'ts for On-Line Communication

1. *Do* make sure that both your modem and telecommunications software are set up correctly for the BBS or on-line system you're calling.

2. *Don't* disconnect your modem from a BBS or on-line service without correctly exiting the system, unless you absolutely must do so. BBS operators don't like this at all, partly because such abrupt exiting can damage their systems.

3. *Do* use the highest baud rate possible when downloading data to reduce your on-line charges; *however*…

4. *Don't* use a high baud rate when talking to another user in real-time on a commercial on-line service; often, the higher speeds are billed at higher rates, and you almost certainly type more slowly than your modem can transmit anyway.

5. *Do* use an automated program to download message headers and messages from CompuServe and other commercial services; reading such messages on-line can run up big phone bills.

6. *Don't* download program files from bulletin boards or Internet sites with which you're not familiar; such files may hide covert computer viruses.

7. *Do* install a separate telephone line for your modem if you can afford it. (It frees up your regular line so that you can talk and type at the same time.)

8. *Don't* configure your modem to use the same COM port as any other device in your computer system, such as a mouse.

9. *Do* make sure that your modem is connected correctly to both your computer *and* your telephone line.

10. *Don't* get too intimidated by all this "information superhighway" jazz; after all, the Internet is nothing more than a giant telephone company with lines strung around the world!

What To Do When Your On-Line Communications Don't Go Right

On-line communications can sometimes give you fits. Everything from incorrect setups to faulty connections to noisy phone lines can make your telecommunicating go awry. Take some time, therefore, to examine the following sections. They describe some of the most common telecommunications problems you may experience and what can cause them.

Problem 1:
Your modem doesn't work—nothing happens

If you attempt to use your modem but it does nothing at all, start by checking all your connections—especially the connection to the phone line. A malfunctioning modem usually results from a bad connection. If you use an external modem, make sure that it's hooked to the correct port in the back of your system unit. Make certain, too, that the modem is plugged into a power source (if necessary) and connected to a phone line. If you use an internal modem, check to ensure that the card is firmly seated in its slot. You should also try hooking a normal phone to the line hooked to your computer, just to make sure that you have a dial tone. After you've taken care of a poor or overlooked connection, you may need to reboot your system to recover from the problem.

Next, start up your communications program and enter its manual mode. Then type AT and press Enter. If you get no response, your modem either isn't working at all or is somehow connected incorrectly. If you receive an OK message, however, your modem is fine, and you can skip to Problem #2 to look for more answers.

If the device still doesn't work, you may have a defective modem on your hands. (Either that, or you configured your communications program incorrectly; check Problem #2.)

Problem 2:
Your modem is working, but it doesn't dial

Okay, using your software's manual mode has confirmed that your modem itself is operational—but you still can't get it to dial a number. If this is the case, check to determine that the phone line your modem is connected to is working. Disconnect your modem and hook a telephone to the same phone line; if the phone doesn't pick up a dial tone, neither will your modem. Try another phone line, or call the phone company for repairs.

It's also possible that you have your phone line plugged into the wrong jack at your modem. Most modems have two jacks—one labeled "line" and the other labeled "phone." Make sure that the phone line is plugged into the one labeled "line."

It's ImPORTant!

If you're running Windows, you should always check the port settings from within Windows to make sure that they're configured correctly. Simply open Control Panel and double-click the Ports icon. From the Ports dialog box you can change various settings for ports COM1 through COM4, including baud rate, data bits, parity, stop bits, and flow control. If you're a real techno-wizard, you can even change certain advanced settings, such as the base I/O port address and interrupt request line.

If your problem persists and it clearly isn't caused by a bad connection, an inoperable phone line, or a defective modem, look to incorrect software or hardware settings as the most likely source of your woes. First, check your telecommunications software. Make certain that you've selected the correct COM port and established the correct transmission protocol for your modem. Check especially the modem initialization string; your modem's documentation lists the correct commands to use for your device. Make sure, too, that your software is configured to transmit at the same baud rate as your modem's own baud capability. And check for any COM port conflicts between your modem and another device, such as a mouse.

If your software is configured correctly (or it wasn't and you've fixed it, but your modem still doesn't dial), check your hardware. Most modems incorporate switches that must be set in certain positions for the device to operate. Refer to your modem's documentation for the correct switch settings for your system.

Problem 3:
Your modem dials, but it doesn't connect

The main causes for this problem are the same as for Problem #2—either your hardware or software is probably set up incorrectly. See Problem #2 for ideas on solving this one.

Problem 4:
Your modem dials and connects, but nothing else happens

Yes! Your modem dials the number and makes contact with the other party—but then it just sits there, doing nothing. What gives? As with the last two problems examined, an incorrect setup is usually behind this one, too.

This particular error, however, may involve the transmission protocols and parameters that enable your computer to talk to the other system. Many on-line services employ their own peculiar settings for stop bits and parity and the like; you may need specific instructions on how to set your system to access any particular on-line service.

Accessing On-Line Services—The Easy Way

Most of the larger on-line services (including Prodigy, Compu-Serve, and America OnLine) provide special introduction kits for new users. These kits include instructions for accessing their systems, first-time user passwords, listings of system protocols and settings, and—more often than not—coupons good for free on-line time. In addition, there are many good computer books (from Que, Hayden, Sams, and other publishers) that include similar types of hookup kits for use with the Internet!

Another common problem stems from setting your system to transmit at a baud rate that the host system can't accept or use. You may have a 9,600-baud modem, for example, but the BBS can only handle a 2,400-baud rate. Try resetting your modem (and your software) to transmit at a slower speed, and see if that works.

If transmission protocol parameters or baud rate incompatibilities aren't at fault, check again for COM port conflicts in your system. Remember that two devices cannot be configured to use the same COM port. Remember, too, that a mouse hooked up to COM1 occasionally interferes with a modem connected to COM3; if you experience this type of trouble frequently, reconfigure your modem's COM settings for another port and see what happens. See Problem #9 for more ideas on COM port conflicts.

Problem 5:
Your modem suddenly stops working in the middle of a call

A sudden modem failure can occur during a call if you have more than one phone in your house hooked to the same phone line. If someone picks up an extension while your modem is on-line, the resulting interruption can scramble the connection. Sometimes the problem can be rectified simply by hang-

Why *Not* To Order Call Waiting...

Call Waiting is not a good service to use on the line you have your modem connected to. When the Call Waiting signal comes down the line, unfortunately, it stands a good chance of either scrambling your modem session or disconnecting your modem completely. The bottom line—*don't enable Call Waiting* on the same line that you connect to your modem! (Of course, you can always temporarily *turn off* Call Waiting while you're using your modem, by dialing *70 right before your on-line session or including this code in your software dial-up script.)

ing up the extension; other times, you must cancel the current modem session and start over again.

Sometimes Windows can cause your modem session to shut down. If Windows is low on memory, it may not have enough resources to let your modem do its thing. If you think this is the problem, try closing a few Windows applications and then restarting your modem. If you have continual modem problems under Windows, you may need to tweak your SYSTEM.INI file a little. Find the line that reads COMxBUFFER=XXXX, and edit the size to a larger number. (The default value is 128, and 1024 works much better.)

Another problem could occur when you're using a Windows telecommunications program and you start up a DOS-based application in a DOS window. This can screw up some Windows protocols, so try to avoid mixing DOS and Windows stuff when you use your modem.

Line noise also can cause random disconnects; see Problem #6 for details.

Problem 6:
Your communications become garbled during an on-line session

Interrupted and Corrupted

If your modem is interrupted while downloading data of any kind, the communication breakdown usually corrupts the data, making it unusable. You'll need to download the file again to ensure that you get a clean copy.

Garbled communications has several possible causes. Using different settings on your system than those required by the host system is one cause. Always make sure beforehand that your setup matches in stop bits, parity, and other such technical settings those of the system you're attempting to access.

Dealing with a Noisy Host

Sometimes, line noise doesn't originate at your end, but in the line feeding the system you're trying to access. If you experience isolated line noise when dealing with a particular BBS, call (using your regular phone, not your modem!) and inform the BBS sysops of the problem.

A second perpetrator of this problem is our old friend, the poor connection. If you haven't done so already, check all your cables—including your telephone cords—to ensure that they're securely fastened. If any older cables are hooked into the line, replace them. Old cables can eventually go bad, resulting in difficulties with your data communications.

The final cause of this type of communications breakdown—and a common one, at that—is line noise on your telephone lines. If you often must endure poor connections when you talk on the telephone, your computer is likely to experience the same poor connections in its telecommunications. Although usually a mere annoyance in person-to-person calls, a similarly poor connection between your computer and another system can totally foul up its on-line transmissions; any lost data that results can destroy a downloaded file or cause an on-line session to end in a disconnect.

Fortunately, you can take several steps to minimize line noise. For example, check your telephone cable from the wall to your computer. Is the cable new and firmly connected? You may try replacing the cable if it's not new. If feasible, remove any nearby electrical devices or appliances from the vicinity of your phone cord. Blenders, TVs, radios, electric shavers—all can create interference that increases line noise. If you've tried these steps but you still have a problem with line noise, call your local telephone company.

If you can rule out line noise as the cause of your download disaster, make sure that you're using the correct protocol for the system you're accessing. If you use YMODEM protocol, for example, and the host system only supports XMODEM, you're not speaking the same language, and you download garbage as a result. Check your transmission rate, too; with some systems you may need to use a lower baud rate than usual to ensure perfect downloads.

Problem 7:
You can't disconnect your modem

Sometimes this really happens—your modem just doesn't seem to want you to hang up. Your first concern is, of course, to break the connection; then you can try to figure out what went wrong. Most communications programs include manual commands that enable you to hang up even when your modem refuses to do so. (Sometimes Scroll+H or Scroll+X initiates this command; read your manual to learn what command your particular program employs.) After you've successfully disconnected, try to exit your communications program and then restart the program; sometimes, this resets the modem. If it doesn't work, you may need to completely reboot your system.

Now to discover why you couldn't hang up. Guess what, folks—the most common cause of this failure is improper software or modem settings. So get out your manuals and look up those settings—your disconnect code is probably incorrect.

Problem 8:
Using your modem causes your mouse to act funny—or vice versa

---

I Hate Meeces to Pieces!

COM port conflicts between your mouse and your modem are explained in more detail back in Chapter 13. Scurry on back there to learn why your peripherals sometimes don't get along together any better than most cartoon cats and mice.

Okay, I warned you, but you did it anyway. You inadvertently set up a COM port conflict. This is actually a common problem and results from weird DOS/hardware bugs that force two different COM ports to use some of the same system resources. As the following paragraphs explain, however, resolving the conflict is simple.

It's as Easy as 1-2-3...

If you're using Windows and running your modem on COM2 and there is no COM1 on your system you may not be able to get your modem to work at all. This is because Windows looks for COM ports in order, and if COM1 doesn't exist...well, you've got problems. Reassign your modem or some other accessory—to COM1, and you'll fix your problem.

First, check the port settings for your mouse and your modem. If they're both configured for the same COM port, change one of the devices' settings so that it can use a different port.

Now, check that they're not both set for COM ports with even numbers (COM2 and COM4). If so, reconfigure one of the devices to use an odd-numbered port.

At the same time, check that the two devices aren't both configured for COM ports with odd numbers (COM1 and COM3). If so, reset one of the devices to use an even number.

Problem 9:
Your computer acts oddly soon after you've completed an on-line session

What now? You've just pulled several files—including a great new game—from the local BBS, and now your computer acts as though it needs to be decked out in an electronic straitjacket. It doesn't seem to have any problems with loose connections, incorrect settings, or excess line noise; your on-line session went without a hitch—flawlessly, in fact. So what's wrong?

Well, along with your nice new files, you could have downloaded a not-so-nice computer virus! Most viruses are transmitted through files passed on via on-line services. Any time you download a file, access the file, and find your computer starting to do strange things (running more slowly, mysteriously losing files, displaying unusual messages on-screen), you may have accidentally infected it with a virus. If the symptoms seem to match, refer to Chapter 9 for what to do next.

Problem 10:
Your DOS communications program doesn't work well from within Windows

DOS communications programs work better if they can get more attention from your system. You'll want to make sure that your program is being run from a PIF file, and then you can tweak some of the PIF parameters. In the Advanced Options dialog box of the PIF file editor, you should set the Background Priority and Foreground Priority higher than the defaults—probably around 200 each. This will give your communications program more Windows resources when multitasking with other applications.

You may also want to run your DOS communications program exclusively in the foreground—and full-screen, not in a window—to protect against potential problems. (Better safe than sorry.) If all else fails, you may need to exit Windows and use your DOS-based program from DOS instead of Windows. Sometimes Windows just won't get along with DOS-based programs that require constant use of various system resources, especially communications ports.

One last thing to try. In the Advanced Options dialog box of the PIF file editor, check the Lock Memory box. This will disable application memory swapping, which may speed up DOS-based communications on some systems.

Problem 11:
You have problems connecting to the Internet

Accessing the Internet opens up a whole new world of telecommunication problems. First, you can have any of the modem and phone-line problems discussed in Problems 1 through 10 in this chapter. Second, you can have problems with your Internet front-end software. Third, you can have problems with your Internet service provider. And fourth, you can have problems with any Internet site with which you're trying to connect.

First things first. If you're having a problem, check Problems 1 through 10 to see if it's something with your hardware or your telephone lines.

Next, make sure you're using your Internet software correctly. Is it configured correctly? Do you have everything you need for it to work (TCP/IP, etc.)? Does it interface smoothly with your chosen service provider?

Now, check your service provider. Does it provide the services you're trying to use? (For example, are you trying to FTP files when the only thing the service provider offers is newsgroup and e-mail access?) Does it carry all the newsgroups you're trying to access? (Some providers—especially on campuses and in corporations—limit access to some newsgroups.) Are the phone lines to your provider clean?

Finally, check the site you're trying to access. Does it have enough capacity to handle a large volume of simultaneous accesses? (If not, you may need to retry your access at nonpeak hours.) Is it well run? (Remember, some newsgroups and e-mail lists are run by individuals, trying to do their best under a staggering workload.) Does it really have what you're looking for? (If you're searching for files, remember to use a search utility—like *Gopher*—before you randomly attempt downloading from an unknown system.)

That said, the Internet can be a lot of fun once you get up and running. Make sure you check out one of Que's fine Internet books to learn more details!

A Few Last Words about the Information Superhighway

The world of cyberspace and on-line communications can be fun and exciting—after you get everything set up and functioning correctly, that is. Make sure you pay attention to detail and closely follow the instructions in your software and hardware manuals, as well as those for any on-line services you decide to access.

Above all else, remember that this is just another form of communication, just like talking or sending a letter. Remember to be courteous and polite, and to use the proper etiquette (also referred to as "netiquette" on the Internet!). If you're unsure of what you're doing, don't be afraid to just watch for awhile (called "lurking" in cyberparlance), or to ask questions of more experienced users. Before you know it, you'll be up and e-mailing like an old cyberpro!

What To Do When...

Your Disk Is Damaged

CHAPTER SEVENTEEN

Files and disks. Disks and files. Both are important, and both can cause problems.

You see, all your data is stored in files, and all your files reside on disks. Your hard disk, because of its size and storage capabilities, stores your permanent data and program files. Data that demands more portability is stored on floppy disks.

Unfortunately, disks are physical devices and, as such, are prone to problems. This chapter is about all the problems you can encounter with your disks.

All You Ever Wanted To Know About Disks

In Chapter 2, you learned that data is stored on disks magnetically. Each disk is divided into tracks and sectors, and clusters of data are placed in each sector. Exactly where each cluster of data resides is recorded in the file allocation table, or FAT. When DOS wants to access a piece of data, it sends the read/write head of your disk drive to the appropriate sector(s).

Different Types of Disks

Your system includes both a *hard disk drive* and one or more *floppy disk drives*. The hard disk can store as much as 200M of data; your floppy disks (which are removable) may store only up to 1.44M. Some new PCs even have 2.88M drives! Both drives work on the same principle, using spinning platters with information stored magnetically.

The Low Down on High Density

It's possible to format a low-density disk as high density, but it really doesn't work well. Low-density disks just aren't of high enough quality to hold the more detailed formatting required of a high-density disk. In addition, high-density disks have an extra guide hole that permits your disk drive to "read" them as high density. Because of this, you can't format a low-density disk as high-density unless you punch a new hole in the plastic sleeve.

Floppy disks come in different sizes and densities. In addition to the two different sizes (3 1/2 inches and 5 1/4 inches), each size can come in one of two different *densities*. A high-density disk has many more tracks and sectors than a low-density disk. Because the high-density disk is made of finer magnetic material, the tracks and sectors are closer together, allowing more data to be stored in the same amount of disk space.

A high-density 5 1/4-inch disk holds up to 1.2M of data, and a low-density 5 1/4-inch disk holds just 360K of data. A high-density 3 1/2-inch disk holds up to 1.44M of data, compared to 720K on a low-density 3 1/2-inch disk. Because most computers today come equipped with high-density drives, most users use high-density disks exclusively.

Essential Disk Information

Before you insert a new disk, make sure that no other disk already occupies the drive. (You really don't want to try to insert two disks into one drive; some fairly serious damage can result.)

Insert the disk with the label side up and toward you. If you're inserting a 5 1/4-inch disk, you must close the little drive latch by moving it into the down position. A 3 1/2-inch disk seats itself when placed far enough into the drive.

To remove a 5 1/4-inch disk, unlatch the drive and pull the disk out. To remove a 3 1/2-inch disk, push the button on the drive, and the disk is ejected.

Formatting Disks

As explained in Chapter 2, all blank disks must be formatted. To format a disk from DOS, use the FORMAT command. The procedure is relatively simple—just type the command, followed by the name of the drive that holds the disk to be formatted. To format a disk in drive A, for example, type the following:

FORMAT A:

A message appears asking you to insert your disk and press Enter; follow these instructions to begin formatting. When formatting is complete, you can assign a name, or *volume label*, to the disk and format additional disks if you want. DOS also displays a short report about the just-formatted disk.

You can also format floppy disks from within Windows. Just open the File Manager, pull down the **Disk** menu, and select **Format Disk**. When the Format Disk dialog box appears, select the proper drive (**Disk In**) and Capacity; if you want, you

Formatting the Hard (Disk) Way

As you learned in Chapter 8, you can also use the FORMAT command to format your hard disk drive. Because most hard disks come preformatted from the factory, you rarely have to do this. Under no circumstances, however, should you use the FORMAT command on a hard disk containing data. Do so and you lose all your data, which is a very serious problem.

can also format the disk as bootable (Make System Disk). When you click OK, you begin the formatting procedure.

Using DISKCOPY To Copy Entire Disks

DOS includes the DISKCOPY command, which lets you copy entire disks at one time. Before you start, you need two disks: your original disk and a blank disk of the same size and density. You cannot copy a disk to a dissimilar disk; for example, you can't copy a 5 1/4-inch disk to a 3 1/2-inch disk or a low-density disk to a high-density disk.

Most users will use a single drive for both the *source disk* (the disk you're copying from) and the *target disk* (the disk you're copying to). You may need to swap disks several times during the copy procedure, as chunks of data from the source disk are stored in your system's memory and then transferred to the destination disk. Because your system's memory can't hold as much data as a typical disk, the copying must be done in bits and pieces.

To use this command, type the following:

DISKCOPY A: A:

More Memory—Fewer Swaps

The more memory you have on your PC, the fewer times you need to swap disks during the DISKCOPY procedure. In fact, if you have enough memory, you may be able to copy the entire contents in one pass!

After you type the command and press **Enter**, you are prompted to insert the source disk. After a time, you are prompted to insert the target disk. Then you're back to the source disk, then the target disk, and so on and so on, until the entire disk is copied. When you're done, the target disk is a mirror image of the source disk.

Using CHKDSK To Analyze Your Disks

Beyond CHKDSK in DOS 6.2

If you're using CHKDSK with DOS 6.2 or later, a message will appear on your screen recommending that you use a new command, SCANDISK, instead. SCANDISK differs from CHKDSK in that it not only checks your disk, but also lets you repair it. If you think you have some serious disk problems, run the following command at the DOS prompt:

SCANDISK /AUTOFIX

SCANDISK will then scan and automatically repair any damage to your current disk drive.

DOS provides the CHKDSK command to analyze disks and fix some basic disk problems. This command looks at the FAT and the directory system to see whether you have any existing or potential problems. It also lets you know how much memory you have on the system and how much of it is unused at the time, as well as how much total disk space you have and how much of that is currently unused.

Issue the CHKDSK command by typing the following:

CHKDSK

DOS then checks your disk and delivers an on-screen report. If CHKDSK finds any problems, part of the report looks like the following:

```
Errors found, F parameter not specified
Corrections will not be written to disk

78 lost allocation units found in 1 chains
159744 bytes disk space would be freed
```

If you see a message like this in your report, you should rerun CHKDSK with the /F switch, which instructs DOS to "fix" any problems (like lost allocation units) encountered during the analysis. To run this procedure, type the following:

Losing Lost Clusters

It's probably a good idea to run CHKDSK—with the /F switch— periodically. Lost clusters are created when programs are exited improperly, and they can eat up valuable disk space unless you use CHKDSK to remove them.

CHKDSK /F

DOS runs its analysis and then gives you the following message:

```
X lost clusters in Y chains
Convert lost chains to files (Y/N)?
```

When you respond affirmatively, DOS takes all the lost clusters and turns them into files with a CHK extension. After the CHK files have been created, you then want to get rid of them by issuing the following command:

DEL C:*.CHK

Using Defragmenter To Speed Up Your Disks

Over time, your hard disk gets all fragmented, so that there is very little contiguous free space available. This slows down your disk access, and therefore your entire system. Fortunately, DOS 6 includes a utility that lets you *defragment* your hard disk.

This utility is called Defragmenter; to run it, just type the following at the DOS prompt:

DEFRAG

Defragmenting from Windows

Normally you can't defragment disks from within Windows. However, the newest version of Norton Desktop for Windows, version 3, includes a Windows-based defragmenter.

Defragmenter launches and does a quick analysis of your disk. (It even displays a real neat map of your hard disk so you can easily see how Swiss-cheesed things are!) There are lots of options available (see Chapter 3 for more details); choose the ones that suit your situation. When you begin the optimization procedure, Defragmenter starts to do its thing, moving data from one part of your disk to another to create as much contiguous free space as possible. When Defragmenter is done, exit the program and reboot your computer.

Using DoubleSpace or DriveSpace To Compress Your Disks

DoubleSpace is a new utility in DOS 6 (but not in DOS 6.21—see Chapter 3 for more details) that compresses the data on your hard disk so that it takes up less space, in effect giving you a bigger hard disk drive. (If you have DOS 6.22, this utility is now called DriveSpace.) This compression takes place in advance of normal operation; the compressed data is decompressed on the fly, as you need it. On most computers DoubleSpace or DriveSpace work invisibly, without a noticeable slowdown in disk access.

You install DoubleSpace by typing the following at the DOS prompt:

DBLSPACE

When DoubleSpace launches, you can choose between the Custom and Express setups. I recommend the Express option.

If you have DOS 6.22, you launch DriveSpace by typing the following at the DOS prompt:

DRVSPACE

All other instructions are the same for DriveSpace as for DoubleSpace.

Once DoubleSpace or DriveSpace is installed, you probably won't even notice that you're using a compressed disk. You should be able to access all your data as easily and as quickly as before. See Chapter 3 for more details on how DoubleSpace and DriveSpace work.

What Can Happen to Your Disks

Your disks are where you store your valuable data. If anything happens to your disks, your data is put in jeopardy. What exactly can go wrong?

- *You can accidentally format a disk that contains data.* Oh, this is the big one! Don't do this! If you're lucky and you're using DOS 5 or 6, you can use UNFORMAT to recover from this, as explained in Chapter 8.

- *You can try to access a disk that isn't there.* If you try to access a disk drive that's empty, DOS gives you an error message. You probably need to insert a disk to proceed.

- *You can insert a disk into its drive incorrectly.* Of course, sticking a disk into a drive upside down or sideways doesn't do you too much good, either. In fact, you could even damage your drive. Try not to do this!

- *You can take a disk out of its drive while it's still being used.* If you remove a disk that's still being accessed, not only will you confuse the system, but you may scramble some data on the disk.

- *Your PC can shut down while a disk is being accessed.* Any time you interrupt a disk access, you run the risk of scrambling data, whether it's with a hard disk or a floppy disk. Do everything you can to avoid doing this.

- *You can format a low-density disk as high density.* Don't be cheap. If you want high-density disks, buy high-density disks. Using a low-density disk formatted as high density just gives you disk errors and headaches.

- *Your hard disk can become fragmented.* A disk gets fragmented when so many files are erased and added and erased and added that whatever free disk space exists is scattered all over your disk—which slows disk access. To *defragment* a disk, you need to use the Defragmenter utility included with DOS 6. If you notice your hard disk slowing down, just type **DEFRAG** at the DOS prompt—in fact, in might not be a bad idea to do this once a month or so just to keep your disk as orderly as possible.

- *DoubleSpace and DriveSpace can cause you problems.* If you're running DoubleSpace or DriveSpace in DOS 6, you may think these programs are causing some hard disk problems. In reality, any DoubleSpace or DriveSpace-related problems probably aren't caused by the utilities themselves, but rather are exacerbated by it. See Chapter 21 for more details on problems you may run into when running DoubleSpace or DriveSpace.

- *The disk itself can go bad.* Yes, it happens. Floppy disks endure a great deal of hard use, going in and out of the drive and back and forth to work. Even hard disks can go bad, especially if your computer is in a space subjected to dirt and dust and cigarette smoke. The cleaner the room and the less abuse, the longer your disks last.

- *A disk can transmit a computer virus.* Be careful about accepting disks from strangers. You never know where that disk has been—or what it carries.

What To Do When Things Go Wrong with Your Disks

Okay, what do you do if you have a disk problem? Read on to examine the most common problems you can experience (or foist upon yourself).

Problem 1:
You accidentally format a disk

Unformatting with Old Versions of DOS

If you don't have DOS 5 or 6, you can still unformat your disks—you just need to buy one of the many third-party utility packages that include unformat utilities. Check out such programs as Norton Utilities and PC Tools Deluxe for their unformat capabilities, which often work quite similarly to the DOS 5 or 6 UNFORMAT utility.

Oh boy, you went and did it this time, didn't you! Fortunately, all hope is not lost. If you have DOS 5 or DOS 6, you can use the UNFORMAT utility to undo that accidental format.

Unformatting a disk is deceptively simple. All you have to do is type the following from the DOS prompt:

UNFORMAT C:

Of course, if you need to unformat a floppy disk, you should replace the C: in the above command with the letter of the drive containing the accidentally formatted disk.

After you press Enter, you are confronted with a series of warnings and technical statements. Answer yes to all of them, and the unformatting process will begin. You will be alerted when the unformat is complete, at which point you should reboot your system.

If you're using DOS 5, the above only works if you were running MIRROR (explained back in Chapter 5). If you weren't running MIRROR with DOS 5, you must run the UNFORMAT command with the /U switch. The proper syntax for this procedure is as follows:

UNFORMAT C: /U

If you're using DOS 6, the unaugmented UNFORMAT command is all you need.

Problem 2:
You can't access a disk

What do you do when your system can't read or write to a disk? First, check and make sure that the disk is really there. If it's a floppy disk, make sure that it's actually inserted into the drive—and correctly. Also make sure that the disk has been formatted.

You should also check to make sure that you typed the right drive letter. If you typed *Q* instead of *C*, naturally your system won't be able to access the drive.

If you can't access your hard disk, you could have major problems. See Chapter 8 for more information.

Problem 3:
Your system shuts down while accessing a disk

This is not good, but is often not catastrophic. You should get your system up and running again, and then try to access the data that was being accessed when the system went down. If the data is okay, then life is wonderful. If the data is scrambled—well, this is what happens: you either have to create that file from scratch or use a backup copy.

Problem 4:
Your disk is running slower than normal

This problem is most often caused by a fragmented disk. As explained earlier in this chapter, you need to run DOS 6's Defragmenter utility (or similar third-party defragmenters) to clean up your disk and get it back up to speed. Just type the following at the DOS prompt:

DEFRAG

See the section on Defragmenter earlier in this chapter for more details on using Defragmenter.

10 Do's and Don'ts for Disk Maintenance

1. *Do* clearly label all your disks.

2. *Don't* type FORMAT C:—*ever*!

3. *Do* use anti-virus software if you're exchanging disks with other computer users.

4. *Don't* format a low-density floppy disk as a high-density disk; it just doesn't work, even if DOS lets you get away with it.

5. *Do* run CHKDSK /F regularly to get rid of lost clusters.

6. *Don't* stick more than one disk into a drive at one time.

7. *Do* use DOS 6's Defragmenter utility to keep your hard disk running up to speed.

8. *Don't* remove a disk from a drive while DOS is still accessing the drive—it's a sure-fire way to scramble your data.

9. *Do* keep your disks far away from magnets and magnetic fields—such as those generated by large audio speakers, monitors, and speakers.

10. *Don't* hesitate to use SCANDISK instead of CHKDSK (in DOS 6.2) if you think you have disk problems.

Problem 5:
You experience problems while running DoubleSpace in DOS 6 (or DriveSpace in DOS 6.22)

Like all disk compression programs, DoubleSpace and DriveSpace can give you fits sometimes. In most cases, it's not really the utility's fault, although I know this is little consolation if trouble happens to you. My advice when using DoubleSpace or DriveSpace is to back up your data early and often, and read Chapter 21 of this book to decipher all sorts of potential problems.

> ### DOS 6—And No DoubleSpace?
>
> Whether or not you have DoubleSpace depends on which version of DOS 6 you have. Microsoft included DoubleSpace in versions 6.0 and 6.2, but was forced to remove it (for legal reasons) in DOS 6.21. Interestingly, the latest version of DOS, version 6.22, adds a similar compression utility called DriveSpace. So if you have DOS 6 and don't have DoubleSpace, you probably have version 6.21 and need to upgrade!

That said, let's look at the most common DoubleSpace and DriveSpace-related problems in DOS 6:

DoubleSpace or DriveSpace trashes some or all of your files

This is generally due to one of three situations:

- *Your drive is old or has surface defects.*

- *You turned off your system too soon.*

- *Your files became cross-linked.*

You see, DoubleSpace and DriveSpace give your hard disk a pretty good workout as it reads and writes compressed data to and from your hard disk. If your hard disk has any defects or weaknesses, DoubleSpace will expose them. In addition, DoubleSpace shows off a weakness in the SmartDrive disk-caching program, which causes problems if you shut off your computer before SmartDrive is done writing data to your disk. Fortunately, DriveSpace solves some of the problems that you may have encountered with Double-Space; it may be a good idea to upgrade to DOS 6.22 to get this newer compression utility. See Chapter 21 for solutions to these problems.

DoubleSpace or DriveSpace slow down your system

Because DoubleSpace and DriveSpace essentially compress and decompress data "on the fly," you may notice a slight deterioration of your system's performance while using a compressed disk drive. If your system has a fast hard drive and a slow processor, running these utilities *will* slow down your system—and there's not much you can do about it.

Some DOS commands don't work under DoubleSpace or DriveSpace

This is true; some DOS commands don't work under DoubleSpace and DriveSpace! See Chapter 3 for more details.

Problem 6:
You get a DOS error message regarding your disk

DOS can generate many error messages when working with disks. Here are a few of the more common messages; see Chapter 28, "DOS Error Messages—What They Mean and How To Deal with Them," for a complete listing of DOS error messages.

```
Attempted write-protect violation
```

You're trying to format a floppy disk that is write-protected. Remove the write-protect tab (on 5 1/4-inch disks) or move the write-protect shutter to close the hole (on 3 1/2-inch disks); then restart the operation.

```
Invalid partition table
Error reading (or writing) partition table
```

You're trying to format a hard disk with a bad DOS partition table. Run the FDISK command before attempting to format again (see Chapter 8 for more details).

```
Cannot read file allocation table
File allocation table bad, drive x:
```

Your FAT is unreadable, meaning that you have major disk problems. You probably need to reformat your disk (refer to Chapter 8 for more details).

```
Current drive is no longer valid
```

DOS attempted to access the current drive, and nothing was there. This probably happened when you removed a floppy disk from its drive before DOS was finished with it. Reinsert the disk to continue.

```
DoubleSpace found Crosslink between files X: and X:
```

This can happen when you run DoubleSpace in DOS 6 if your drive is *too full* (90% or more utilized), or if your EMM386 command line in the CONFIG.SYS file has a HIGHSCAN parameter. To correct the cross-linked entries, run the CHKDSK /F command (or the DBLSPACE /CHKDSK /F command) from the DOS prompt. (DOS 6.22 can generate a similar message when you're using DriveSpace.)

```
Insufficient disk space
```

Your disk is full. You need to delete some files before you can use the disk again. (You also may get this error message when copying a file to a disk if the file is bigger than the disk. In this instance, use the BACKUP command or DOS 6's Microsoft Backup utility to copy this extra-large file onto multiple disks.)

```
Invalid disk change
```

You removed a disk before DOS was finished with it. Reinsert the disk to finish the operation.

```
Invalid drive or file name
Invalid drive specification
```

You either mistyped a drive letter or entered the same drive for both source and destination in a COPY operation. Check your mistake and try again.

```
Invalid media or Track 0 bad - disk unusable
```

This message is generated when you're trying to format a disk that is damaged. Try running FORMAT a second time; if you continue to get this message, the disk is bad and should be thrown out.

```
No target drive specified
```

You tried to use the BACKUP command without specifying a target drive. Retype the command correctly.

```
Non-System disk or disk error
Replace and press any key when ready
```

You tried to boot your system with a nonbootable disk in drive A. Remove the disk and reboot.

```
Non-DOS disk
```

The FAT (File Allocation Table) on the specified disk is invalid. Reformat the disk to make it usable.

```
Sector not found
```

Your disk drive couldn't find the specified sector. This usually signifies a
bad disk, although a defective drive can also cause this problem.

```
Not ready, reading drive x
Drive not ready
Read fault
Write fault
```

The specified drive was not ready for the operation you selected. Either you
forgot to insert a disk, or you didn't insert the disk correctly.

```
TARGET disk bad or incompatible
Target disk may be unusable
Target disk unusable
```

Something is wrong with your target disk in a backup or copy operation. It's
possible that the disk has not been formatted; in this case, format the disk
and then try the original operation again. It's also possible that the disk is
bad. If so, throw it away.

```
Write failure, disk unusable
```

In formatting a floppy disk, bad sectors were found in the FAT area.
Throw away the disk.

```
You must specify the host drive for a DoubleSpace drive
```

In DOS 6, you tried to use SmartDrive to cache only the DoubleSpaced or
DriveSpaced drive. Sorry, but it doesn't work this way; the entire drive,
compressed portion and noncompressed portion, must be cached together.

Problem 7:
CHKDSK or SCANDISK indicate you have damage to your disk

The first thing to try is letting
SCANDISK try to fix your problems. Just type the following at
the DOS prompt:

SCANDISK /AUTOFIX

SCANDISK will attempt to scan
your current disk for errors, and
then repair any errors or damage, automatically.

Undoing SCANDISK Changes

If, for some reason, you want to "unfix" whatever SCANDISK
repaired, just type the following at the DOS prompt:

SCANDISK /UNDO

Note that any undoing done after you've saved any new
information to your hard disk will have unpredictable results.

If this doesn't fix your problem, you're in bigger trouble. You'll probably need to run a third-party utility, like Norton Disk Doctor, or consult someone more technical for help.

A Final Word on Disks

Despite their appearances, disks are fragile. Treat them with care. And, more important, make copies of them if they contain valuable data. Where your data is concerned, you're better safe than sorry. If you don't believe me, read Chapter 7; then do everything I advise there. Some day—maybe not tomorrow but soon, and for the rest of your life—you'll thank me for it.

Your CD-ROM Doesn't Spin Right

CHAPTER EIGHTEEN

One of the biggest buzzwords in personal computing circles is *multimedia*. For most folks, this means using CD-ROM drives and add-in sound cards to get moving pictures and sound through their PCs.

Well, we'll discuss sound cards (and associated problems) in the next chapter. *This* chapter deals with CD-ROM drives and how to get them to work as promised!

What's All This Noise about Multimedia?

The thing about multimedia is, no one can really define *what* it is. By some definitions, multimedia is anything that involves interactivity, full-motion video, and audio. Of course, that describes a Nintendo game as much as it describes *Compton's Multimedia Encyclopedia*, but that's the trouble with definitions. For our purposes, let's think of multimedia as anything that adds sound and pictures to your PC through a CD-ROM disk. (This may not be the *perfect* definition, but it's mine—and I like it!)

Naturally, you need a little more than a basic PC to run multimedia applications. For one, you need a CD-ROM drive. You also need sound capabilities beyond that supplied by that tiny little speaker built into most system units.

A few years back, a bunch of computer software and hardware manufacturers got together and came up with a minimum specification for what they called the *Multimedia Personal Computer* (or *MPC* for short). Those specs, now a few years old, dictate that an MPC computer include the following:

- 80386-based (or higher) PC running at 33MHz or more

- 4M RAM or more

- 120M hard disk or more

- CD-ROM drive with 150K/second transfer rate or more

- Sound card with 8-bit digitized sound and MIDI playback

- Windows 3.0 with Multimedia Extensions or Windows 3.1

Getting Up to Speed

There are two ways to measure the speed of a CD-ROM drive. The *transfer rate* measures the amount of information that can be transferred from the CD-ROM disk to the CD-ROM drive buffers; 150K is a minimum transfer rate, and 300K is better. The *access speed* measures the amount of time it takes to find specific data; 800ms is the bare minimum, and 400ms is much better.

In today's world, I would recommend something even more powerful to run the current batch of multimedia programs. In particular, aim for an 80486 PC, 8M RAM, and a CD-ROM with 300K transfer rate—and don't forget the add-on speakers for your sound card!

Looking at CD-ROM Drives

CD-ROM stands for *compact disk read-only memory*. This doesn't mean that CD-ROMs are memory devices; they're storage devices, just like hard or floppy disks. The difference is that you can't write data to CD-ROM disks—you can only read data from them.

Is a CD-ROM a CD?

Both audio compact discs (CDs) and computer CD-ROMs store data in the same manner, and both types of drives use laser beams to read the data. But you can't play a CD-ROM disk in an audio CD player because the computer data is stored in a different format than normal audio data. You can think of a CD-ROM as an extension of basic CD technology, kind of a superset of the basic compact disc.

The other difference between a CD-ROM disk and a normal disk is that information is stored on a CD-ROM *optically*, while a normal disk stores data *magnetically*. In essence, a CD-ROM disk is composed of concentric circles filled with numerous pits. A laser beam in the CD-ROM drive reads these pits and converts the information into data that can be used by your computer system.

Hooking It Up to Your System—and Making It Run

When you add a CD-ROM drive to your system, it can be added internally or externally. Both function identically; they just hook up differently. An internal drive hooks up into a spare drive bay in the front of your system unit. An external drive hooks up to a spare port on the back of your system unit. An external unit also needs external power; an internal unit gets its power directly from your system unit.

After your CD-ROM drive is installed, you need to load a device driver (normally included with your CD-ROM drive) into system memory so your system can recognize the presence of the new peripheral. This is normally done via a line in your CONFIG.SYS file. In addition, there is a DOS program called MSCDEX.EXE that must be run before the drive can be operated; this program is normally loaded via a line in your AUTOEXEC.BAT file.

Once your drive is installed, and the correct drivers and programs are loaded, it's time to use the darned thing. After you reboot your system, your computer sees the CD-ROM drive as just another disk drive. So if your hard disk was drive C, your CD-ROM drive is now drive D. You can insert a CD-ROM disk into the drive, switch to the drive, and then start the new program the same way you'd start any program. The difference is that a CD-ROM can hold over 600M of data—which means CD-ROM-based software is normally a lot more sophisticated than normal disk-based programs!

Something New—Photo CD!

As if laser-generating CD-ROM drives weren't exotic enough, there's a new development in the world of optical storage that you may want to be aware of. Kodak, the photographic film company, has introduced a new CD-ROM technology called *Photo CD*. A Photo CD works more or less like a CD-ROM, but stores high-quality photographic images (transferred from photographic film). While Kodak is selling dedicated Photo CD players that hook up to your normal television set, many new CD-ROM drives are coming equipped with the capability of playing Photo CDs as well as normal CD-ROM disks. If you think this may be important to you (and Kodak will do its best to convince you so), make sure that your CD-ROM drive is Photo CD-capable.

What Can Go Wrong with Your CD-ROM Drive

> ### Don't Interrupt My Request!
>
> An add-on device uses something called an *interrupt request* (abbreviated IRQ) to interrupt your PC and get its attention so that it can do what it needs to do. Most systems have 16 available IRQs; your sound card and CD-ROM drive (along with other peripherals) can be set to use any of these interrupt settings.

The bad thing with CD-ROM setups is that they don't always work right! Just look at the things that can go wrong when you add a CD-ROM drive to your system:

- *Things might not be hooked up right.* Remember to seat all the cards and connect all the cables—including power cables for external CD-ROM drives!

- *Things might not be loaded right.* Don't forget to load the device drivers for your CD-ROM drive into system memory.

- *Things might be in conflict—in particular, ports (also called input/output addresses), interrupts, and DMA channels!* It's *very*

> ### What's the Channel?
>
> Peripherals use direct memory access (DMA) channels to route information directly to your system's memory, bypassing the microprocessor. Most systems have eight DMA channels available.

  important to make sure that your CD-ROM drive is set up so that it doesn't use ports, channels, or interrupts assigned to other devices on your system. If you have conflicts, you might find that *several* devices don't work right!

- *Things might not be compatible.* Believe it or not, not all CD-ROM drives are compatible with all sound cards. Check with your dealer or manufacturer to make sure all your equipment really can work together—don't assume that everything will work with everything else!

Make sure you check all these things *before* installing or using your CD-ROM drive. You may also want to check out my advice on upgrading your system hardware in Chapter 25.

Fixing CD-ROM Problems

Okay, you have your new CD-ROM drive installed and ready to spin. But what do you do if it doesn't spin right? As usual, it's time to sift through the potential problems and offer a few timely solutions.

Problem 1:
Your CD-ROM drive doesn't work—nothing happens

First, have you inserted a CD-ROM disk into your drive? Do you have the disk inserted *properly* (label side up)? If you're using an external drive, is it plugged in and powered on? Have you accessed the disk properly?

If you think you're doing everything right, you probably have some sort of power problem with your CD-ROM drive. If you're using an internal drive, you should check all the connections inside your system unit; not only should the drive be plugged into a drive controller, but it should also be plugged into your computer's power supply. If you're using an external drive, make sure all the connections are solid and that the drive actually has power (make sure the power light is on).

If you do have power and still can't get the drive to work, see Problem 2.

10 Do's and Don'ts for Using Your CD-ROM Drive

1. *Do* make sure your CD-ROM drive has Photo CD capability; trust me, you'll want to use this someday.

2. *Don't* assign your CD-ROM drive to ports, channels, or interrupts used by other devices in your system.

3. *Do* make sure your CD-ROM drive is compatible with your sound card.

4. *Don't* assume that your CD-ROM drive can play normal compact disks—most CD-ROM drives need special drivers and programs to play audio CDs.

5. *Do* make sure your system conforms to MPC standards *before* you install the CD-ROM drive.

6. *Don't* forget to load the proper device drivers for your CD-ROM drive via your CONFIG.SYS and/or AUTOEXEC.BAT files.

7. *Do* invest in the fastest CD-ROM drive you can afford.

8. *Don't* forget to treat your CD-ROM disks with care; damage and debris can affect playback.

9. *Do* check out the wide variety of multimedia games and programs available on CD-ROM—some of this stuff is pretty neat!

10. *Don't* get concerned if your CD-ROM drive appears slow— CD-ROM access *is* slower than normal hard disk drive access.

Problem 2:
Your CD-ROM drive doesn't work—the drive spins, but you can't access the disk

Let's assume that you have power to your drive and have a CD-ROM disk inserted properly. If you can't access the disk, you probably don't have the correct driver loaded into system memory. Make sure that your CONFIG.SYS file is loading the proper CD-ROM device driver (the one that came with your drive). Then make sure that the driver is where your computer thinks it is—make sure that the file actually exists in the directory specified. If not, you'll need to recopy the driver to your hard disk and then reboot your machine.

Also make sure that you have the MSCDEX.EXE file loaded. You can load the file via a line in your AUTOEXEC.BAT file or just type **MSCDEX** at the DOS prompt. Without this file loaded, your system won't recognize your CD-ROM drive.

If you're trying to load either your device drivers or the MSCDEX.EXE file into high memory (via the DEVICEHIGH or LOADHIGH commands), try loading them into conventional memory instead. Sometimes these CD-ROM drivers and programs don't work well in higher system memory.

Finally, check for IRQ, DMA, and port conflicts. Make sure that you have the right assignments selected, and then try changing the assignments to make sure that they don't conflict with the assignments of other devices.

Problem 3:
Your CD-ROM drive doesn't work—you receive an error message on-screen

Error messages generally result from IRQ, DMA, or port conflicts. Make sure that your assignments are not used by other devices, and then change them if they are.

Problem 4:
Your CD-ROM drive freezes your system

Again, the culprit is most likely a DMA, IRQ, or port conflict. Check your assignments and change any conflicting ones.

A less likely, but still possible, cause of this problem occurs when you load the CD-ROM device driver and/or MSCDEX.EXE file into high system memory. Change your CONFIG.SYS and/or AUTOEXEC.BAT file to load these items into conventional memory, and then reboot your system.

Problem 5:
Your CD-ROM drive doesn't generate sound through your system speaker(s)

This problem sometimes occurs when you don't have the correct CD-ROM or sound card driver loaded. Make sure you have the latest versions of these drivers installed.

This problem also can occur if you didn't hook up your speakers, hooked them up incorrectly, or didn't turn them on. Check the obvious stuff, okay?

Believe it or not, some CD-ROM-based programs just don't utilize sound-card capabilities. They either don't have sound at all, or ignore the sound card and direct their sound to the headphone jack on the front of your CD-ROM drive. If this is the case, plug your headphones into your CD-ROM headphone jack and get on with it!

Finally, some CD-ROM drives are incompatible with some sound cards. See Problem 6 for more information.

Problem 6:
Your CD-ROM drive doesn't work with your sound card

First of all, if everything is hooked up properly (and don't assume that it is!), you may have a port, channel, or IRQ conflict between your CD-ROM drive and your sound card. Check these specific assignments to make sure they're as they should be.

It's likely that your CD-ROM drive isn't compatible with your sound card. I know that sounds crazy, but since there are no standards in this insane world of multimedia, you sometimes get devices that don't work with one another. Check with the manufacturers of both your CD-ROM drive and sound card to make sure that they can work together. If not, you'll need to buy one or more new devices—or forgo sound with your CD-ROM!

Problem 7:
Your CD-ROM drive doesn't play audio CDs

Some CD-ROM drives just can't play normal audio compact discs. Sorry.

On the other hand, your drive might be okay, but you need special software to play compact discs. Check with your local computer dealer or BBS to obtain this special CD software.

Problem 8:
Your CD-ROM drive doesn't play Photo CDs

This is true, sometimes. In fact, *most* current CD-ROM drives can't play Kodak's new Photo CDs. Check with your CD-ROM drive manufacturer to see if your drive is Photo CD-compatible.

If your CD-ROM drive will play Photo CDs but doesn't, then you probably lack the correct software to perform this function. Again, check with the manufacturer of your CD-ROM drive to obtain the proper Photo CD software.

Problem 9:
Your CD-ROM drive is slow

Yeah, that's true. CD-ROM drives *are* slow—much slower than most hard disk drives—and about as sluggish as a good floppy disk drive. There are a few things you can do to speed up your CD-ROM performance, however, including the following:

- *Add more memory to your system.* All data transfer utilizes system memory at some point, and the more you have, the faster things go.

- *Add a disk-caching utility.* Disk caches store frequently accessed data in your system's memory and can really speed up disk-drive access—including CD-ROM access. While normal disk caches such as DOS 6's SmartDrive do a pretty good job, you should look into a caching program specifically developed for CD-ROM use.

- *Get a faster CD-ROM drive.* Some newer drives operate at 300K transfer rate and 400ms access speed—which is a lot faster than older 150K/800ms drives.

- *Get a faster computer.* Yeah, it's drastic, but a faster computer will make all your peripherals *seem* faster, at least.

Problem 10:
Your CD-ROM doesn't always read data accurately

Inaccurate data can result from several problems. Most likely, you have a scratched or dirty CD-ROM disk. You can buy commercial CD cleaners that will remove surface dirt and debris; scratches are less easily fixed—if at all.

It's also possible that the laser beam inside your CD-ROM drive is dirty or out of alignment. You can try to "blow" the dirt out of the drive with compressed air, or—in some cases—wipe the laser lens with a cotton swab. However, your best bet is to see a repair person ASAP to get this puppy fixed.

Problem 11:
Your CD-ROM drive causes another peripheral to malfunction—or vice versa

No doubt about it—you have a conflict! One or more of your port, IRQ, or DMA channel assignments is used by another device on your system. If you have a listing of all your assignments, you can easily determine the conflict and fix it. If you don't have such a listing, then you have to use the old trial-and-error method. Begin by changing the port assignment; then reboot your computer and see what happens. If that doesn't do it, change the IRQ assignment (or try another port assignment), and so on and so on. I know, this can get tedious, but it's just about the only way to figure out what is conflicting with what—short of calling in a professional computer guru-type (which isn't a bad idea, actually!).

A Last Word on CD-ROMs

Adding a CD-ROM drive to your system really adds a lot of value to your computer system. There's a whole world of cool games and useful programs available only on CD-ROM—and most have great graphics and sound. If you can get past the normal setup difficulties, your CD-ROM drive should give you many hours of entertainment and education!

What To Do When...

Your Sound System Doesn't Sound Right

CHAPTER NINETEEN

In the last chapter we talked about part of what makes a multimedia system, the CD-ROM drive. Now we'll examine the other part—*sound*.

Of course, this isn't a simple thing to examine. This is because sound concerns your basic system unit, a sound card you insert into your system unit, and add-on speakers that hook up to your sound card. With all this going on, it's not hard to imagine something going wrong.

Looking at (or Listening to) Multimedia Sound

To add sound to your computer system, you actually add two things—a sound card, and a pair of external speakers. Without these, the only sound you have is what you get through the tiny, tinny built-in speaker.

Pick a Card, Any Card

A *sound card* is just like any card you add to your system. In this case, the card provides the ability to play back high quality audio—in other words, sounds and music. You install a sound card the same way you would any other add-in card—open up your system's case and slide the card into an open slot. It's pretty simple, really.

Once the sound card itself is installed, you also need to load the appropriate device driver for the card into your system's memory. Most cards come with their own driver files, which are generally loaded via your AUTOEXEC.BAT file; some cards come with utilities that do this chore for you automatically.

Crank It Up!

Most sound cards come with utility programs that let you set the volume for your audio playback. Some sound-capable programs include their own volume controls, as well.

Most major sound cards conform to the MPC specification. Some cards even let you *record* sounds, with an optional microphone. You probably want to use a card that's compatible with the SoundBlaster card because many games use the SoundBlaster as a standard.

Don't Forget the Speakers!

Now, a sound card in and of itself won't do you much good—you need some way to listen to the wonderful sounds it creates. Most sound cards come with a jack (sticking out the back of your system unit) to connect headphones. But if you really want the whole audio experience, spend a few bucks and hook up a pair of *powered speakers*. (The speakers are "self-powered" because they don't draw power from your system unit.) These speakers will normally hook up to your sound card's headphone jack and provide high-quality stereophonic playback of system audio.

Maximizing MIDI

If you *really* want to get into high-quality audio, look into something called MIDI. MIDI, which stands for *musical instrument digital interface*, is a standard used by professional musicians to record and play back music digitally. Most sound cards come with

---
Music without MIDI

Of course, you don't need a complete MIDI setup to get basic musical instrument playback capabilities. The Software Toolworks makes an add-on piano keyboard called The Miracle Keyboard, which is compatible with SoundBlaster audio cards. The Miracle functions just like a normal piano and can also be used (with accompanying software) to teach you basic piano techniques.

---

basic MIDI capabilities; pro musicians might opt for more fully-featured dedicated MIDI cards, most of which are compatible with the Roland MPU-401 standard. With a MIDI setup, you can connect your computer to digital keyboards and other synthesized instruments—and use your computer to "sequence" and play back music through the attached musical instruments.

What Can Go Wrong with Your Multimedia Sound

The most common problems with sound cards are often the same problems you find with CD-ROM drives.

FYI, IRQ—A-OK?

All add-on devices—including your sound card—use something called *interrupt requests* (abbreviated IRQs) to interrupt your PC and get its attention so that it can do what it needs to do. Most systems have 16 available IRQs; your sound card can be set to use any of these interrupt settings.

- *Things might not be hooked up right.* Remember to seat all the cards and connect all the cables—including the power cables for your powered speakers!

- *Things might not be loaded right.* Don't forget to load the device drivers into memory for your sound card.

- *Things might be in conflict—in particular, ports (also called* input/output addresses*), interrupts, and DMA channels!* It's *very important* to make sure that your sound card is set up so that it doesn't use ports, channels, or interrupts assigned to other devices on your system. If you have conflicts, you might find that *several* devices don't work right!

- *Things might not be compatible.* Believe it or not, not all sound cards are compatible with all CD-ROM drives. Check with your dealer or manufacturer to make sure all your equipment really can work together—don't assume that everything will work with everything else!

Direct Memory for Your Sound

Your sound card, like most peripherals, uses a *direct memory access (DMA)* channel to pipe information directly to your system's memory, bypassing the microprocessor. Most systems have eight DMA channels available.

When you're adding a "standard" sound card to your system, you run into a basic problem—there really is no such thing as a "standard" when it comes to multimedia computing. Every sound card seems to work with a different set of parameters than other cards, and there's no way to know which card really does what. This means that installing a sound card requires more trial-and-error than most other add-on devices. I wish it were different, but it's not. Sorry.

Fixing Audio Problems

Okay, you have your new sound card and speakers all fired up and ready to go. But what do you do if they *don't* go? Well, let's take a look at the most common sound problems you may encounter.

Problem 1:
Your sound card doesn't work—you don't get any sound

Let's look at the simple stuff first. Is the card installed properly in your system unit? Are speakers (or headphones) hooked up to the card? Are the speakers plugged in and turned on? (And are they plugged into the correct jack? You don't want to plug your speakers into your microphone jack!) Are you running a program that produces sound? Is the sound part of the program activated? Is the sound turned up loud enough (both on your speakers and in the program in question)? Is your sound card compatible with the program you're trying to run?

Okay, now that the easy stuff is out of the way, let's turn to something more difficult. The most likely cause of no sound is some sort of conflict. One by one, change your card's DMA, IRQ, and port settings. (This may entail resetting some jumpers on the card itself, as well as making some software-based changes.)

10 Do's and Don'ts for Multimedia Audio

1. *Do* hook up a good pair of powered speakers to your sound card; it's a lot more convenient than using headphones!

2. *Don't* assign your sound card to ports, channels, or interrupts used by other devices in your system.

3. *Do* make sure your CD-ROM drive is compatible with your sound card.

4. *Don't* hesitate to spend a little more money for a better sound card; the result will be higher-quality playback.

5. *Do* make sure your entire computer system conforms to MPC standards—*before* you install your sound card!

6. *Don't* forget to load the proper device drivers for your sound card via your CONFIG.SYS and/or AUTOEXEC.BAT files.

7. *Do* order your new PC with sound card and CD-ROM pre-installed; it will save you a lot of trouble if you want to add multimedia capability later on.

8. *Don't* forget to check out all of your sound card's capabilities, including hookups for MIDI keyboards.

9. *Do* check out the so-called "multimedia upgrade kits" that include both a sound card and CD-ROM drive; they're often better integrated and easier to set up than separate components.

10. *Don't* waste too much time playing with Windows sound files—these WAV files sound way cool through a sound card and a good pair of stand-alone speakers!

Problem 2:
Your sound card freezes or crashes your system

If you've just installed your sound card, you may not have the card properly installed. Check your installation (is the card properly seated and connected?) and then reboot your system.

If this doesn't fix it, you have something wrong in your setup. Check your software setup to make sure you have the same DMA, IRQ, and port assignments as selected on your sound card itself (usually via DIP switches or jumpers). If the settings are right, then you probably have a conflict of some kind. You should methodically change the DMA, IRQ, and port assignments so that they don't conflict with the assignments for other devices on your system.

Problem 3:
When you launch Windows, you get an error message about your sound card

There are a number of error messages you can receive about your sound card when you launch Windows. Perhaps the most common is one that looks something like this:

```
SOUNDCARD ERROR: DRIVER.XXX not installed
```

This error message occurs for one of three reasons:

- The driver file for your sound card is not being installed when Windows is launched.

- The driver file for your sound card cannot be found.

- There is no entry for your sound card driver in your SYSTEM.INI file.

The obvious fix is to make sure the driver is being loaded properly. There are two things to check.

First, is the driver file where Windows thinks it is on your hard disk? Check your Windows system directory (normally C:\WINDOWS\SYSTEM); if the driver file is not there, you may need to copy it from your sound card's installation directory or from your sound card's installation diskette. You may even need to reinstall your sound card software.

Second, is your sound card sharing an interrupt with another device? If so, change the IRQ setting for one of the two devices.

Problem 4:
Sound from your sound card skips or plays continually

This problem generally results from an IRQ conflict. Change the interrupt setting for your sound card to one not used by another system device and then reboot your system. You may want to change the sound card's interrupt to one between 3 and 8; in some cases using a higher interrupt (between 9 and 15) may cause problems with some systems.

Problem 5:
You only get sound from one channel of a stereo setup

The most likely cause of this problem is using the wrong kind of plug for your powered speakers. It's possible that you're using a mono plug; you need a stereo plug to connect to your sound card's stereo jack.

This problem also can occur if you don't have the proper driver for your sound card loaded into memory. Check your setup to make sure that the driver is loaded in either your CONFIG.SYS or AUTOEXEC.BAT file.

Problem 6:
The volume level from your sound card is too low or too high

This is normally a simple problem with a simple solution. First, try adjusting the volume on your powered speakers. If this isn't the problem, you need to adjust the volume of your sound software. Read the instructions that come with your sound card to find out how to adjust this software-driven volume level.

Problem 7:
Sound from your sound card plays too fast

This is a tough one and generally results from your PC being too fast for your particular sound card. In many cases, you can change sound drivers or "turbo down" your computer (to run at a slower speed) and fix the problem. In other cases, your PC and your sound card are just plain incompatible, and there's nothing you can do about it. Try calling the technical support line of your card manufacturer for more help.

Problem 8:
Sound from your sound card is of poor quality

First, check your setup to make sure you have the right sound driver loaded. Next, try moving your speakers farther away from your video monitor; electrical noise from your monitor might be affecting the speakers' sound. Finally, try moving your sound card to another slot inside your system unit. Sometimes proximity to another card can cause your sound card to generate poor quality sound.

Of course, poor quality sound can simply be the result of using poor quality speakers with your system. You may want to invest in some better speakers if you're really picky about this sort of thing.

Problem 9:
Your CD-ROM drive doesn't work with your sound card

First of all, if everything is hooked up properly (and don't assume that it is!), you may have a port, channel, or IRQ conflict between your CD-ROM drive and your sound card. Check these specific assignments to make sure they're as they should be.

If all that checks out, you probably have a CD-ROM drive that isn't compatible with your sound card. Check with the manufacturers of both your CD-ROM drive and sound card to make sure that they can work together. If not, you'll need to buy one or more new devices—or forgo sound with your CD-ROM!

A Last Word on PC Sound

Fortunately, most newer sound cards—especially those that come as part of "multimedia upgrade kits" that also include CD-ROM drives—make setup a breeze. For example, I just added MediaVision's "Memphis" kit to my personal system, and all the IRQ and DMA settings were done automatically through a software-based installation program. If your sound card is just as easy to set up, congratulations! If not... well, that's why you just got done reading this chapter, right?

What To Do When...

Your Files Are Funky

CHAPTER TWENTY

Back in Chapter 17 you learned all about disk problems. But what if you have trouble with the individual files on your disk?

You see, all your data is in files. All the good things you do with your computer involve files, and some of the bad things do, too. This means you must be careful when working with your files, because any mistake you make can cause your files—and your valuable data—to disappear.

The Least You Need to Know About Files

The next few sections are like a refresher course in DOS file management. Feel free to skip these pages if you're comfortable with your DOS skills.

As explained in Chapter 2, files are composed of data. Every file has a file name, consisting of an eight-character (maximum) name, an optional period, and an optional three-character (maximum) extension. A typical file name looks like the following:

FILENAME.EXT

File Management in Windows

If you're using Windows, you use the File Manager for most of your file tasks. To open File Manager, just double-click on the File Manager icon in the Main program group. You'll see a two-pane display; a directory tree is on the left, and files for the selected directory are on the right.

When you specify a file, you must use its correct full file name. Sometimes you even have to list its path (see "Setting the Path," later in this chapter). The reason you must list the path is simple—you can have multiple files with the same name on your disk. Unless you list the directory a file is in, DOS won't know which file to pick.

Managing Your File Directories

Files are stored on your disk in directories. A *directory* is like a master file; each directory can contain both files and additional directories, called *subdirectories*. The main directory on your disk is called the *root directory*, and all other directories branch off of it.

With all the possible branches, the directory structure on any given disk is called a *directory tree*. In fact, if you look at the directories on your hard disk, they look something like a tree with the root directory and its many branches and sub-branches.

Setting the Path

When you specify a directory, you must use its entire *path*, which is a list of all directories and subdirectories leading to that directory. The path of the root directory on drive C is specified as:

C:\

The path of DIR01 off the root directory is specified as:

```
C:\DIR01
```

And the path of DIR02 off DIR01 is specified as:

```
C:\DIR01\DIR02
```

Sometimes you have to include the path when you're specifying a file. A file name with its path looks something like the following:

```
C:\DIR01\DIR02\FILENAME.EXT
```

In Windows, the entire path is shown in the directory pane on the left side of the File Manager window.

Changing Directories

If you're in one directory and need to get to another, you need to change directories. DOS lets you do this with the CD command. Just type the command, followed by the full path of where you

> **Space, the Final Frontier**
>
> When you type a DOS command, you must always insert a space between the command and anything that comes after the command. If you don't, DOS thinks the whole multi-word jumble is one long command—and not one that it recognizes, either!

want to go. To change to the root directory on drive C, for example, type the following:

CD C:

You also can change to subdirectories within a specified directory. Just make sure that you type the entire path after the command. To change to subdirectory DIR02 under directory DIR01, for example, type the following:

CD C:\DIR01\DIR02

Naturally, Windows makes this a little easier. When you're in the File Manager, all you have to do is click on a subdirectory in the directory pane to access it.

Making and Deleting Directories

If you need to make a new directory from the DOS prompt, use the MD command. Just type the command, followed by the name of the new directory, as follows:

MD C:\NEWDIR

In Windows, it's a simple matter of opening the File Manager, selecting the directory to be the "parent" of the new directory, pulling down the File menu, and selecting Create Directory. When the Create Directory dialog box appears, type the Name of the new directory, and click OK.

To delete an old directory from the DOS prompt, use the RD command. (The directory you're deleting must be empty of all files and subdirectories before you can delete it, however.) Just type the command, followed by the directory to delete, as follows:

> **RD C:\NEWDIR**

To delete a directory in Windows, just select the directory in File Manager's directory pane, pull down the File menu, and select Delete.

Good Things You Can Do with Files

DOS includes many commands that let you manipulate your files and directories. If you use Windows, you can perform many of these same operations from File Manager. The theory is the same, even if the procedures are a little different.

The next sections list a few of the useful tasks you can perform on files.

Copying Files

Copying files is the most common task you'll do with files, and it's easy. From the DOS prompt, type the COPY command, then the name of the source file, and then the destination to which you want to copy. For example, suppose that you want to copy a file from the current directory to drive A. Type the following:

> **COPY FILENAME.EXT A:**

To copy a file from drive A to a directory on drive C, type the following:

> **COPY A:FILENAME.EXT C:\DIR01**

In Windows, you do all your copying from the file pane in File Manager. Just select a file, and use your mouse to drag it to a new directory in the directory pane. Alternatively, you can select a file, pull down the File menu, and select Copy. When the Copy dialog box appears, type in the name of the To directory, and then click OK.

Deleting Files

DOS lets you delete any file you want with the DEL command. You issue this command, followed by the name of the file you want to delete. A typical delete command looks like the following:

```
DEL FILENAME.EXT
```

Think Twice Before You DEL

The DEL command can be a dangerous one, especially when used with wild cards. For example, the command cited in the text (DEL A:*.*) deletes all the files on drive A. That's pretty powerful—and pretty dangerous. Make sure that you really want to delete everything listed when you use the DEL command, or you could end up missing files you will really need at a later date!

Naturally, you can also use wild cards to delete groups of files at one time. You can delete all the files on your A drive, for example, by typing the following:

DEL A:*.*

In Windows, deleting a file is as simple as selecting it in File Manager, and then pressing the Delete key on your keyboard. (Alternatively, you can pull down the File menu and select **Delete**.)

Moving Files

DOS 6 features a new command, MOVE, that lets you move files from one directory or drive to another, without first copying and then deleting the original file. (If you don't have DOS 6, you have to copy the file to the new location, and then delete the old file.)

A typical MOVE command looks like this:

MOVE C:\OLDDIR\FILENAME.EXT C:\NEWDIR

You can also use wild cards to move multiple files at one time. (Be careful *not* to use wild cards in your destination, however!) For example, to move all your files from the DIR01 directory of drive C to drive A, you type the following:

MOVE C:\DIR01*.* A:

Windows features a similar command. Just select a file in the File Manager, pull down the File menu, and select **Move**. When the Move dialog box appears, type the new destination in the To box and click OK.

Renaming Files

Changing Names with MOVE

You can use the MOVE command to change the name of a file while you're moving it. Simply type in a new file name as part of the destination, and your original file will be moved and given a new name in one fell swoop. The syntax looks like this:

MOVE C:\DIR01\OLDFILE.EXT

C:\DIR02\NEWFILE.EXT

DOS enables you to rename files with the REN command. Just issue the command, followed by the original name, and then the new name. A sample command looks like the following:

```
REN OLDFILE.EXT NEWFILE.EXT
```

You can even use wild cards to rename entire groups of files.

Suppose that you want to rename all your DOC files to have the BAK extension. Just type the following command:

REN *.DOC *.BAK

To rename a file in Windows, begin by selecting the file in File Manager. Then pull down the File menu and select Rename. When the Rename dialog box appears, type the new file name in the To box and click OK.

Listing Files

The DIR command lets you display a list of files in a given directory. Just type the command, followed by the directory, as follows:

DIR C:\DATA

DIR lists all the files in the directory, along with information on each file. Also listed are any subdirectories of the selected directory.

If you're using Windows, directory listings appear naturally in the file pane (right-hand side) of File Manager.

Searching for Files

If you can't remember where a file is on your hard disk, you can look for it with the DIR command. All you have to do is use the /S switch with the command; this switch tells DOS to search your disk for the specified file(s), instead of merely giving the normal directory listing.

For example, suppose that you want to find all the files with a DOC extension on your hard disk. Simply type the following command:

DIR *.DOC /S

After you press Enter, DOS lists all files matching the wild card, and tells you in what directory you can find them.

To find a file in Windows, you need to open File Manager, pull down the File menu, and select Search. When the Search dialog box appears, type the file you want to look for (including wild cards, if need be) in the Search For box. Then type the *highest-level directory* in your search in the Start From box; if you want to search all subdirectories, check this box, as well. When you click OK, Windows will search for the files in question and display any "finds" in a Search Results dialog box.

Looking at File Contents

You can look at the contents of a file by using the DOS TYPE command.

This command displays the contents of a file on your computer screen. The command is useful if you want to view a file that's in a format you can actually read. For that reason, the TYPE command is great if you want to view the contents of a text file, but less than great if you

> ### More! More! More!
>
> The MORE switch is used with some commands (such as DIR and TYPE) to break long lists into screen-sized chunks. When MORE is activated, a long display stops when a screen is filled up; press any key, however, and another screen full of information is displayed. Notice that the | character must be used before the MORE switch. This is different from the normal / character and is unique to MORE.

want to view the contents of a program file. For example, to view the contents of a particular file in a particular directory, type the following:

TYPE C:\DIR01\FILENAME.EXT

If you're viewing a rather long file, you will find that it scrolls rapidly off your screen. You can prevent this by using the MORE switch, as follows:

TYPE FILENAME.EXT | MORE

> ### No Viewing in Windows
>
> Unfortunately, Windows does not include any automatic file viewers. If you want to view file contents from within Windows, you need to invest in a third-party solution, such as Norton Desktop for Windows, which includes all sorts of automatic viewers for different types of files.

Bad Things You Can Do with Files

After the last section, you know all the basic good things you can do to files by using DOS commands. Now take a look at some of the mistakes you can make when working with files.

- *Accidentally deleting files.* This is really bad. Fortunately, DOS 5 and 6 enable you to recover accidentally deleted files with the UNDELETE command.

- *Typing the wrong file name.* If you type the wrong name, DOS doesn't know which file you mean. Garbage in, garbage out.

- *Misplacing files.* Sometimes you type a file name and the file isn't there. What did you do with it? What directory is it in? DOS can't help you if you don't know where your files are.

- *Creating duplicate files.* If you copy files from one directory to another, you can have two or more files on your disk with the same name. Which file is the one you really want to use? Again, DOS can't help you unless you know what you're doing.

- *Forgetting the path.* This is like forgetting where your file is. Sometimes you have to type the entire path leading to your file, or DOS won't know where it is.

- *Misusing wild cards.* Using wild cards (explained in Chapter 2) is a powerful way to select multiple files. But it can also be a powerful way to mess up multiple files. Be very careful whenever you use wild cards.

What To Do When You Have File Problems

Most file problems are caused by you. Either you mistype something, use the wrong command, or just plain mess up an operation. The most important information you need to know about file problems, then, is how to recover from your own mistakes!

Problem 1:
You accidentally deleted an important file

Deleting an important file can be one of the most disconcerting errors you will make in the course of using your computer. How could you do that? Deleting a file you didn't want to delete! Just what do you know?

UNDELETE at Once!

You can undelete a file only if its data has not been overwritten by newer data on your disk. For that reason, you should undelete any files as soon as you notice the accidental deletion.

When you're done berating yourself, you can get down to the business of bringing that file back from the dead. As explained in Chapter 7, when you delete a file, that file isn't *really* deleted. The data still exists on your hard disk, although all reference to the data in the file allocation table (FAT) has been removed. Fortunately, the UNDELETE utility with DOS 5 and 6 can restore the file's reference in the FAT, thus undeleting the file.

10 Do's and Don'ts for File Management

1. *Do* use UNDELETE (with DOS 5 and 6) as soon as you discover a file has been accidentally deleted and before that file's data is overwritten by new data.

2. *Don't* use wild cards indiscriminately; you can mess up too many files at one time if you're not careful.

3. *Do* keep backup copies of your important files (refer to Chapter 7).

4. *Don't* turn off your computer while you're in the middle of a file operation; the data probably will be scrambled.

5. *Do* get rid of old files periodically; they just clutter your disk and take up valuable space.

6. *Don't* delete files you don't really want to delete; although you can use UNDELETE in DOS 5 and 6, it's easier if you don't make the mistake in the first place.

7. *Do* create separate directories and subdirectories for various types of data; putting everything in one large directory makes it hard to find things.

8. *Don't* use any of the following characters in a file name:

   + = / [ ] ' : ; , ? * \ < > |

9. *Do* use the DIR command to find important file information without actually opening the file.

10. *Don't* hesitate to use Windows File Manager for all your file chores while you're in Windows; you don't have to drop back to DOS to do all this stuff!

If you're running Windows 3.1 and DOS 6, however, it's easiest to use the Windows-based undelete utility. Just open up the Microsoft Tools program group and double-click on the Microsoft Undelete for Windows icon. When Microsoft Undelete launches, select the drive and directory where the undeleted file resides (by clicking on the **Drive/Dir** button), and click on the file to be undeleted. When you click on the **Undelete** button, you'll be asked to Enter (the) First Character of the file (shown as a "?"). Do so, and click OK. Your deleted file will now be automatically undeleted!

If you *don't* have Windows, you'll have to use the slightly more complex DOS-based undelete utility. The command syntax for UNDELETE is simple but has several variations. The simplest version is to invoke the command alone, as follows:

UNDELETE

Supplying File Names

You may find that the first character of the file name has been replaced by a question mark (?). If so, you need to enter the real first character of the file name before it can be undeleted. If you supply the wrong character, DOS will go ahead and undelete the file anyway—it'll just have a different name than it had before.

When you issue this command, DOS attempts to undelete all deleted files in the current directory.

You can specify a particular file to undelete by typing the path and file name after the main command. This variation looks something like the following:

```
UNDELETE C:\DIR01\FILENAME.EXT
```

You can also instruct DOS to undelete all files in a specific directory by typing a command such as the following:

UNDELETE C:\DIR01

If you're not sure which files you accidentally deleted, use the /LIST switch to list all deleted files that can be recovered. That command looks like the following:

```
UNDELETE /LIST
```

When you invoke the /LIST switch, DOS displays a list of files that have been deleted from the current directory. Any files listed with an * or ** are probably not recoverable; all other files on the list can be recovered. Once you locate the file you want to recover, note its name and use the UNDELETE command with the file name specified.

If you've used DOS 6's Delete Tracker (explained in Chapter 3), issue the following command to undelete tracked files:

> **UNDELETE /Tdrive**

If you used DOS 6's Delete Sentry (also explained in Chapter 3), issue the following command to undelete sentry-protected files:

> **UNDELETE /Sdrive**

When you finally run UNDELETE (whichever variation you choose), you're presented with some technical information, as well as a prompt to recover the file. Answer yes and hang on tight; DOS will go through a few gyrations and ultimately bring the file back to life.

Undeleting with Old Versions of DOS

If you have a version of DOS prior to DOS 5, it's still possible for you to undelete files. Many third-party utility programs include undelete utilities. Check out such programs as Norton Utilities and PC Tools Deluxe for their undelete capabilities, which often work quite similarly to the DOS UNDELETE command.

When DOS has restored a file, it gives you the following message:

```
File successfully undeleted
```

If DOS cannot restore the file, it tells you so. Your only option at this point is to restore the file from your most recent backup disk, as explained in Chapter 8.

Problem 2:
You can't find a file

Is it possible to actually lose a file on your hard disk? Of course it is. When you have thousands of different files in dozens of different directories and subdirectories, you can easily forget where you stashed a certain file.

Fortunately, you can use the Search command in Windows to find any files on your hard disk. Just open File Manager, pull down the File menu, and select Search. When the Search dialog box appears, type the file you want to look for (including wild cards, if need be) in the Search For box. Then type the *highest-level directory* in your search in the Start From box; if you want to search all subdirectories, check this box, as well. When you click OK, Windows will search for the files in question and display any "finds" in a Search Results dialog box.

If you don't have Windows, you'll have to use the DOS DIR command to find your file. Just issue the DIR command, followed by the file name you've lost, followed by the /S switch, as follows:

DIR FILENAME.EXT /S

DOS lists all occurrences of files with that name and their directories.

If these procedures don't find the file you're looking for, the file may actually be on another disk (maybe on a floppy disk instead of your hard disk), or you may have accidentally deleted the file. To look for a possibly deleted file, you first have to determine which directory you think the file was in. Then issue the UNDELETE command with the /LIST switch, as follows:

UNDELETE C:\DIR01 /LIST

DOS lists all recently deleted files in that directory. If you find the file you lost, refer to Problem #1 to learn how to undelete a file. If the file isn't there—well, maybe you were hallucinating?

Problem 3:
You can't tell which is the most recent copy of a file

You find two files with the same name on your hard disk (in different directories, of course). Which is the newer file? The answer is simple—look at the date and time stamp in the File Manager file pane or in the DIR listing. The newest file is the one with the most recent time listed.

Problem 4:
You can't delete a file

You tried using the Windows Delete operation or the DOS DEL command on a file, but it won't delete. This problem occurs for one of three reasons:

- *You typed either the wrong command or the wrong name of the file.* Try it again.

- *You're trying to delete a file from a floppy disk that is write-protected.* If you're using a 5 1/4-inch disk, uncover the square notch on the side. (If no notch is present, you're out of luck—the disk is permanently write-protected.) If you're using a 3 1/2-inch disk, slide the tab in the lower-left corner so that the hole is closed. Then try the procedure again.

- *The attributes of the file have been set so that you can't delete it.* DOS might even tell you that the file is write-protected. (Every file has attributes, which are set by DOS; one attribute makes a file read-only, meaning that you can't delete it or write to it.) To change a file's attributes, you use the ATTRIB command at the DOS prompt, followed by the -R parameter, followed by the file name, as follows:

ATTRIB -R FILENAME.EXT

If you're using Windows, you can change attributes directly from File Manager. Just select the file, pull down the File menu, and select Properties. When the Properties for *FILE* dialog box appears, unselect the Read Only box in the Attributes section, and then click OK.

Now you can delete the file, like you wanted to in the first place.

Problem 5:
You try to access a file and find that its data is scrambled or incomplete

Scrambled data can be caused by a number of factors. The most likely reason is that you accidentally rebooted or turned off your system while that file was being accessed, causing the file to become corrupted. Another cause for scrambled data is a bug in a software program or a computer virus. Whatever the cause, you can't do much about it—once data is scrambled, it's scrambled.

> ### Restoring Those Scrambled Programs
>
> Of course, if a program file gets scrambled, you can always reinstall the program from your original program disks or copies thereof. Just turn to your handy-dandy PC Survival Kit (remember this from Chapter 7?), pull out your copies of your original program diskettes, and rerun the installation program. Voila! New, unscrambled program files!

If you have a backup copy of the data on another disk (or on a backup disk), however, you can always use that copy to replace your scrambled copy. See Chapter 8 for more information on restoring backup data.

Problem 6:
You type a file command and get a DOS error message

When you work with files, get used to seeing DOS error messages. Most of the time, they result from incorrectly typing something, so if you get a message, the first action is always to type the command again. However, even when you type it correctly, you can still get error messages. Chapter 28,

"DOS Error Messages...What They Mean and How To Deal with Them," gives a more complete listing of error messages; the following messages are those you're most likely to encounter when working with files.

```
Access denied
```

You tried to work with a file marked read-only. See Problem #4 for details on how to change a file's read-only attribute.

```
Bad command or file name
Bad or missing file name
File not found
Invalid drive or file name
```

You either mistyped the command or file name, or you typed a file name for a file that doesn't exist. Try typing the command again. If you still get the message, you may have to type the complete path for the file. It's also possible that the file really isn't where you think it is; see Problem #2 for more details.

```
Cannot move multiple files to a single file
```

You tried to use the DOS 6 MOVE command with wild cards for the source file and a specific name for the destination file—in other words, you tried to move multiple source files to a single file destination. You can't do that, so go back and retype the command, either without the wild cards or with a directory destination instead of a file destination.

```
Duplicate filename or File not found
```

This message is generated when you use the REN command to rename a file and something goes wrong. The problem is often a mistyping of either the old or new file name. The message can also be generated when the new name you try to assign already exists for another file.

```
File cannot be copied onto itself
```

You used the COPY command and inadvertently tried to copy the file on to itself. The command you typed looked something like the following:

```
COPY THISFILE.EXT THISFILE.EXT
```

Plain and simple—you can't do that. Issue the command again, but this time give a different destination file name.

```
File creation error
```

For some reason, DOS doesn't want to create a new file. Perhaps you tried to create a file name that has the same name as an existing directory or an existing read-only file. If this mistake is the culprit, assign a different name to your file.

You can also receive this error message if your disk or directory is so full that nothing else can be added to it. In this case, you need to delete some files *pronto* before you can do much of anything else.

```
Insufficient disk space
```

You get this message when your disk is so full that nothing else can be added to it. The only action to take is to delete some unused files from your disk to make room for anything else you care to save.

> ### Copying Large Files to Small Diskettes
>
> If you're trying to copy a really large file to a diskette, where the file is larger than the free space left on the destination diskette, you probably need to consider something other than the normal COPY operation. I recommend backing up the file with either the BACKUP command or the Microsoft Backup utility. This way a single large file can reside on multiple diskettes. Just remember that before you can use the file, you have to restore it to its original state on your hard disk with either the RESTORE command or Microsoft Backup.

```
Invalid directory
Path not found
```

You specified a directory that doesn't exist. More than likely, you simply mistyped a directory name. Try retyping it—but more slowly and more carefully this time. It's also possible that you got the path wrong. Double-check exactly what it is you're supposed to be typing, and type it right next time. It's possible, too, that the directory you specified really doesn't exist. You might have removed that directory. Check your disk's directory tree before you proceed.

```
Invalid drive in search path
Invalid drive or file name
Invalid drive specification
```

Very simply—you typed the name of a drive that doesn't exist. Maybe you meant to type *A* and typed *Q* instead. Check what you just typed, and retype it correctly.

```
Invalid path or file name
```

You typed either a directory path or file name incorrectly. Check your directory tree and files and retype the name correctly this time. (It's also possible that you typed the name of a file you accidentally deleted; see Problem #1 on how to undelete files.)

```
Unable to create destination
[Unable to open source]
Unable to read source
Unable to write destination
```

In DOS 6, an error occurred as you used the MOVE command. You may have an illegal character in the file name, or you're trying to move an entire directory instead of a single file, which you can't do. If this isn't the problem, you may have to use the COPY and DELETE commands to execute the operation.

Problem 7:
You attempt a file operation from File Manager and get a Windows error message

When you're working with files, you'll get error messages—even in Windows! As with DOS error messages, Windows messages often result when you incorrectly type something, so if you get a message, the first action is always to try the operation again, typing more carefully this time. However, even when you type it correctly, you can still get error messages. Chapter 27, "Windows Error Messages...What They Mean and How To Deal with Them," gives a more complete listing of error messages; the following messages are those you're most likely to encounter when working with files.

```
Cannot find file
```

The most common cause for this message is that the file in question is either missing or corrupted. Use File Manager to search for the file; reinstall the program in question, if necessary.

```
Cannot read from drive x
```

Windows is looking for a file on drive x:. If no diskette is in drive x:, insert an old diskette to end the Windows look loop. If a diskette is in drive x:, you either have a bad (or unformatted) diskette, or a bad diskette drive.

```
Directory xxx does not exist
```

You have specified a directory that does not exist. Check the spelling of the directory and path name. If you are using File Manager, select the **R**efresh option from the Window menu to refresh the current directory tree.

```
File already exists. Overwrite?
```

You're trying to create or save a file with a name that already exists. Windows is asking if you wish to overwrite the existing file. If so, answer yes. If no, answer no, and assign a new name to your file.

```
File is missing
```

When Windows loads, it tries to load any programs that are included in the StartUp program group. This message is generated when one of these files no longer exists or has been entered incorrectly. Open the StartUp group and check all programs and associations, removing or editing those that are not correct.

```
Not a valid filename
```

You typed an invalid file name for a file operation. Try typing a different file name. Remember, all files can have eight characters before the dot, and a three-character extension afterwards.

```
The specified path is invalid
```

You typed an incorrect directory path for a file operation. Check the path and retype the command.

```
Write protected disk
```

You're trying to perform a file operation on a floppy disk that is write-protected. Change disks, or uncover the write-protect notch (on 5 1/4" disks) or slide the write-protect tab into the down position (on 3 1/2" disks).

A Final Word on Files

As you can see, you can cause a lot of problems with files just by typing something wrong. This fact speaks volumes when it comes to taking as much time and care as you need to do things right the first time. Although DOS and Windows enable you to recover from a great many of your mistakes, it's much quicker not to make the mistakes in the first place.

Your DOS Doesn't

CHAPTER TWENTY-ONE

Just about every IBM-compatible computer today has DOS. Even if you're running Windows, you're still running DOS. (Windows sits *on top of* DOS, you see.)

DOS is just another piece of software—but a *very important one.* What makes DOS important is that it's an *operating system* that acts as a bridge between you and your hardware; DOS (that's *Disk Operating System*) makes your system operate.

Unfortunately, because DOS is involved with just about everything your system does, it too can actually cause some of your problems. Read on to find out how.

Miller's Very Brief DOS Refresher Course

Okay, here's the nickel-and-dime refresher course on DOS. DOS consists of four parts: the BIOS, the command interpreter, the utilities, and the Shell. You never see the BIOS; it's the part that translates your commands into a form your hardware can understand. You do, however, use the command interpreter (otherwise known as the DOS prompt), the DOS utilities (miniprograms that perform specific functions), and—if you have a version of DOS prior to 6.2—the DOS Shell (the semigraphical interface that's far easier to use than the DOS prompt). Reread Chapters 2 and 3 for more detailed information, or pick up one of the DOS books published by Que for really detailed information.

Starting DOS

Windows vs. DOS

If you use Windows, you may think you're not using DOS. Well, you're wrong! Windows isn't really an operating system, but rather an operating *environment* (or shell) that still requires an operating system (DOS) to operate. Windows sits on top of DOS and uses the pretty Windows graphical interface to isolate you from the nasty DOS command prompt. So if you're using Windows, you're still using DOS—and you can still have DOS problems (which is why you're reading this chapter)!

DOS loads as soon as you turn on your computer. As explained in Chapter 10, your computer's system undergoes an elaborate startup procedure, during which it loads the COMMAND.COM file. The COMMAND.COM file contains the command interpreter, several DOS system files, and two DOS startup files (CONFIG.SYS and AUTOEXEC.BAT). All this programmed data enters your system's memory, where it works behind the scenes to operate your computer. All you have to do to start DOS is make sure it's installed on your hard disk and, of course, turn on the machine.

Different Versions of DOS

In the years since its inception, several different versions of DOS have made the rounds of computer users. Each new version has built on the previous one, improving its functionality and adding many useful new commands and capabilities. The latest version, as I write this book, is DOS 6.

If you haven't yet installed DOS 6 on your machine, I recommend that you upgrade as soon as possible. DOS 6 performs much better than any of the previous versions and introduces many useful commands and functions that weren't available before.

Command Line DOS

Most computers drop you right into the DOS prompt after you start your system. But that's okay—you can handle it. I have confidence in you!

It's Polite to Point

Actually, there are several *subversions* of MS-DOS 6 released by Microsoft, each of them called *point releases*. Version 6.0 (six point oh, hence the name "point release") is the original DOS 6 version, and includes DoubleSpace and all those other neat new utilities. Version 6.2 was next out the gate, and included some bug fixes and patches to make installation and use of DoubleSpace a lot easier. (This version also pretty much did away with the DOS Shell.) Version 6.21, however, did away with DoubleSpace, for legal reasons. The latest release (well, the latest *as of this writing!*) is version 6.22, which adds DriveSpace, a disk compression utility kind of sort of like DoubleSpace. Got all that?

The *command line*, located immediately to the right of the DOS prompt, is where you type all your DOS commands. These commands enable you to work with disks, manipulate files, set system parameters, run various utilities, and load your favorite programs. Working from the DOS prompt is easy—if you know what you're doing, of course. Fortunately, any good book about DOS can teach you the important DOS commands and how to use them.

A Double Dose of DOS

It's actually possible to start DOS from DOS, which can cause some problems if you're not aware of what you're doing. All you have to do to run a double DOS session is to type **COMMAND** at the DOS prompt—or start a second DOS window from within Windows. This loads a second copy of COMMAND.COM into your system's memory. Because running two versions of DOS at the same time can eat up system memory and cause problems when you try to run other programs, you don't want to do this. If you think you may have a second copy of COMMAND.COM loaded, just type **EXIT** at the DOS prompt. This closes the second command interpreter and returns you to your original DOS prompt.

You must be careful, however, to issue these commands correctly. If a command requires a certain switch or parameter, you'd better use it if you want the command to work. If you don't, DOS tells you, via an on-screen *error message*, just how wrong you are. DOS employs these error messages to tell you, in no uncertain terms, that you messed up. (Well, actually the terms aren't always all *that* certain. But if you're reasonably computer-savvy, you can usually decipher a particular error message enough to find your mistake and correct it. See Chapter 28, "DOS Error Messages…What They Mean and How To Deal with Them," for more details on reading DOS error messages.)

Oh, one other thing about the command line: if you type the command wrong, you get an error message. It's the old garbage in, garbage out routine; DOS knows to do only what you tell it. So be careful what your fumbling little fingers tell it to do.

The DOS Shell

If you prefer not to work from the DOS prompt (and you are using DOS version 4 or later—but not version 6.2 or later), you can skip the command line entirely and go straight to the DOS Shell. To load the Shell from the command line, just type the following:

DOSSHELL

Be careful to type *both* S's in the command; leaving one out is a mistake I often make, and DOS stubbornly refuses to acknowledge a single-S-ed shell. You may not even have to worry about starting the Shell, however, as many computers are now set up to load the Shell automatically at system startup. To have the Shell load automatically on your computer, just add the following as the last line in your AUTOEXEC.BAT file:

DOSSHELL

Now, whenever you start your system, you're dropped right into the DOS Shell. (Of course, if you leave the Shell for any reason, you still must type **DOSSHELL** to return to the Shell.)

The Shell features a series of pull-down menus that make performing the most important DOS operations easier than with the command line. Instead of typing **COPY** at the DOS prompt, for example, the Shell enables you to pull down the File menu and select the Copy option.

No More Shell

The funny thing about the DOS Shell is, well, nobody used it. Or, rather, less than 10% of all DOS users used it. So, beginning with MS-DOS 6.2, Microsoft did away with it. (Actually, they made it an "option" you could special order direct from Seattle.) So if you have DOS 6.2, 6.21, or 6.22, you don't have the DOS Shell—not that you'd have used it, anyway.

You can operate the Shell either with the keyboard or with a mouse. When you use a mouse, performing most operations is as simple as pointing and clicking. Many users prefer to use the Shell, along with a mouse, and deal with the DOS prompt only long enough to type **DOSSHELL**. I certainly recommend the ol' Shell game to everyone I know.

DOS 6—The Latest and Greatest

As I discussed way back in Chapter 3, "The Do's and Don'ts of DOS," DOS 6 includes lots of new features. Let's take a minute to go back over the most important new stuff in DOS 6.

DoubleSpace (or DriveSpace)

DoubleSpace is a utility that essentially increases the size of your hard disk by compressing the data so that it takes up less space. DoubleSpace works by compressing and decompressing your data into a special hidden file; all this work is done "on the fly," so you never see the process, just the results. (Remember, DoubleSpace is only in DOS 6.0 and 6.2, *not* in version 6.21; if you have version 6.22, you have a DoubleSpace-like utility called DriveSpace.)

MemMaker

MemMaker is a utility that optimizes your system's use of memory. When you run the MemMaker program (from the DOS prompt), it automatically analyzes your system. Then it makes appropriate changes to your CONFIG.SYS and AUTOEXEC.BAT files and loads files and drivers into upper memory whenever possible.

Defragmenter

Defragmenter is a utility that defragments data that has become fragmented on your hard disk. When your data is defragmented, all free space is placed in contiguous areas, which speeds up disk access speeds.

Undelete

Undelete is an enhanced version of a utility originally included with DOS 5 that "undeletes" deleted files. In DOS 6, the utility works much better (and doesn't require the Mirror utility to be run in the background). Undelete is now available in both DOS and Windows versions.

Microsoft Backup

Microsoft Backup is a special stand-alone utility that automates your backup operations and works in place of the normal DOS BACKUP command. You can run either the DOS or Windows version of Microsoft Backup.

Microsoft Anti-Virus

Microsoft Anti-Virus is a utility that protects your system from computer viruses and can be run in either DOS or Windows. DOS 6 also includes a memory-resident program called VSafe that stays in memory and constantly scans for new viruses.

Microsoft Diagnostics

Microsoft Diagnostics is a utility that analyzes your system and reports on its configuration. It's great for keeping track of system options and settings if you're having major problems.

SmartDrive

SmartDrive is an advanced disk-caching utility that maximizes extended memory use. With DOS 6, SmartDrive is called SMARTDRV.EXE and is loaded automatically by a line added to your AUTOEXEC.BAT file. The DOS 6 version of SmartDrive works more efficiently than the older SMARTDRV.SYS driver included in previous versions of DOS.

New Commands

DOS has a few new commands that will make your life a little easier. The two most important commands are:

- **MOVE** is a new DOS command that enables you to move files from directory to directory (or disk to disk) without using the **COPY** and **DELETE** commands.

- **DELTREE** is a new DOS command that enables you to delete entire directories (and their contents) from your disks in a single step.

What Can Go Wrong with DOS

A great deal can go wrong with DOS, I'm afraid. Fortunately, however, a scant few causes create these many problems. First—and foremost among these causes—is when you type something wrong. You can mistype a command, for example, or leave out required switches or parameters. You can enter the name of a drive that doesn't exist or a file you erased a week ago. You can even accidentally delete a file or reformat your entire hard disk. To put it bluntly, most of your DOS problems are caused by *you*.

So how can you use DOS to minimize potential problems? Above all, *be careful*. Read each command after you type it and *before* you press the Enter key. Type more slowly and more carefully than usual, especially when you are entering important commands. Look up the correct command syntax in a reliable DOS manual, and make certain that you're using the commands correctly. Think twice before you do anything irreversible, such as deleting files and formatting disks. And never be afraid to ask someone for help if you need it. It's okay—using DOS is difficult for *everybody* at first.

What To Do When You Have DOS Problems

When you boil everything down to the basics, DOS problems really aren't all that plentiful. Generally, DOS either starts or it doesn't—or you get an error message. (Unfortunately, error messages *are* plentiful—which is why I include in this book Chapter 28, "DOS Error Messages...What They Mean and How To Deal with Them." Feel free to skip directly to that chapter right now if you so desire; I won't be offended at all if you don't read anything else between here and there. After all, this is your book—you bought it and you can do whatever you like with it!)

What's more, many of the so-called DOS problems you encounter actually are problems concerning disks and files. Because disk and file problems were covered earlier in this book, this section focuses on problems that are strictly DOS-derived dilemmas.

10 Do's and Don'ts for DOS

1. *Do* upgrade to DOS 6 if you have an earlier version of DOS; the benefits far outweigh the hassles!

2. *Don't* install *all* the new DOS 6 utilities at once. Install MemMaker, Defragmenter, and DoubleSpace (or DriveSpace) one at a time; verify that each one is working correctly before you add the next utility.

3. *Do* retype any DOS command if it doesn't work or if an error message appears on-screen; it probably *was* your fault!

4. *Don't* run DoubleSpace until you've defragmented and backed up your hard disk.

5. *Do* look in Chapter 28 to find out about the DOS error messages that appear on your screen.

6. *Don't* run more than one copy of COMMAND.COM at a time from the DOS prompt; sooner or later it'll cause you problems.

7. *Do* use Windows if you have it; it's much easier than using the DOS command line!

8. *Don't* erase your CONFIG.SYS and AUTOEXEC.BAT files; DOS requires these startup files to configure itself correctly.

9. *Do* keep a Bootable Emergency Diskette on hand (as discussed in Chapter 7), just in case DOS doesn't want to run from your hard disk.

10. *Don't* feel like a failure when you must choose the F option after you're prompted with the `Abort, Retry, Fail?` message—it's really not a reflection on you personally.

If you have DOS 6, the most commonly reported problems involve the use of DoubleSpace. Some users have experienced major data loss when using DoubleSpace—most caused by bad hard disks (or hard disks *in the process* of going bad). DoubleSpace puts more wear and tear on your hard disk than normal disk access, so it stands to reason that disk defects become evident under DoubleSpace. If your disk is flaky, it'll be even flakier under DoubleSpace. (Note, however, that the version of DoubleSpace in DOS 6.2 is more stable than the version in DOS 6.0; also note that DOS 6.22's DriveSpace is also more stable than the original DoubleSpace.)

It's also possible that using SMARTDRV.EXE and DoubleSpace together can cause problems if SmartDrive is not set up or used correctly. The nature of a disk cache (like SmartDrive) is that it holds some information in memory (rather than immediately writing it to disk), so problems may arise if you turn off your computer *before* this cached information is written to your DoubleSpaced disk.

If you want to use DoubleSpace, keep the following things in mind:

- *Back up your hard disk completely before running DoubleSpace.* Then if you run into DoubleSpace problems, you can always restore your disk to its pre-DoubleSpace condition.

- *Before running DoubleSpace, run CHKDSK /F from the DOS prompt, which finds and eliminates any lost clusters.* Then use the DEL command to delete files with the CHK file extension that were created by CHKDSK. This action frees up valuable disk space.

- *Run Defragmenter before running DoubleSpace.* DoubleSpace works best on a defragmented drive.

- *Before running DoubleSpace, free up as much disk space as possible by deleting any unnecessary files.* DoubleSpace *doesn't* work best if your disk is completely full beforehand. Give yourself some extra free disk space and DoubleSpace will be happier.

Any and all of the previous recommendations also apply to DOS 6.22's DriveSpace compression utility.

Getting Rid of DOS 6

What do you do if you don't like DOS 6? You can always uninstall it! During the DOS 6 installation a special safety disk (or disks) is created. Just insert the first safety disk into drive A and reboot your computer; a special UNINSTAL program runs automatically that removes DOS 6 from your system and restores your previous version of DOS. (This assumes that you haven't used the DELOLDOS command to delete your old version of DOS from your hard disk!)

All in all, however, the best advice when you install DOS 6 is to *keep backups of everything* and *don't do everything at once!* To be safe, you should first install DOS 6 and use it for awhile; then run MemMaker and use the new setup for awhile; next run Defragmenter and use your system for awhile. Finally, activate DoubleSpace or DriveSpace. Don't do everything at once; give your system a chance to settle down (and give any problems a chance to surface) before you make the next major change. If you try to do everything at once, you'll never know what hit you if a problem does occur!

You might also run into problems when you run MemMaker. It's possible that it could misanalyze your system and suggest a memory setup that freezes your system. It's always a good idea to keep a copy of your Bootable Emergency Diskette (which should have copies of your AUTOEXEC.BAT and CONFIG.SYS files) handy just in case you need to reboot from drive A following a MemMaker freezeup.

Problem 1:
DOS doesn't start

If DOS doesn't start, your computer doesn't start—it's that simple. You may receive an error message, or your system may simply freeze up. The most common cause of this problem is a bad or missing COMMAND.COM file. To rectify the situation, you must reboot, using your Bootable Emergency Diskette, and copy COMMAND.COM from that disk to your hard disk. Of course, you also may have a bad disk or be facing some other startup problem. Refer to Chapter 8 for more details about getting out of this sticky situation.

Problem 2:
You get a DOS error message

What can I tell you? Hundreds of DOS error messages exist, each caused by a different set of circumstances. The first thing to do, always, is to take a look at the command you just typed. (It should still be on your screen.) Is this the command you meant to type? Did you include the necessary switches and parameters for the command to execute correctly? Does the command refer to any files or disks that don't exist? In other words, *did you type it correctly?*

If you didn't type the command correctly, take this opportunity to retype it, slowly and more accurately, and then try executing it again. If the command still results in an error message, either you're a bad typist or something else is wrong. See Chapter 28 for a complete listing of DOS error messages, what causes them, and how to fix what's wrong.

Problem 3:
You get a DOS error message followed by the secondary message Abort, Retry, Fail?

If the message Abort, Retry, Fail? appears on your screen, look closely at the first part of the error message and see if it suggests anything that you can correct. If so, correct it and press **R** (Retry). If Retry doesn't work, press **A** to Abort the operation. The last choice is to press **F** (Fail), which continues the operation but with possible errors. I can't think of any good reason to use the Fail option unless trying the other two options first doesn't do you any good.

Problem 4:
DOS runs slowly, or error messages about low memory appear on-screen

The most common cause of a sluggish system or a low-memory error message is that you're running two copies of DOS at one time. Either you accidentally loaded a second version of the command interpreter by typing **COMMAND** at the DOS prompt, or you're actually still in an application program and you've just "shelled out" to the DOS prompt. (Many programs include an option that enables you to temporarily leave the program to issue DOS commands; these programs often implement these options by starting a second version of DOS.) Regardless of how two copies of DOS happen to be running, this is not a good situation. One copy of DOS requires more than enough memory, and two copies just bog down your entire system. To exit the second command interpreter, type **EXIT** at the prompt.

It's also possible that you're running DOS from within Windows. You can start a DOS window in Windows, so it's quite easy to maximize the DOS window to full-screen size, and then forget that you're actually running Windows! DOS runs much slower from within Windows than DOS by itself, so this could be your problem. If you think this has happened to you, type **EXIT** at the DOS prompt to close the DOS window and return to Windows.

Another possibility is that you're experiencing memory conflicts among the other programs you're running simultaneously or that your current programs are consuming most of your system's existing memory. Try running fewer programs at one time. You may want to jump ahead to Chapter 23, "What To Do When…Your Software Is Hard To Use," for detailed information on dealing with memory conflicts among programs.

Problem 5:
You can't load the DOS Shell

Hmm, now this is a puzzler. What could cause this?

Well, first, make sure that you typed the command correctly. That's **D-O-S-S-H-E-L-L**, with two *S*'s and two *L*'s. (It's so easy to leave out the second *S*!) Next, make certain the DOSSHELL.EXE file actually is in your current path or directory. You may have to switch to the DOS directory (by typing **CD\DOS**) and retype the command from there. It's possible, too, that the file isn't even on your hard disk. Are you certain you have Version 4, 5, or 6 of DOS installed on your system? (Check your version number by typing **VER** at the command prompt.) DOS Shell didn't even exist prior to Version 4 (and isn't included with DOS 6.2 or later), so if you're running Version 3.3, for example, you can't load the Shell because you don't have it. If you *are* running the appropriate version of DOS and the DOSSHELL.EXE file is not in your DOS directory, you may have to reinstall DOS to copy the file to your hard disk.

Problem 6:
DoubleSpace or DriveSpace trashes some or all of your files

This is not a good thing. As a good Monday-morning quarterback, I'll use this opportunity to remind you that this is one of those occasions for which you keep a backup of your important data. (If you *didn't* have a backup… well, maybe you'll learn from this experience!)

DoubleSpace and DriveSpace have been known to trash files under one or more of the following situations:

Your drive is old or has surface defects

DoubleSpace and DriveSpace give your drive a good workout, so they can exacerbate any existing problems; and, drive defects, whether you're running disk compression or not, always have the potential for trashing data. Try running a good disk fix program, such as Norton Disk Doctor in Norton Utilities (Version 7 is specifically designed for use with DOS 6), or have a technician take a look at your system. You have major problems unrelated to disk compression that you need to have fixed!

You turn off your system too soon

Actually, this is not a problem with DoubleSpace but with the new version of SmartDrive (SMARTDRV.EXE) included with DOS 6. SmartDrive is a disk-caching program that holds some information in

> ### Disk Caching—Fixed!
>
> With DOS 6.2, Microsoft fixed this disk caching conflict between DoubleSpace and SmartDrive. (It's also fixed in 6.22 with DriveSpace.) So if you have DOS 6.0 and experience this problem a lot, upgrade to the most recent point release!

system memory before it writes it to your hard disk. If you turn off your system (or if circumstances turn it off for you) *immediately* after certain disk operations, this information doesn't get the chance to make it from memory to your hard disk. This unfortunate occurrence interferes with DoubleSpace and causes you to lose data.

If you find yourself in the preceding situation, you have three choices:

- Don't use SmartDrive (not an option if you're using Windows).

- Disable write-caching by including the *X*: parameter in the SMARTDRV.EXE command line in your AUTOEXEC.BAT file (in which *X* is your hard disk drive, as in SMARTDRV.EXE C:).

- Wait a bit (ten seconds or so) before you turn off your computer after performing any disk operations.

For most of us, the last option is the easiest to implement and most preferable.

Your files become cross-linked

DoubleSpace may display the following error message:

```
DoubleSpace found Crosslink between files X: and X:
```

(If you're running DriveSpace, you can get a similar message.)

This message appears if your drive is *too full* (90% or more utilized) or if your EMM386 command line in the CONFIG.SYS file has a HIGHSCAN parameter. This message displays drive letters rather than file names because there are cross-linked entries in the FAT (file allocation table), and DOS can't figure out which file is which.

To avoid cross-linked files, try any one, or all, of the following tactics:

- Decrease the size of your compressed drive with the **DBLSPACE** (or **DRVSPACE**) command (see Problem #4).

- Remove the HIGHSCAN parameter from the EMM386 line in your CONFIG.SYS file.

- Free up excess space on your compressed disk by eliminating unused files.

- Run DEFRAG (or DBLSPACE /DEFRAGMENT) on your hard disk.

What Is a Cross-Linked File?

MS-DOS organizes your disk's data area into sections called clusters or allocation units. Your disk's FAT includes an entry for each cluster. Cross-linked files occur when two or more files are marked as "owning" the same cluster; one or both of the files may contain information belonging to the other. The only way to fix the FAT is to run the **CHKDSK /F** command—which means you lose all the data included in both cross-linked files.

To correct the cross-linked entries, run the **CHKDSK /F** command (or the DBLSPACE /CHKDSK /F command) from the DOS prompt.

When you run DoubleSpace or DriveSpace, it's best to make frequent backups of your data (so that you can restore a file just in case it gets trashed) and to check your disk frequently for any pending problems.

Problem 7:
Some DOS commands don't work under DoubleSpace or DriveSpace

This is true; some DOS commands *don't* work (or don't work *the same*) under Microsoft's disk compression utilities! Note the following:

- *The DIR command won't always accurately represent the amount of remaining free space on your compressed disk.*

- *CHKDSK doesn't work on a compressed drive.* You have to use the following command: **DBLSPACE /CHKDSK [/F]** (or **DRVSPACE /CHKDSK [/F]** if you're running DOS 6.22).

- *DEFRAG won't defragment a compressed drive.* You have to use the following command: **DBLSPACE /DEFRAGMENT** (or **DRVSPACE /DEFRAGMENT**).

- *FORMAT won't format a compressed drive.* You have to use the following command: **DBLSPACE /FORMAT_X** (or **DRVSPACE /FORMAT X**), where *X* is the drive to format.

- *You can't delete a compressed drive using the normal DOS DELETE commands.* You have to run the following command: **DBLSPACE /DELETE_X** (or **DRVSPACE /DELETE_X**), where *X* is the drive to delete.

If you're using DoubleSpace or DriveSpace, be sure to factor the preceding information into your normal system operations.

Problem 8:
MemMaker freezes your system

Sometimes MemMaker can misanalyze your system and propose a memory setup that just doesn't work and also freezes up your system! If this happens to you, you may be able to answer a few on-screen questions and get MemMaker to reset itself automatically. If your system is completely frozen, however, you have to revert to Plan B.

> **MemMaker Fixes Its Own Problems!**
>
> In actuality, it's nearly impossible to screw up MemMaker. If the utility has trouble rebooting after it changes your system configuration, it simply resets things, starts again, and lets you know what's happening. Pretty foolproof, which is very unique in the DOS world.

Plan B involves the following steps:

1. Grab your Bootable Emergency Diskette (created way back in Chapter 7).

2. Insert it into drive A.

3. Reboot your system.

4. Copy the AUTOEXEC.BAT and CONFIG.SYS files from drive A to drive C.

5. Remove the Bootable Emergency Diskette.

6. Reboot your system again.

These steps set things back to normal. At this point, you can try running MemMaker again—perhaps using the Custom setup and juggling whatever options are necessary to ensure a clean booting situation.

Problem 9:
Defragmenter is stopped in the middle of an operation

Sometimes this is a big deal, sometimes not a big deal. I'm not sure why, but sometimes you can reboot your computer when you're in the middle of defragmenting and nothing terrible happens—you're simply returned to the pre-defragmented version of your hard disk. Other times, however, your FAT is completely screwed up, because it was left in a half fragmented/half defragmented condition. If the latter is the case (and you'll know it; either your hard disk will be totally screwed up, or half your files and directories will be missing!), your only recourse is to restore your hard disk from your backup disks. (Quite an argument for backing up before defragmenting, isn't it!)

A Final Word on DOS

You use DOS every day, whether you know it or not. When you follow the precautions and advice in this chapter, your DOS experience doesn't have to be painful!

What To Do When...

Your Windows Are Broken

CHAPTER TWENTY-TWO

In the last chapter, I discussed problems you can experience with DOS. But most computer users—you included, I bet, if you're reading this chapter—run Microsoft's Windows on top of DOS.

What added problems does *that* cause?

Well, whatever the problem, this is the right chapter. So turn the page and let's examine some common Windows woes!

Your Window on Windows

Unlike DOS, Windows is not an operating system; Windows is an operating *environment*. This means that Windows doesn't talk directly to your hardware; it injects yet another operating layer between you and your hardware: you talk to Windows, Windows talks to DOS, and then DOS talks to your hardware. That's right. It's one more element in the equation—one more thing to go wrong. (Oh well, it does provide a friendly face.)

No Mouse? Hard Windows!

If you don't own a mouse, reconsider using Windows; it's extremely difficult to use effectively with only the keyboard. If your mouse develops problems, refer to Chapter 13 for possible solutions.

To use Windows to its fullest capabilities, you must master the mouse. A mouse enables you to click on objects or options to select them, double-click to activate them, and drag them around the screen. (In Windows 3.1, you can even *drop* items onto other items to initiate actions.)

So how exactly does Windows work? To find out, take a peek now at the various parts of Windows, as described in the following sections.

Basic Windows Operations

Opening More Windows

I can't tell you everything you need to know about Windows in a few short pages. Sorry. To really learn a lot more about Windows, buy one of Que's top-selling Windows books, such as *Using Windows,* 3.11 Edition, Special Edition.

Instead of relying on the normal, obtuse DOS commands for its operations, Windows employs a series of *icons*. An icon is merely a little picture that represents something bigger. In Windows' case, each icon represents a software program or utility. Every icon is contained in what Windows calls a *program group*. Each group is like a drawer in a file cabinet, and each icon like a file in that drawer. You can create as many groups as you like and stuff as many icons into each group as pleases you.

After Windows starts up, it displays the Windows *Program Manager*. The Program Manager holds all the Windows groups. (Notice that program groups not only *contain* icons but that they are *represented* by icons as well. So don't get confused and think that a group is already open when the Program Manager splashes a set of icons across your screen.) After you double-click a group icon, that group is *opened*. This means that the group icon is replaced by a window containing all the program icons in that group. Double-clicking one of these program icons initiates the program.

Windows itself contains several utility programs, termed *applets* by diehard Windows users. Applets control various segments of Windows and perform utility functions in the Windows environment.

One of the most important features of Windows is its *File Manager*. This utility is available from the Main program group and enables you to manipulate your disks and files. You perform most of the chores normally associated with DOS, such as formatting, copying, and deleting from the File Manager.

> ### Too Much of a Good Thing
>
> When it comes to creating program groups, however, you can overdo it. Each group you create takes up system resources. If you have too many program groups, you use up too many of your system resources, which slows Windows down. So hold the number of groups you create down to a half-dozen or so to keep Windows running at full tilt.

Two other important applets are the *Control Panel* and *Windows Setup*, also located in the Main program group. These two utilities enable you to set up and configure Windows' many options. Get to know these guys; you'll use them often.

Starting and Stopping Windows

Starting Windows is easy. From the DOS prompt, simply switch to the Windows directory (using the **CD\WINDOWS** command), and type the following:

WIN

Windows starts up and displays the Program Manager on your screen. If you want Windows to load every time you start your computer, just add the following two lines to the end of your AUTOEXEC.BAT file:

CD\WINDOWS

WIN

Windows now loads whenever you boot up your system, bypassing the DOS prompt altogether.

Exiting Windows is equally simple. Just pull down the File menu and select the Exit option. Windows closes all operations in progress, shuts itself down, and returns you to the DOS prompt.

> ### Making a Clean Break
>
> Of course, nothing is really that simple, not even leaving Windows. If you're running a DOS application in a window when you try to exit Windows, you can't exit. Windows sends you an error message informing you that the DOS application is still running and then aborts the exit procedure. You must switch to the DOS application, close it, and then try to exit Windows again.

Windows Requirements

Despite its ease of use, Windows does have its drawbacks. In particular, it demands of your computer some fairly hefty system-performance requirements to run at all. For the latest version of Windows, Version 3.11, you must own an 80286 or higher computer, with a minimum of 2M RAM even to start the program.

In reality, you should have an 80386 machine that runs at 20 MHz or more, and you probably should have at least 4M of memory available. Of course, you need a mouse and a video card/monitor combination capable of displaying VGA color. (SuperVGA is even better because you can fit more windows on the screen with 800 x 600 resolution.)

If your system doesn't meet these basic requirements, Windows runs slowly, if at all. Not only that, but many Windows problems and peccadilloes result from having too little memory on your system. If you experience a lot of problems with Windows, you may need to buy a more powerful computer or to install more memory on your existing system.

Different Types of Windows

As with DOS, several versions of Windows have been released over the years. The original version of Windows (1.0) and its replacement (2.0) really weren't that good, and not many people used them. But Windows 3.0 (released in May, 1990) changed all that because it did what it was supposed to—and did it well.

In April 1992, Microsoft released Windows 3.1, and the Windows juggernaut rolled on. Windows 3.1 added several new features (such as sound), improved the capabilities of others (particularly the File Manager), and fixed numerous bugs and performance problems.

The very latest version of Windows is version 3.11. It basically includes some more bug fixes and performance enhancements. In addition, Microsoft now sells something called *Windows 3.11 for Workgroups*, which is a special version of Windows designed to run in networked environments. (It also includes some changes in File Manager, which makes it easier to run.) If you're on a network, this is the version to get!

Possible Cracks in Your Windows

So Windows is now installed on your system, and you're mousing away as you please, just dragging and dropping icons to your heart's content. What, pray tell, can go wrong in this GUI paradise? Welllll…

First (yes, you know the drill), *you* can do something wrong. I must admit, however, that in the Windows environment, the user is much less likely to make mistakes than when working with DOS. (Just using a mouse instead of typing commands eliminates the possibility for countless potential errors.)

Second, you may have configured Windows incorrectly for your system. The Windows setup procedure provides you numerous options, and you can all too easily select settings that fail to optimize your computer's performance.

Third (and this is quite common), Windows and the various Windows applications can eat up so much of your computer system's resources (memory and disk space in particular) that they create a plethora of problems. If enough memory isn't available, for example, some programs simply won't run; and, even if they do run, they don't run well. If your system can't handle it, Windows can be your window on computing hell.

Some Windows applications are not particularly well-behaved either and may fight bitterly with other Windows programs over available memory. This memory conflict can have even further consequences: all programs use memory when they're running, but some Windows applications continue to hoard memory even after you've closed them! That's right—when you exit them, many Windows programs refuse to release all the memory they consumed when they were running—leaving even less memory available for other applications. (An easy way to guard against this problem, however, is to exit Windows from time to time; exiting the entire environment clears all system resources, freeing up the stockpiled memory.)

The behavior of Windows itself, unfortunately, can be erratic, too; Windows generates errors of its own accord with an uneasy regularity. This flaky behavior crops up less frequently in Windows 3.1 than in 3.0, but the program still is not a totally perfect environment. So even if you do everything right, Windows can still blow up in your face at the most inopportune of times. Well, you'll just have to get used to it. That's part of the trade-off you make for Windows' increased ease-of-use (and it's one that most true Windows aficionados seem more than happy to make).

10 Do's and Don'ts for Windows Use

1. *Do* make sure that Windows is installed and set up properly for your system and applications.

2. *Don't* get overly frustrated if you run Windows on an 80286 or a lesser machine; it just doesn't work as well on one as on a more powerful system.

3. *Do* add enough memory to your system to run Windows effectively; 2M is okay, but 4M is much better (and 8M is *superb!*).

4. *Don't* be embarrassed about having to shell out to DOS to perform certain operations; some users prefer the command line, and that's quite all right.

5. *Do* exit Windows periodically to free up uncleared system resources and memory.

6. *Don't* try to run an old Windows 3.0 application under Windows 3.1; pick up an upgraded version of the program.

7. *Do* upgrade to Windows 3.11 (or Windows 3.11 for Workgroups) if you're currently using Version 3.0 or earlier.

8. *Don't* try to convince a diehard command line freak that Windows makes things easier; some people just won't get GUI, no matter how much you try to convince them!

9. *Do* feel free to customize your screen as much as you want with wallpaper, screen colors, and sounds.

10. *Don't* run a DOS program directly from the File Manager; use a PIF file to launch the DOS program with the correct options and parameters.

What To Do When You Have a Windows Problem

As may be evident by now, you can experience many problems when using Windows—more than I can cover in one chapter. I've tried in the following pages, however, to isolate the most common Windows problems and to offer solutions to them.

Problem 1:
Windows doesn't start

This is not good. Many factors can keep Windows from starting on your computer. The following are the top 10 reasons why Windows won't start:

1. *You may not be in the right directory when you try to start Windows.* Switch over to the Windows directory (by typing **CD\WINDOWS**), and then type **WIN**. (*Don't* type **WINDOWS**—you can only start Windows by typing **WIN** at the prompt!)

2. *Your system may be incapable of running Windows.* Check Windows system requirements against your system's performance capabilities to determine whether you have the horsepower to run Windows. (A word of advice—if you own an 8086 computer, forget it.) Most important, make certain that you have enough memory to run Windows (a minimum of 2M, although 4M is recommended); without sufficient memory available, Windows can't even start.

3. *You need access to high system memory for Windows to run.* Make sure that you're running the HIMEM.SYS memory management driver; the following line (or one similar) should reside in your CONFIG.SYS file:

Get High!

Various kinds of memory are available on your system, and you probably don't care much about them. Despite that, you should know that Windows can access a type of memory called "high" memory, which is located just above the normal 640K memory area. The HIMEM.SYS memory manager enables your system to access this high memory.

DEVICE=C:\WINDOWS\HIMEM.SYS

If this line isn't in your CONFIG.SYS file, add it. Then reboot your system and restart Windows.

You may want to verify that the version of HIMEM.SYS you're using is the one that came with Windows; this is the most up-to-date version of the driver available. Unless you're using DOS 6, *don't* use the HIMEM.SYS file that came with DOS; the DOS 6 HIMEM.SYS file is more up-to-date than the one that ships with Windows. If in doubt, just load the HIMEM.SYS file listed in the Windows directory.

4. *You're attempting to run Windows in the wrong operating mode for your system.* Windows has several modes of operation, each generating different levels of performance and requiring different standards in hardware. If Windows doesn't start on your machine, you may need to force Windows to start in *standard mode*. If you have Windows 3.1, type the following command (with the S switch) to invoke standard mode:

   WIN /S

If you're running Windows 3.0, the situation becomes a little more complicated. If specifying standard mode doesn't get you up and running, try starting in *real mode* by typing the following command (using an R switch this time):

   WIN /R

One of these modes may enable you to run Windows, even on a lower-powered machine.

The preferred mode, however, and the one that Windows always tries to use as its default, is *enhanced mode*. This mode provides access to several features not found in the other modes. If you can't start Windows in enhanced mode, you probably need to add more memory to your system or to buy a more powerful system.

Get Smart!

SMARTDRV.EXE is a disk-caching utility used to speed up Windows operations. Disk caches enable your system to store information temporarily in high system memory and make some programs (such as Windows) run faster.

---

5. *You may not have reserved enough of your system's resources for Windows.* Make sure that the FILES statement in your CONFIG.SYS file is set to at least 50 and that your BUFFERS statement is set to at least 20. (If you've installed SMARTDRV.EXE, the BUFFERS statement should be set to 10.) If you must edit your CONFIG.SYS file for these values, make sure that you reboot your system before trying to restart Windows.

6. *Make sure that you have enough free memory to run Windows.* If you're running any DOS programs—particularly *memory-resident* programs—close them before you try to restart Windows.

7. *Your system may have sufficient memory but not the right type of memory to run Windows.* System memory must be configured as *extended memory* for Windows to access it. If you use memory-management software (such as the DOS EMM386.EXE manager or the third-party QEMM386.EXE manager), make sure you have allocated at least 1M RAM to extended memory. See the instructions included with your memory manager on how to do this.

8. *Make sure you have enough free space on your disk to run Windows.* Run the **CHKDSK** command from the DOS prompt; it will tell you how much free disk space is available. If you have less than 10M free, delete some files on your hard disk before you try to restart Windows.

9. *Another likely cause of startup problems is an upper memory conflict between Windows and one or more DOS device drivers.* You need to systematically remove any device drivers from upper memory to discover which may be in conflict with Windows. Check your AUTOEXEC.BAT and CONFIG.SYS files and, one-by-one, change all DEVICEHIGH statements to DEVICE statements, and all LOADHIGH statements to normal *.EXE statements. You may also need to change the EMM386.EXE line in your CONFIG.SYS file to read:

    DEVICE=C:\EMM386.EXE NOEMS X=A000-FFFF

10. If you're running an older version of the QEMM third-party memory manager, it may not work with your version of Windows. You may need to install a different version of QEMM, or you may not be able to use QEMM at all. (Sorry!)

If you check out all the preceding possibilities and try the suggested fixes but none seem to work, call in a pro. Something weird is happening, and even I have no idea what it is.

Problem 2:
A Windows application crashes

When a program crashes, you may be presented with several options. If you have a choice between a Close and an Ignore option, always try Ignore first. In most cases, however, Ignore doesn't work, so you have to Close the program. (And you lose all work in progress for that program, unfortunately.)

Sometimes the program just freezes, and you can't do anything with the mouse or the keyboard. If you're in Windows 3.0, you must reboot your entire system. If you're in Windows 3.1, however, you can press Ctrl+Alt+Del to reboot only the problem application. You're presented with a screen asking whether you want to exit this application or to exit Windows itself. Press Enter to reboot only the application.

After you finally manage to close a problem application, it often leaves behind some cluttered memory. The application itself may not even work if you immediately try to relaunch it while you are still in Windows. The better course to take, after you've closed the problem child, is to exit Windows and reboot your system from the DOS prompt. You then can restart both Windows and your application, and everything should be fine.

Unfortunately, programs crash with annoying frequency in Windows. The causes are myriad and often difficult to pin down. They include the following:

1. Your system may have run out of memory. Try running the program while no other Windows programs are running, or add more memory to your system.

2. The program may be getting caught in a memory conflict with another Windows program. Try running the program by itself.

3. The program may be an older version that's incompatible with Windows 3.1. Upgrade the program to its latest version.

4. Windows was just feeling cantankerous. Start the program again and hope for the best.

If your Windows applications crash on a regular basis, the situation probably can be attributed to insufficient memory. See your computer dealer about adding more RAM to your system.

Problem 3:
A DOS application running under Windows crashes

Those Pesky PIFs!

To run correctly, each DOS application should be started from a Windows program information file (PIF). The PIF file contains configuration information that enables your DOS program to run effectively in Windows. You edit a PIF by using the PIF Editor applet, located in the Main program group.

You handle a DOS program crashing under Windows slightly differently from the way you deal with a Windows program crashing. First, if you can close the DOS application normally, do so. If not, try to temporarily leave the DOS program and save any pending Windows applications by pressing Alt+Esc, Alt+Tab, or Ctrl+Esc to return to Windows. Then close all other Windows applications and click on the icon for the DOS application. (The application actually is still running, even if it has crashed or frozen.) After you click once on the icon, a control menu appears. Select the Settings option, and choose Terminate. This kills the DOS application. Finally, exit Windows, reboot your system, and start over again.

DOS programs can crash in Windows for the same reasons as those cranky Windows programs, so refer back to Problem #2 for ideas on how to alleviate the problem. Also, check the PIF file for the DOS application (see the sidebar) to ensure that it's configured correctly. Sometimes, too, a DOS application crashes more frequently when displayed in a window rather than on the full screen, so you may want to select Full Screen mode whenever you're running DOS programs in Windows. And you may want to provide a DOS program with Exclusive Execution (as set up in the PIF file) to prevent potential memory conflicts.

Yes, a DOS application can crash in Windows because of a memory conflict. DOS programs that use extended memory may not get along with Windows because Windows too uses extended memory. If this occurs, check the Advanced options in the program's PIF file, and turn off the Memory Option for Uses High Memory Area. This should fix your immediate problem.

Problem 4:
Windows won't let you exit

The most common cause for this is that you have an open program—and probably an open DOS program, at that. You need to close all your programs (and save all your documents) before Windows will let you close up and go home.

If you're not sure what's running and what isn't, you can always refer to the Windows Task List. You access this neat little utility by double-clicking anywhere on the open Windows desktop. (You may need to minimize

Closing from the Task List

You can even close your Windows applications directly from the Task List. Just highlight the application you want to close, and then click on the End Task button. Voila! The application closes automatically. (Note that this doesn't work with DOS applications—you still need to close them in the regular fashion.)

an application or two to clear off some desktop space to click on.) When you do this, the Task List dialog box appears, listing all open applications. You then can access any open application just by double-clicking its name in the Task List. This is a great way to get a list of all open applications—and find those pesky programs you need to close before you can exit Windows!

But what happens if you can't close an application? Sometimes a bug in a program will freeze the program and won't let you close it, and you need to get out of there and get out of Windows. Your only option at this point is to reboot the application itself. (*Note:* You can only do this under Windows 3.1; attempting this procedure under Windows 3.0 may result in your rebooting your entire system. Also note that you can't do this with programs that aren't frozen—you can still close them in the normal fashion.)

Begin by switching to the offending application. Then press **Ctrl+Alt+Del** simultaneously. When you get the big full-screen warning message, press the Enter key. The offending application closes down and you're returned to Windows. Now close all your other applications, exit Windows, and reboot your entire system. If you try to continue using Windows (or any other application on your system) after this kind of forced reboot, instability may result.

Problem 5:
Windows crashes

Unfortunately, even Windows itself can crash. And when it does, you lose all work in progress. *OOPS!*

So just what happens when Windows crashes or freezes? Well, you could be dumped unceremoniously back to the DOS prompt. If so, pick yourself up, dust yourself off, reboot your system (to clean up any loose ends that might be floating around), and restart Windows.

If you run Windows 3.0, you may find yourself facing the ubiquitous Unrecoverable Application Error message (or UAE for short) on-screen. (Windows 3.0 users are probably used to getting UAEs by now—that version of Windows was a tad unstable on some systems.) About all you can do with a UAE is press Enter to close down Windows, reboot your system, and restart Windows.

If you run Windows 3.1, however, you needn't worry about UAEs. For this version, Microsoft changed the Unrecoverable Application Error to a General Protection Fault, so now you get GPFs instead. If a GPF appears on-screen, well, you can always try to ignore the problem and hope that it goes away. But if that doesn't work, which it doesn't, select the Close option, reboot your system, and—once more, with feeling—restart Windows.

If your system freezes in Windows 3.1, the fault may lie in a specific program and not in Windows itself. Try returning to Windows by pressing Alt+Esc, Alt+Tab, or Ctrl+Esc. If you make it, close the offending application by clicking on its icon and selecting the Exit option. If you can't return to Windows, try pressing Ctrl+Alt+Del from within the frozen application; if you're lucky, you get a message asking whether you want to close this program or all of Windows. Press Enter to close this program and return to Windows.

What causes Windows to crash? Any number of problems, among them the following:

1. You may be running an application that isn't compatible with your version of Windows. If so, upgrade the program.

2. You may not have enough memory to run Windows effectively. Upgrade the amount of RAM in your PC.

3. A memory conflict may exist between applications or between an application and Windows itself. Make certain that you're not running any memory-resident programs from DOS; check for any you may have started before you launched Windows and any you may have started from within Windows, either by a DOS application or from a DOS window. And try running programs one at a time to avoid potential memory conflicts.

If your system crashes frequently, call in a pro. These kinds of problems can be tough to track down by yourself when you're dealing with Windows.

Problem 6:
Certain Windows applications don't run

Several factors can cause a Windows application to refuse to run, including the following:

1. *The program may not be compatible with your version of Windows.* If you run Windows 3.1, make sure that all your programs are the newest versions. If you use Windows 3.0, the newest versions of many programs can't run on your system, so you probably need to upgrade to Windows 3.1.

2. *Your system may not have enough memory available to run the program.* Try closing other Windows applications before you start this one. Be sure, too, that HIMEM.SYS is loaded so that Windows can use high memory to run programs.

3. *Your computer may not have enough disk space to run the program.* Windows employs free disk space as extra memory (called *swap files*) on some systems. Try deleting unused files from your hard disk before you restart the program.

4. *You may not have configured the program correctly.* Click on the program's icon, pull down the File menu in the Program Manager, and select the Properties option. Review the program's configuration to ensure that it's correct. (One common problem is to have missed a path or listed a wrong path for a program.)

Getting into Swapping

If you have your swap file settings too high, you may not have enough disk space for the swap file. If you experience continued trouble with Windows or Windows applications not running, use the Control Panel to lower your swap file settings a little.

So if you've tried everything the preceding list suggests but the application still doesn't run, exit Windows. Then reboot your system, restart Windows, and try launching the program again. You'd be surprised how often this works.

Problem 7:
Certain DOS applications don't run under Windows

As is true of Windows applications, DOS applications may not load for any number of reasons. These include the following:

Configuration Options—Check?

While you're in the Properties option or the PIF Editor, check the program's other configuration options. Incorrect options can prevent a DOS program from loading or cause it to behave erratically.

---

1. *The program may not be where you think it is—that is, it may actually be in a different directory.* (This isn't a problem, however, when you launch programs from the File Manager.) Click on the program's icon, pull down the File menu in the Program Manager, and select the Properties option. Review the program's configuration to make sure that it's correct. If you're running the program from a PIF, use the PIF Editor to review the program's PIF settings. You may have specified the wrong path in either of these two places.

2. *Your computer may not have enough memory to run the program.* Try closing any other open programs, and then restart the DOS program. Examine the program's PIF file to be sure that you've set its KB Required option high enough. Consult the application's manual for recommended settings. (Most DOS programs require at least 512K to run efficiently.)

3. *You may be running the program in a window when it needs to run full screen.* Change its setting in the Properties dialog box, which you access from the File menu.

4. *You're not using a PIF file.* Okay, sometimes you can run simple DOS applications without PIFs. But many DOS programs are relatively complex; they require the extra control over their operation that a PIF contributes. Use the PIF Editor to create a PIF file for your application, and then double-check the PIF's settings in the Properties dialog box (accessed from the Program Manager's File menu). Make sure that the settings are correct for this particular program, as detailed in the program's documentation; especially check that the KB Required setting is high enough.

It's a simple fact of computing that the more memory your computer possesses, the easier you'll find it to run DOS applications under Windows. If you own a PC with insufficient memory, you may want to exit Windows whenever you need to run your DOS programs.

Problem 8:
You can't launch a program file

There are numerous reasons why double-clicking a program file (with an EXE, COM, or BAT extension) may not launch the program. These include the following:

> ### DOS Programs Windows Hates
>
> There are some types of programs that just won't run under Windows because they need full control of your system to do their jobs. These programs—such as Norton Disk Doctor for DOS and SpinRite—simply shouldn't be used under Windows. To use these programs, exit Windows first and then run them from the DOS prompt.
>
> In addition, many DOS-based anti-virus programs work by checking all read/write activity taking place on your hard disk. Because Windows does a lot of reading and writing (and even a little arithmetic!), some of these anti-virus "shield" programs go nuts when you run Windows. You may get a lot of error messages (from either Windows or the anti-virus program), or Windows may lock up and not run at all. The solution is simple— buy a Windows-based anti-virus program!

1. *The file may not really be there.* Pull down the Window menu and select the Refresh option to get an updated listing of available files.

2. *The program may not be compatible with your version of Windows.* If you run Windows 3.1, make sure that you have the newest version of the program that's compatible with Windows 3.1. If you use Windows 3.0 (or earlier), the newest versions of many programs can't run on your system, so you need to upgrade to Windows 3.1.

3. *Your system may not have enough memory to run the program.* Try closing other Windows applications before you try starting this one again. Also, be sure that HIMEM.SYS is loaded so that Windows can use high memory to run programs.

4. Your computer may not have enough disk space to run the program, since Windows uses free disk space as virtual memory while running programs. You may need to delete some unused files to free up disk space. You also may want to lower Windows' use of virtual memory. Open the Control Panel, double-click the 386 Enhanced icon, click the Virtual Memory button, and Change the New Size to something smaller than the old size.

5. *You may be trying to run a DOS program.* Lots of things can go wrong when running DOS programs under Windows. Because of this, you should avoid launching DOS programs from the File Manager. Instead, create a PIF file for your DOS files and add them to a program group.

Problem 9:
You can't launch a document file

When you double-click a document file, it should launch the associated program, with the selected document pre-loaded. It's possible that, however, Windows may display a dialog box with this message:

```
Cannot Run Program
No application is associated with this file.
Choose Associate from the File menu to create an association.
```

If you receive this message, that means you need to create an association for the particular document type at hand. Do this by pulling down the File menu and selecting the Associate option. When the Associate dialog box appears, type the three-letter document type extension into the Files with Extension box, and then scroll through the Associate With box to select the associated program. Select OK when you've set up the association, and try the launching operation again.

If you still can't launch the file, then something is probably screwy with the program file itself.

Problem 10:
Windows runs slower than normal

The most likely culprit behind a system slowdown is memory—or rather, the lack of it. Have you changed any part of your setup that may result in less memory being allotted to Windows? Are you running any new applications—or upgrades of older applications—that may consume more memory? Are you running more programs than usual at the same time? Any of these factors consumes more memory and forces Windows to slow down. If you're dissatisfied with the performance of Windows on your system, the answer is simple: *add more memory!*

Something else to check: do you leave Windows running all the time? If so, your computer may have a great deal of *unreleased memory*. As already discussed, not all Windows programs release all the memory they've used after they're closed. (Ami Pro and Word for Windows are notorious for this.) This tendency leaves little chunks of unreleased memory floating around in RAM. Other programs can't access this hoarded memory, which in turn slows down your system. After you exit Windows, the "lost" memory is released for use when you next load Windows. If you never exit Windows, however, all those little unreleased memory clots begin to accumulate, clogging up your system and deteriorating its performance. I make it a habit to exit Windows at least once a day just to free up this unreleased memory.

Problem 11:
Your Windows display doesn't look right

You can experience many different kinds of display problems. Some of the more common ones are listed as follows:

1. *You're using the wrong video display driver.* (This is the most common source of display problems.) You may be using a SuperVGA driver, for example, even though you have only a normal VGA video card. For the best results, you must install the correct driver in Windows—the one that matches your system's card/monitor combination. To check your driver, open the Windows Setup dialog box, which is accessed from the Main program group in the Program Manager. This dialog box lists all your primary settings; your display driver is among them.

To change drivers, pull down the Options menu and select the Change System Settings option. Then pull down the Display list and choose a new driver. Windows asks whether you want to use the Current driver (assuming you have a driver already installed on your hard disk) or a New driver. You can generally choose the Current driver; in fact, choose New only if you actually have a new version of that driver to install. (If you do choose New, you must insert a disk containing the new driver.) After making your choice, choose OK. Then install the driver (if necessary), and reboot Windows for the new driver to take effect.

2. *Your video display is set up incorrectly.* As a result, you may see nothing but video garbage on-screen when you start Windows. If so, you can't even access the Windows Setup dialog box to change your settings. You must do it from DOS. From the DOS prompt, change to the Windows directory (by typing **CD\WINDOWS**), and type **SETUP**. This loads the DOS-based setup program, from which you can change your video display driver.

3. *Your selected video driver is the correct one, but you need an updated version to work with your current version of Windows.* If so, contact your video card manufacturer to obtain the latest version of the proper driver, and then install it according to steps 1 or 2.

4. *You're using a screen saver that Windows doesn't like.* Screen savers sometimes can cause display problems. Some screen savers leave garbage on-screen when you close them. Try disabling your screen saver, and see if that rectifies the problem.

5. *Windows isn't configured correctly for your system.* If this is the case, you can experience major display problems. Have a pro look at your SYSTEM.INI file to make sure the correct screen grabber is installed. If you don't have access to a pro, you can solve many setup problems by reinstalling Windows from scratch.

6. *You have incorrect fonts installed for your system.* If you're having problems with the way fonts are displayed, you may need to check your Windows font setup. Open the Control Panel (from the Main program group), and then open the Fonts applet. From here, check to ensure that the correct fonts for your system are installed. If not, change them.

7. *You have a loose connection or a bad cable.* Check all your connections and cables. Any display problem possible with DOS also can inflict Windows. Make it a rule always to be certain that everything is hooked up and set up correctly.

Many other problems can affect your video display, but most of those are too technical for anyone but a technician to identify and correct. So if you can't fix your own video problem, call your local repair shop. Someone there undoubtedly can help you.

Problem 12:
Your fonts don't display properly

It's possible that you may have the wrong fonts installed in Windows. Open Control Panel and then double-click the Fonts icon. From here, check to make

> ### Good on Paper, Bad on Screen
>
> Even though Windows uses MS Sans Serif for any small size TrueType font on-screen, it always uses the correct font when you print your document.

sure that you have the right fonts installed for your system. (You might try uninstalling all the fonts, then reinstalling them one at a time.)

If you're trying to view TrueType fonts at a very small type size, you may be disappointed. TrueType is not optimized for small type sizes, so Windows substitutes the generic MS Sans Serif font for whatever TrueType font you selected below a specific size.

Also note that most fonts displayed at very large sizes will look somewhat jagged on your screen. This is just a function of how Windows handles fonts and won't affect how the fonts are actually printed on paper.

Problem 13:
You can't find fonts you *know* are installed

This is a common problem with certain Windows applications, including Word for Windows and Ami Pro. You have a font installed, and yet you can't access the font from your application. You check your font setup and verify that the font is really installed—yet it still doesn't show up in your application. What's the deal?

The deal is simple. You have to have a printer selected in your application before it will display all your available fonts. That's right, if you don't have a printer selected, Word for Windows and other applications won't let you use all your pretty screen fonts. So use Control Panel to select a printer, and all your fonts will show up in your application's font selection list.

Installing vs. Selecting

You can actually install multiple printers on your system, but you run the risk of having the wrong one selected at any given time. Use the Printer setup dialog box to set your current printer as the Default Printer.

Problem 14:
You have trouble printing from Windows

Printing also can be a problem in Windows. Just look at what calamities can occur:

1. *You may have the wrong printer driver installed.* Check the Printer setup in the Control Panel. And while you're there, check all the options to make sure they're configured correctly. After all, if you tell Windows you own a laser printer when you have a dot-matrix connected to your computer, you can forget about getting the output needed for your device.

2. *You may not have enough disk space to print.* I know this sounds strange, but Windows sometimes uses temporary disk space to store information while a print job is in progress. Try deleting some old files to free up disk space.

3. *Your system ports may not be configured correctly for Windows.* Check the Ports setup in the Control Panel and make any necessary corrections.

4. *Your programs may not be configured correctly.* Some Windows programs provide additional printer configuration options that go beyond those available on the Windows Control Panel. Check your programs to make sure they're set up correctly.

5. *You could be trying to print from both a DOS and a Windows program at the same time (or even from two DOS programs).* You can't do this because the output becomes garbled. Stop printing, and then restart with just one program at a time.

6. *You could have the wrong fonts installed on your system.* Check the Fonts setup in the Control Panel. You may need to reinstall some fonts. It's possible, too, that the fonts don't match those you're trying to use in your program. Check your program to make sure you're only using available printer fonts.

7. *You may be out of paper.* If you receive an error message to this effect, reload your printer, and select the Retry option to restart the print job.

8. *Your printer connections may be faulty.* Remember to check all your cables, and make certain that the printer is plugged in and turned on. If bad connections can cause problems when you're working in DOS, they can do so in Windows as well.

Whew! That's quite a bit that can go wrong! But if anything does, just keep your head and check all the usual suspects. If none of the standard fixes work, call in a pro to scope out the offender.

Problem 15:
You receive a Windows error message

Windows can display literally hundreds of error messages, depending on the context in which the error occurred. In most cases, the message is (or tries to be) self-explanatory. If you receive a Windows error message, write it down, try to figure it out, ask for help from a pro if necessary, and try to get on with your normal computing. (If that's possible!) Plus, you should see Chapter 27, "Windows Error Messages... What They Mean and How to Deal With Them."

There are, however, two *very* common error messages you may encounter in your day-to-day Windows use.

If you're running Windows 3.1, the most common error message is

    General protection fault

This message normally accompanies a Windows program crash, more often than not caused by a memory problem. When this message appears, you normally have the option of closing the offending application or ignoring the problem. Since ignoring the problem generally leads directly to the problem occurring again, you probably ought to resign yourself to closing the program. Then, after Windows has shut down the program, exit Windows, reboot your system, restart Windows, and relaunch the naughty program.

The Windows 3.0 equivalent of the GPF is the UAE:

    Unrecoverable application error

Like GPFs, UAEs usually are caused by some sort of memory problem. Unlike a GPF, a UAE doesn't give you any options and generally dumps you out of Windows right to the DOS prompt. So when you encounter a GPF, reboot your system, restart Windows, and relaunch the program at hand.

Problem 16:
File Manager isn't displaying correctly

If File Manager isn't displaying the right files for a given disk, that means you need to refresh its display. Pull down the Window menu and select the Refresh option. Voila! You should see the right files for your selected disk.

It's also possible that you have File Manager configured to list only certain types of files. Pull down the View menu and select the By File Type option. When the By File Type dialog box appears, make sure that *.* is typed in the Name box and that all the File Types are checked. When you select OK, all files should be displayed in the drive window.

If File Manager is only displaying part of the drive Window, you need to reconfigure File Manager. To display both halves, pull down the View menu and select the Tree and Directory option. This should solve your problem.

It's also possible, of course, that you've resized either half of the drive window so that it's too narrow to view. If that's the case, use the mouse to drag the center divider into a more appropriate position for practical use.

Problem 17:
Your mouse doesn't work right

First, make sure that your mouse is connected correctly to the back of your system unit. It's quite easy to connect a mouse to the wrong port on your machine.

Next, make sure that you have the right mouse driver selected in the Windows Setup program. (If in doubt, select Microsoft Mouse; nearly every mouse is Microsoft-compatible.) Then make sure you have the latest driver for your mouse—an older driver might cause erratic or nonexistent operation. Finally—and perhaps the most common problem—your mouse driver might be in conflict with some other device on your system. The solution is simple—you need to reconfigure one or more of your devices so that they're on adjacent ports.

If you can see the mouse pointer on-screen but your mouse doesn't move it, Windows can't correctly detect the kind of mouse you're using. During Setup, Windows attempted to determine which mouse was connected to your system and loaded the appropriate mouse driver. However, sometimes Windows gets it wrong. (Surprise!) If this is the case, you'll need to run Setup (from the Main program group in the Program Manager). When the Setup dialog box appears, pull down the Options menu and select the Change System Settings option. When the Change System Settings dialog box appears, pull down the Mouse list and choose a more appropriate driver for your brand of mouse.

If your mouse quits working after you initiate a print job or use your modem, chances are you have this peripheral on a conflicting interrupt with your mouse. (It's the old COM1/COM3 problem again.) You'll need to change the port assignment of either your mouse or your other peripheral to resolve this conflict.

If your mouse works in Windows but not in a DOS program running within Windows, there could be several causes. First, you have to have a separate mouse driver loaded for your DOS programs—that is, just loading a Windows mouse driver won't make you mouseable in a DOS program. Make sure that you load a DOS mouse driver *before* you launch Windows. Normally, this is done by including a line in your AUTOEXEC.BAT file like of the following:

    C:\MOUSE\MOUSE.COM

Note that, depending on your system, you'll load either MOUSE.COM or MOUSE.SYS. If you have a choice, use MOUSE.COM; it works better from within Windows.

If you have a DOS mouse driver loaded, you could have other problems. Try running your DOS program full-screen instead of in a window; this will work sometimes. Also, your DOS mouse won't work in Windows if it's hooked up to COM2 and there's no COM1 active on your system. You may need to reassign your mouse to COM1 to get things moving.

Finally, if you have Windows 3.0 or earlier, you simply can't use your mouse with DOS windows. Upgrade to Windows 3.1 to get mouseability within your DOS windows.

Problem 18:
Your Program Groups disappear

This sometimes happens because the group files themselves get damaged or erased. (This doesn't mean that the actual program files in the group are gone—just the files that track the contents of each group!) Fortunately, Windows has a secret way to rebuild your program group files. Just pull down the File menu and select the **Run** option. When the Run dialog box appears, type **SETUP /P**, and the Windows Setup program will rebuild your program groups. (You have to use the /P switch for this procedure to work!)

A Last Word on Windows

Running Windows on your computer can help make your computing both easier and more fun in many ways, but it *can* cause you problems as well. Most users, however, consider its pluses worth the trouble. Just be sure to keep this book—and the number of a good computer technician—handy, just in case problems do pop up.

Your Software Is Hard To Use

CHAPTER
TWENTY-THREE

Hardware is important. No doubt about it.

Hardware by itself, however, is nothing more than a collection of useless chips and transistors inside a fairly ugly off-white case, topped off by a blank, staring picture tube.

No, even though hardware is important, it's not much without software. Software, after all, makes your computer go.

So let's get going and figure out what kinds of problems you can encounter with your software...and how you can fix 'em!

What You Need To Know about Software

Software is a part of your system that you can't touch directly. Software comes in a package and is encoded on floppy disks. You insert the disks into one of your computer's floppy drives to transfer the program files to your hard disk, where your computer can access them and load them into its system memory. You interact with the programs with your keyboard and mouse, and you follow your progress on the computer screen. When you're done, you can print out the results on your printer. Put simply, software is how you get stuff done. Without software applications, you wouldn't have any need for DOS, Windows, your mouse—or anything else that makes up your computer system.

Running Software from the DOS Prompt

It's easy to start a software program—if you have all the keys (and I don't mean those on the keyboard). The first key is knowing the name of the executable program file. To load the program, you must type its name at the DOS prompt. The executable file for WordPerfect, for example, is WP.EXE, and the executable file for Lotus 1-2-3 is 123.EXE. To load these programs, just type the file name (minus the extension) at the DOS prompt, like this:

WP

or

123

Executing a Batch of Extensions

Nearly all executable program files have an EXE extension. Some programs may combine several program instructions into a multiline batch file; batch files load just like executable (EXE) files, but have a BAT extension.

With some programs, you can add to the program name certain parameters or switches that enable you to launch the program under special conditions or with a predefined configuration. Check your program's documentation to learn any special switches or parameters you may want to use when you load the program.

Running Software in Windows

If you're in Windows, you can start a program in one of several ways. One way is to pull down the **File** menu and select the **Run** option; this displays a dialog box in which you type

> ### Start in the Right Directory
>
> You want to be sure that DOS knows where to look for your program before you start it. It's best to change to the program's directory before you type the startup command.

the name and path of the program you want to load. Another way is to open the File Manager and double-click the file name of the program you want to load. Or you can create an icon for that program and then double-click the icon to launch the program. (Many programs, however, save you the trouble of creating an icon; they create their own when installed.)

Making Your Software Programs Work Together

If you're working in DOS, you really can't run more than one application program at a time. You can, however, load several *memory-resident programs* at the same time as a single application program. Memory-resident programs are small utilities loaded into memory. You access them with a special key combination (sometimes called a *hot key*); otherwise they remain in memory, waiting to be accessed.

Unfortunately, some programs may not work with other programs. Memory-resident programs are especially troublesome in this regard. It's best, therefore, to use as few memory-resident programs as possible so as to reduce the chance of their causing memory conflicts with other programs.

If you're working in the Windows environment, you can run many applications at one time. This is called *multitasking*, and Windows does it relatively well. Again, however, memory can be a problem. Your computer may not possess enough memory to run all the programs you want to at one time. Or two or more programs running simultaneously may attempt to use the same memory space, resulting in memory conflicts. If you frequently run up against these types of problems, try running fewer programs at the same time.

10 Do's and Don'ts for Software

1. *Do* use the most up-to-date version of a software package.

2. *Don't* expect your software to read your mind; make sure *you* read the documentation manual so you can tell the program what you want it to do.

3. *Do* keep your original software disk and documentation in a safe place for future reference.

4. *Don't* attempt to run multiple copies of the same software at one time; you're just asking for trouble.

5. *Do* make backup copies of all your original software disks.

6. *Don't* pirate software; if you're using a program, pay for it. It's the right thing to do.

7. *Do* install and configure your software correctly for your specific system's setup.

8. *Don't* forget to read the README files included with most packages before installation.

9. *Do* buy a Que book for each software package you own—two, or three, if you can afford them!

10. *Don't* confuse DOS and Windows versions of the same program; if you're using Windows, you're probably better off using the Windows version of the program.

Other Things That Can Go Wrong

In addition to memory conflicts, you can experience several other problems, such as:

- You may mistype the program's name when you're trying to start it.

- You may need to include the program's directory path in the start-up command or change to the program's directory before starting it.

- The program may not be configured correctly for your system.

- The program may have system-performance requirements that your system doesn't provide or require components your system doesn't incorporate.

- The program itself may contain bugs that keep it from operating correctly.

- And finally, you just may not know how to operate your software. (Really!)

Any of these problems can be darned annoying. Read on for hints on how to drastically reduce your annoyance level.

What To Do When You Have Software Problems

It's impossible in the course of a few pages to discuss everything that can go wrong with every software package currently available—so I'm not even going to try. Instead, I'll simply examine a few common problems shared by all software programs.

Problem 1:
Your software doesn't work

If you can't get a certain program to run, first make sure you typed the correct command to load the software. Sometimes the name of the executable program file—and thus the command that starts it—isn't self-evident. Next, make certain that you're in the right directory to start the file. Which directory you start in may not matter to some programs; with others, however, you may have to switch to that program's own directory to coax it to load. Next, check to ensure that the program is installed correctly. (If you're in doubt, reinstall the program, and don't forget to make any necessary alterations to your AUTOEXEC.BAT or CONFIG.SYS files.) Also, make sure that you don't have two programs with the same name: if you have both PROGRAM.EXE and PROGRAM.BAT files, for example, you may accidentally start the wrong one when you type PROGRAM. Finally, be certain that the program is compatible with your computer's particular hardware configuration. Your machine may need more memory, a faster microprocessor, or a higher-resolution video card before your finicky new program consents to run on it.

If all else fails, consult the instruction manual for this particular piece of software, or call the software publisher's technical support line.

Problem 2:
Your software crashes

Everything works fine, but then—all of a sudden—your software bombs! What can cause this software-specific disaster?

First, look for conflicts with other programs. Are any memory-resident programs loaded? (Don't forget to check your AUTOEXEC.BAT file for any memory-resident programs that load automatically at startup.) If so, unload them, and then try running your program again. Are you running any other programs at the same time? If so, don't.

Next, check the memory in your system. Does it have enough to run the program? Is it configured correctly? (Your RAM may be configured as extended memory when your program uses expanded memory—have a pro check this out for you.)

Taking Advice

When you call a software manufacturer's technical support line, be prepared for their questions. Have all pertinent information about your program handy, including which version you're using. Also be prepared to answer questions about your system setup—what kind of PC you have, what peripherals you have hooked up, and so on. And finally, be prepared to jot down any instructions they give you for future use. The folks on these lines can be really helpful—if you give them a little help, too!

Finally, the cause of the crash may be a bug in your software or even a corrupted program file. If nothing else pans out, try reinstalling your program from scratch. If this doesn't fix the problem, call the knowledgeable folks at the software publisher's technical support line for assistance. After all, that's what they're there for.

Problem 3:
Your software doesn't look right on-screen

Okay, your program runs fine, but somehow the display looks wrong! First, make sure that the program is configured correctly for your system. Don't simply assume that an upgrade can use your old configuration information. That isn't necessarily the case.

Next, check to see that the program can run with your video card. If you own an older EGA or CGA system, some of the newer graphics-intensive programs may not run on it. If necessary, upgrade your video card and monitor.

Finally, make certain that you have the latest device driver for your video card installed. If not, you may need to order an updated driver file from your card's manufacturer or from the publisher of the software.

Problem 4:
Your software doesn't print

You've finished all the important work on a file in your program, and you're ready to print it. But the printer does diddley. What's wrong? Did you re-member to configure your new software for your existing hardware? Please, please, check the setup for your new program to make sure that it's config-ured correctly for your hardware setup. You may even need to obtain a newer device driver to use your existing printer with some newer programs. Check with the software publisher or your printer's manufacturer for more information.

Check, too, to see if your printer still works with your other programs. If not, you have printer problems that probably can be eased by following the advice in Chapter 15. If it does work with everything but the new program, back up and check that configuration again.

Still having problems? If you haven't already done so, check your program's documentation for further ideas.

A Final Word on Software

When you have specific software problems—that is, problems that don't appear when you use other programs—your best bet may be to call the technical support line for that software manufacturer. Their software-specific experts can generally determine your problem and get you up and running again in no time. Look in your software instruction manual for the manufacturer's phone number!

Your New Software Causes New Problems

CHAPTER TWENTY-FOUR

The only thing worse than trying to get your software to work right is getting *new* software to work right! When you install new software on your system—even if it's just a new version of a current program—you introduce the opportunity for lots of *new problems*!

So, if you really have to install new software on your system, this is the chapter for you. Read on and figure out how to do it right—or fix it if it's wrong!

What You Need To Know about Installing New Software

Installing new software doesn't have to be hard. Just take things nice and easy, and things should go okay!

Things to Do *Before* You Upgrade Your Software

Before you install any program, there are a few precautions you should take.

First, make sure you back up all the information on your hard disk. (Yes, that's right, *all of it*!) You'll remember how to back up your hard disk from Chapter 7, of course. The reason for this is simple—new software will re-write certain common files, and may even (if things don't go right) trash files and perhaps even your hard disk. So, be safe—rather than sorry—and do a backup before installation.

Next, make copies of your key system files. Remember, new programs will often rewrite these files, so it's nice to have copies you can return to in case the installation goes south. I recommend you make copies of these files:

Current Filename	New Filename (Copy)
AUTOEXEC.BAT	AUTOEXEC.OOP
CONFIG.SYS	CONFIG.OOP
WIN.INI	WIN.OOP
SYSTEM.INI	SYSTEM.OOP

The last two files exist only if you're running Windows, and should be found in your Windows directory (normally C:\WINDOWS). The first two files are found in your hard disk's root directory (C:\).

(Some of the more technically-minded among you may wonder why I didn't recommend copying the files to backup files with *.BAK extensions. This is because some upgrade installations create their own backups with this extension, and it's best to have your own copies, just in case.)

Finally, be sure to read all the documentation from the new software, including some special documentation that you will normally find tucked away on the software's main program disk. This last-minute documentation often

> ### Recovering from a Bad Installation
>
> If your new software installation, for whatever reason, doesn't work out right, the first thing to do is to rename these backup files (the ones with the "OOP" extension) back to their original names. If you still have troubles, you may need to restore the data from your hard disk backup. (See Chapter 8.)

is contained in a file named README, README.TXT, or READ.ME. These files (set up in ASCII format) contain information about the program that cropped up *after* the printed documentation was completed. You often discover a few last-minute installation instructions in these files, as well as information on any known bugs in the software. To read these files, load them into a word processor or the DOS Editor, or display them as ASCII text by typing the following command:

> **TYPE A:README.TXT |MORE**

(The |MORE tells DOS to display only one screen at a time; press any key to move to the next screen of information.)

Installing New Software

Loading new software usually is a very simple task. When loading a DOS application, for example, you merely insert the first disk in your drive and type INSTALL, or SETUP, or something similar at the DOS prompt. (Each program's documentation provides the specific installation command.) Most software packages come with an actual installation program that auto-mates the process; all you have to do is answer the few questions it asks about your system and shuffle the disk in and out of the disk drive as directed.

Some programs, however, don't include automatic installation programs. To install such programs, you first must create a new directory on your hard disk (using the DOS MD command) and then copy the program files from the disk to that directory.

If you're installing a new Windows application, the installation process is similar to that of a DOS application, but you usually have to perform the installation from within Windows. To run an installation program, you can pull down the File menu and select the Run option. After the dialog box prompts you for the name of the program, type the installation program's name (accompanied by the drive letter, of course) and click OK.

Upgrading Your Current Software

Installing a software upgrade normally is just like installing brand new software. There is one extra precaution you may want to take, however.

If you think you may ever want to erase the new software version and return to your original version, you'll need to save the old version—because most upgrades install right over the old software. The thing to do here is to make a new directory (call it OLDSOFT or something like that) and copy all the files from your old software into this directory. You can then install the new version over the old version, because you have the duplicate (in the OLDSOFT directory) you can return to if necessary.

New Isn't the Same as Old

One more thing to watch out for—new versions of old programs often work differently from the old programs. Make sure you read the manual (or appropriate Que book) to learn all the program differences before you proceed blindly into the software upgrade!

New Things That Can Go Wrong

The list of things that can go wrong with a software upgrade is only slightly longer than the list of what can go wrong with a new installation:

- The new program may have a different name or extension, so it doesn't start with the same command as the old version.

- The new program may be installed in a different directory than the old version.

- The new program may be configured differently than the old version for your system.

- The new program may have system-performance requirements different from the old version, and your system may not be compatible or sufficient anymore.

- The new program's installation procedure may alter your CONFIG.SYS or AUTOEXEC.BAT files in such a way that the operation of other programs is adversely affected.

- The upgrade may not accept files created with the older version.

10 Do's and Don'ts for Software Upgrades

1. *Do* keep a copy of the old software version, *just in case!*

2. *Don't* install the new program without making copies of your AUTOEXEC.BAT and CONFIG.SYS files (and your key *.INI files if you're running Windows).

3. *Do* keep both your original and upgrade software disks and documentation in a safe place for future reference.

4. *Don't* attempt to run the old version and the new version of your software at the same time; your system probably won't know how to handle this.

5. *Do* make backup copies of all your original software disks for the software upgrade.

6. *Don't* expect the new software to work just the same as the old version; most new versions upgrade their operations as well as their features.

7. *Do* change any appropriate system configurations necessary for the new software.

8. *Don't* forget to read the README files included with most packages before installation.

9. *Do* buy a Que book for your new software version—don't expect the old Que book to work with the new software!

10. *Don't* let this new program intimidate you; most programs use a similar logic in the way they operate.

- As usual, the program itself may contain bugs that keep it from operating correctly.

- And, finally, you just may not know how to operate the new software—especially if it's radically different from the old version.

And you thought upgrading an existing program was simple!

What To Do When You Have Upgrade Problems

In addition to the normal software problems discussed in Chapter 23, take a look at these potential problems that can happen when you add new software to your system.

Problem 1:
You installed new software, and now your other programs don't work

New programs can affect the way older programs work—usually for the worse. If you've recently installed a new program and can't get existing programs to run correctly (or run at all), first check your AUTOEXEC.BAT and CONFIG.SYS files; the new program may have altered them in a way that adversely affects some of your existing programs.

It's possible, too, that the new program has introduced a memory conflict with an existing program. If only one of your older programs is affected, it's relatively easy to isolate the problem. If several programs are affected, however, the problem may be more widespread. Unfortunately, such multiple-program conflicts are the most difficult problems to diagnose and solve; you may have to call in professional help on this one.

Problem 2:
After installing the new version, you can't use (or find) the pre-upgrade version of your software

This is normal. In most cases, the upgrade is installed *over* the old version of the software—meaning it just doesn't exist anymore. (This is why you should have made a copy of your old version before you upgraded!) If you want to revert to your old software version (and you didn't make a copy), you'll have to *delete* the new version from your hard disk and reinstall the previous version from scratch!

Of course, if you want to keep your old version around after you install the upgrade version, you'll want to install the upgrade to a *new* directory—a directory different from your existing program directory. In most cases, you can instruct the software installation program to use a different directory for the upgrade.

Problem 3:
Your new software doesn't work with files from a previous version

Sometimes when you upgrade a program to its latest version, it turns out that the newer version uses a file format different from that of the older version. If so, your old files won't run in the new version. If this happens to you, check the upgrade's documentation or check with the software publisher for instructions on how to convert your older files to the new format.

Another possibility is that the new version of the program simply doesn't know where to look for your old files. Remember, just because you had configured the old version to your liking doesn't mean that the new version is using the same configuration information. Check the program's setup to make sure it knows where to look for all your files.

A Final Word on New Software

In dealing with new software problems, the main thing to keep in mind is to trace your steps. If you've installed a new program and now something else in your system refuses to work, trace your steps back to see if you can deduce how the new program may have affected your wayward software or hardware. Even if you must call in a pro to untangle things for you, this little piece of detective work can help you help your rescuer identify—and fix—the problem that much faster.

Your Hardware Upgrade Downgrades Your System

CHAPTER TWENTY-FIVE

For some reason, you've decided to upgrade your computer system. You want to add more memory, or a CD-ROM drive, or a sound card, or a new monitor, or... well, one or more of a dozen possible things. If you're like me, you're a little daunted by the thought of taking your system unit apart, and a trifle anxious about what sort of problems you may encounter.

As well you should be.

Let's face it, any time you poke around inside your computer you're just asking for trouble. So if trouble is what you find when upgrading, turn the page, and we'll explore what you can expect—and how you can fix it!

Why Should You Upgrade Your Computer?

You upgrade your computer when you want more of something—more speed, more memory, more storage, more capabilities—and you don't want to buy a whole new computer system. It's often easier (and a lot less expensive!) to add exactly what you want to your present computer than to buy a brand new $2,500 PC.

What sort of things can you upgrade on your computer system? Take a look at this list:

- Microprocessor chip (and numeric co-processor chip)
- Memory chips
- Video card
- Sound card
- Game card
- Hard disk drive
- Floppy disk drives
- CD-ROM drive
- Tape drive
- Modem (or fax modem)
- External speakers
- Monitor
- Keyboard
- Mouse
- Joystick
- Scanner
- Printer

In short, just about anything on your system you can unplug or unscrew, you can upgrade!

Before You Upgrade— Taking Precautions

Step-by-Step Upgrading—for Normal Folks!

If you're thinking of upgrading your system, check out Que's *Upgrading Your PC Illustrated*. This is, quite simply, the best book I've read on upgrading your hardware. It uses hundreds of color photographs—and plain-English language—to lead you step-by-step through common upgrading procedures. It's a must-buy if you're adding to your system!

Now, I won't even pretend to show you how to upgrade your computer in this single chapter. However, I will point out some things you'll want to do *before* you upgrade, to reduce your chances of experiencing major problems!

Prepare a PC Survival Kit

I won't bore you with the details of this again. (However, if you don't mind getting a little bored, just turn back to Chapter 7 for more information.) Suffice to say, you need to create a Bootable Emergency Disk, in case you knock out your key system files while upgrading.

Back Up Your Important Data Files

Again, before you do anything major to your system, you need to back up any important files from your hard disk. (In fact, I always recommend a complete hard disk backup in situations like these.) See Chapter 7 for instructions on backing up in DOS or Windows.

Record Your CMOS Information

Some critical information about your system is stored on a special chip inside your computer. This battery-powered chip is called a *CMOS* chip, and it holds all the configuration information about your system in permanent memory. You need to record the information from this chip, *just in case* something goes south during your upgrade and fries this chip (or its battery).

To record your CMOS information, follow these steps:

1. Most newer PCs have a setup program available in ROM. One of the very first messages you see when you turn on your computer will indicate how you access this program. (This message will typically occur before or during the memory check—when those numbers flip by real quickly on your screen—but before accessing any of your disk drives.)

2. Now you need to access this setup program. Note that different computers use different keystrokes to access this setup program. Some manufacturers require you to press the Del key when your system is booting (during the memory check); other vendors require you to press Ctrl+Alt+S, and still others require Ctrl+Alt+Esc. If these don't work, you may need to refer to your system documentation or call the vendor where you purchased the system.

3. When you access your setup program, you'll see your CMOS information displayed on-screen. Now you should either write it down or press the Print Screen key to print it out on your printer. Put the information in a safe place so you can get it when you need it.

If, while upgrading, your CMOS chip loses its memory, you'll need to access the setup program again. Referring to the information you gathered in step 3, reset all your CMOS parameters.

Obtain the Proper Tools

To do the upgrade right, you'll need the right tools. (It just won't do to use an old butter knife in place of a proper screwdriver!) Take a look at the contents of Miller's Recommended Minimum Upgrading Toolkit:

- Phillips-head screwdriver—a #2 (or "medium-sized") is the preferred size.

- Flat-blade screwdriver—try to find one with a blade about an eighth of an inch wide.

- Pliers—the needle-nose type, small enough for prying things loose inside your PC.

- Tweezers—the kind for plucking eyebrows will work just fine.

> **More Power!**
>
> If you think you will be working on your PC system quite a bit, invest in a small power screwdriver. It will make your life a lot easier—and, besides, we all need *more power!*

- Chip-pulling tool—but only if you're really serious about this sort of thing. (Otherwise, the pliers or tweezers will do an adequate job.)

- Large, soft cloth—a good place to put all your delicate parts.

Turn Off the Power!

It goes without saying—*Don't mess with your computer until you turn off the power and unplug the system unit!*

Enough said.

Reduce the Risk of Static Electricity

Another danger in poking around inside your PC is damaging the very sensitive chips by giving them a jolt of static electricity. (You can build up enough static electricity walking across a carpet to do hundreds of dollars' worth of damage to your system unit!) Use an anti-static "strap," or anti-static spray, or an anti-static mat, or anything else to ground yourself and drain the static electricity from your body *before* you touch those expensive chips!

After You Upgrade—Common Problems

Okay. You've plugged in your new card, or new memory chips, or new peripheral. You put your computer back together, plug it in, turn it on, and…

Something goes wrong.

Such as:

It's a Test!

Before you reassemble your system, you should fully test everything related to what you upgraded. If, for some reason, something doesn't work, you should retrace your steps to try and figure out what you may have done wrong. It's good procedure to remove the last device you installed and then restart your system. Going backwards step-by-step will help you identify which component is causing your current problems.

- You forgot to plug your computer back in—or plug everything back into your system unit.

- You didn't connect something properly.

- You need to change your system configuration to recognize your new upgrade.

- Your new component conflicts with an existing component, either in memory or IRQ assignment.

- Some part of your system isn't compatible with your new component.

- You broke something while you were inside your system unit.

- You left something loose inside your system unit, like a wire or a screw.

If things are really screwed up, you probably ought to bring in expert help—like a good computer technician.

Before you do that, however, finish reading this chapter and see if you can fix it yourself.

10 Do's and Don'ts for Hardware Upgrading

1. *Do* use the proper tools when disassembling your system unit.

2. *Don't* forget to plug everything back in properly when you're finished upgrading.

3. *Do* take proper precautions before upgrading your system— such as making a PC Survival Kit and backing up the contents of your hard disk.

4. *Don't* be afraid to call in expert help if you're having big problems.

5. *Do* remember to reconfigure your system to recognize your new components.

6. *Don't* forget to ground yourself so you don't release a static charge and fry your computer chips.

7. *Do* record your CMOS information, just in case.

8. *Don't* be a total klutz and break anything inside your system unit!

9. *Do* buy a copy of Que's *Upgrading Your PC Illustrated*; it's a great book for everyday upgraders like you and me!

10. *Don't* even attempt a difficult upgrade if you're not totally confident of your abilities; it's better to be safe than sorry, and let a professional do the dirty work.

Fixing Upgrade Problems

Just as I couldn't cover all the details about upgrading in one chapter, I also can't cover all the problems you might encounter in this limited space. Some upgrading problems are actually covered in other, more specific sections of this book. I'll just try to cover the most common problems here.

Problem 1:
Your upgrade doesn't work

This could be one of a number of things. If you installed a new card, it may not be properly seated in the slot. You may not have all your cables connected properly. You may have broken something while you were diddling about inside your PC. You may have a bad part. You may not have completed the installation or setup. (A lot of components require some software-based setup to work properly, often modifying your CONFIG.SYS or AUTOEXEC.BAT files.)

Retrace your steps backward through your installation, and try to determine if everything was done correctly. If all else fails, call the technical support line for your new component, or consult with a technical professional.

Problem 2:
After you upgrade, an existing part of your system no longer works properly

This is probably caused by some sort of resource conflict between your new and old components. The most common resource conflicts involve IRQ and/or port settings.

If you're adding an external component, you may be able to fix this by simply changing ports. If this doesn't fix it (or if you installed an internal device), you'll need to change IRQ settings for one or both of the devices in conflict.

Also note that conflicts can occur when devices hooked up to two nonconsecutive ports are used at the same time. In other words, if you have two devices trying to use COM1 and COM3 (or COM2 and COM4) simultaneously, both could freeze up. (I've had this happen with a mouse hooked up to COM1 and a modem hooked up to COM3.) If this is your problem, change the port for one of the devices.

Problem 3:
After you upgrade, your existing software doesn't work right

This is normally a simple setup problem. You'll need to tell your software about your new hardware or system configuration. If you're in Windows, you'll use the Windows Control Panel and Windows Setup utility to do this. In DOS-based programs, you'll need to refer to specific setup/installation instructions. In any case, you'll probably need to reboot your system for these changes to take effect.

It's also possible that your old software simply won't work with your new hardware. If you suspect this is the case, put in a call to the software manufacturer and see if they have a quick solution; if not, you may have to upgrade to a newer version of your software.

Problem 4:
You installed new memory, and now your entire system doesn't work (you may receive an error message on system startup)

When you added memory, you didn't tell your computer about it. The solution is simple—tell your computer!

Getting the Jump

On some older PCs you may need to adjust jumpers or switches on the motherboard to get your system to recognize your new memory.

You do this by accessing your CMOS information (discussed earlier in this chapter) via your system's startup program. When you've accessed the CMOS info, you need to change the settings to reflect your new memory settings. (Fortunately, many new systems will automatically recognize the new memory setup during the power-on procedure.)

Problem 5:
You installed a new component, and now it doesn't work (your system doesn't recognize it)

Depending on what you installed, you may have to do one of several things to get your system to recognize its new component:

- Change CMOS settings (most common for memory and disk drives)

- Load new drivers via your CONFIG.SYS and/or AUTOEXEC.BAT files

- Adjust specific jumpers or switches on your motherboard or other specific component

Remember, after you make any of these changes you'll need to reboot your system in order for the changes to take effect.

Problem 6:
You added a new video card, and now your monitor doesn't seem to work right

The problem here could be one of two things. Thing one: You didn't set up your card right to work with your monitor, or with some specific software program. Check the setup program (or the documentation) for the card for more information.

Thing two: Your monitor isn't compatible with your video card. It's more likely than not that you have a higher-resolution card (SVGA, perhaps) and a monitor that can only display a lower-resolution picture. If this is the case, can the new card or buy a new monitor.

A Final Word on Upgrading

Fortunately, most common upgrades (sound cards, CD-ROM drives, etc.) come with very explicit instructions, and automated software setup routines. Because of this, it's a lot easier to upgrade your system today than it was a few short years ago.

That's not to say it's always a walk in the park, of course. Just try to keep one important thing in mind—if you do get in over your head, there are thousands of qualified technical repair people out there just waiting to help you out. (For a price, of course!) Don't be afraid to call in a pro when you need to; it's better than ending up with less of a computer than you started with before the upgrade!

A Quick Course in Problem Solving

Hardware

or

Software

Problems

When you're trying to troubleshoot a particularly pesky problem, it helps if you can narrow the problem down to one specific area of your system. Is your problem caused by your hardware, by your operating system, or by a specific software program? Turn the page and I'll share some hints on how to isolate your problems to a particular part of your system.

First, a Few Troubleshooting Tips

Before we look at specific types of problems, it might help to get a little advice on troubleshooting the problems with your computer system.

My first tip, stated simply, is—*DON'T PANIC!* In the grand cosmic scheme of things, a malcontent microcomputer just doesn't register on the significance scale. Besides, if anything major went wrong, there's not much you can do about it *after* the fact. The thing to do is keep your cool and use the advice in this book to minimize the damage and get things back to normal as soon as possible.

Next, you should try to reproduce the problem. After all, if it only happens once, it's not really that bad of a problem, is it? If you can't reproduce the problem, it means that something fixed itself automatically (unlikely), or that your problem was caused by a one-time user error (quite common).

If you *can* reproduce the problem, the next thing to check is your entire installation and setup. You need to examine every cable going into and out of your system unit, the installation of any add-in cards, the setup of specific software programs (including Windows), and anything else you can think of that might cause the problem. After you've checked everything out, exit to the DOS prompt and reboot your system. (Sometimes correcting a poorly connected cord or misselected option won't register with your system until it starts up again—hence, the reboot.)

If you still have problems, it's time to start thinking methodically and logically. Begin by tracing the steps that led to your problem. Did you do anything wrong—or different from normal? Have you recently added anything new to your system—or changed anything old? It's common for new hardware or software to induce changes in your system's behavior— even of software programs seemingly unrelated to the new items. If you can isolate the cause of the problem, it's easy enough to remove the new peripheral or program and get your system back to pre-problem operating status.

Finally, if you can't fix the problem—and none of the suggestions in this book make things any better—it's time to call in a professional. Don't get discouraged if you can't figure it out yourself; there are just some problems that are beyond the abilities of mortal men (and women). That's why computer technicians exist. If you need to, call one. It's okay.

Hammering Out Hardware Problems

Hardware problems are fairly easy to identify. First, they generally affect everything you try to do on your system. For example, if you have a printer problem, all your programs will print poorly—the problem isn't isolated to specific programs.

Second, hardware problems generally affect specific operations related to the piece of hardware itself. That is, a problem video card will affect your video display—*not* your ability to print.

Third, you can generally assume a hardware problem when something weird happens after you upgrade your system with a new peripheral or other hardware component. The new part of your system may even cause old parts of your system to act funny!

Finally, hardware problems are relatively easy to troubleshoot. All you have to do is replace the suspected culprit—if it was a hardware problem, a new part will get things going again, lickety-split. For example, if you're having trouble with your keyboard, replacing the keyboard with a new one will fix the problem automatically.

All that said, there are some hardware problems that are more difficult to track down. Specifically, problems with ports can give you fits. As I've noted in various places of this book, assigning two peripherals (such as a mouse and a modem) to the same port (or even consecutive ports) can cause one or both peripherals to misbehave. When in doubt, have a professional look at your hardware configuration; it's easier for a pro to sense when things are wrong (and make the requisite fixes) than it is for us average folk.

Dealing with DOS Problems

Actually, there are very few problems that are caused by DOS itself. Oh, you can *make* DOS do something wrong, but that's classified as human error. More often than not, you don't have to worry about DOS problems.

There are certain situations, however, where DOS can cause problems. If you have problems starting your computer, you could have a problem with the DOS startup files (CONFIG.SYS and AUTOEXEC.BAT). If you have problems related to memory use (most notably, a lack of available memory), you also have DOS to blame. (In particular, the configuration of your system's memory in your CONFIG.SYS and AUTOEXEC.BAT files.) Finally, some disk problems are actually DOS problems—particularly if you have problems with the DOS 6 DoubleSpace disk-compression utility.

Other than those, you probably won't experience problems with DOS.

Winnowing Out Windows Problems

Windows, on the other hand, can cause you lots of problems. This is because Windows sits on top of DOS and adds overhead to your system. Overhead means increased problems, in most cases.

How to tell if you have a Windows problem? First, the problem occurs only when you're using Windows—*not* when you're using a DOS program. Second, the problem occurs in more than one Windows program. Finally, you can affect the nature of the problem by changing the way you use Windows—by closing some programs or by changing Windows setup options.

There is one problem that may seem like a Windows problem but can actually be a DOS problem. If you keep running into situations where Windows is low on memory, you may have a problem with your DOS memory setup in the CONFIG.SYS and/or AUTOEXEC.BAT files. Of course, you could also have a Windows problem, but in this one instance I'd look at your DOS setup files first.

Sorting Out Software Problems

Software problems are normally easy to spot. If you only have problems when using a specific program—that is, if you can't duplicate the problem in other programs—you probably have a problem with that software program. If your problem only occurs when using two programs at the same time, the problem probably lies in one of the two programs—or in the interaction of the two. If your problem occurs in *several* programs, then your problem most likely lies elsewhere—probably in your system hardware.

A Last Word on Troubleshooting

It's not easy to figure out what exactly is causing a specific problem on your personal computer system, but it is necessary if you're going to fix the problem. For a more visual approach to tracking down problems, turn to Chapter 30, "The Great Troubleshooting Road Map."

What They Mean and How To Deal with Them

CHAPTER TWENTY-SEVEN

Windows uses error messages to try to tell you why something bad has happened. Sometimes the messages are easy to decipher. Sometimes they're not.

Because Windows can display literally thousands of error messages—some of them fairly obscure—I've tried to whittle it down to the most common messages you're likely to encounter with Windows and sort them in alphabetical order. (I've avoided including program-specific error messages, or else this book would expand by a few hundred pages or so.) If your message isn't in this list, don't despair—it just means you have something *really weird* happening with your system. Write down the message and call a competent computer technician. They'll be glad to help you out.

The Major Messages—GPFs and UAEs

The most common error messages you'll encounter are called *General Protection Faults (GPFs)* and *Unrecoverable Application Errors (UAEs)*. These are particular types of error messages that are displayed when an application crashes—or when Windows itself crashes.

General Protection Faults

GPFs are displayed by Windows 3.1 when serious system errors occur—that is, when something crashes. GPFs seldom shut down Windows itself, but more often alert you to a problem that has frozen a Windows application. You are most often presented with an option to close down the offending application, which you should do. Then you can exit Windows properly, reboot your system, restart Windows, and then relaunch the application in question.

Unrecoverable Application Errors

UAEs are the equivalent of GPFs for the older 3.0 version of Windows. UAEs are displayed when serious system errors occur—that is, when something crashes. Most often UAEs are caused by memory conflicts or program bugs. More often than not, a UAE will drop you out of Windows back to the DOS prompt—where you should reboot and then restart Windows.

All the Other Messages

What follows is an alphabetical listing of some of the most common general Windows error messages.

    A TSR is installed

Windows does not work with many DOS-based terminate-and-stay-resident (TSR) programs. If you receive this message, remove any TSRs from your system's memory and edit your AUTOEXEC.BAT file so that TSRs are not automatically loaded when your system is booted.

    Abnormal termination

This message occurs when a Windows application crashes unexpectedly, most often due to memory problems. Sometimes this kind of program crash will also crash Windows itself. You'll need to reach the DOS prompt, reboot your computer, and then restart Windows and the offending application.

```
Adobe Type Manager ATM fonts and Postscript printer fonts
don't match on XXX
```

In this case, *XXX* is the name of a specific font. You get this message when you try to use an ATM font with the same name as a font preinstalled in your PostScript printer. There is no effect, positive or negative, on what gets printed, so feel free to ignore the message.

```
Another application is using communication port
```

You are running two programs that are both trying to access a single communication port, such as two communications programs. Close one of the two programs to avoid the current conflict.

```
Application execution error: Cannot find file
Check to ensure path and filename are correct
```

This message results when Windows tries to load a program that either doesn't exist or isn't located where Windows thinks it is. If this message appears when you start Windows, it means you have an incorrect file inserted in your Startup program group. Check all the icons in this group to make sure the filename and path are correct. You can also check your WIN.INI file to make sure there are no errors in the RUN= or LOAD= lines.

```
Application execution error: No association exists for this
file
```

If no program file is associated with a data file you're trying to launch, you receive this message. To associate a program file with a data file extension, pull down the File menu, select the Associate option, and click on the Associate dialog box.

```
Application execution error: Unexpected DOS error #11
```

This message appears if either your video grabber or the WINOLDAP.386 files are missing or corrupted. Try the procedure to reinstall the grabber file discussed above. If that doesn't work, reinstall Windows from your installation disks.

```
Application is still active
```

You're trying to exit Windows while a DOS application is still running. Close the DOS program and then exit Windows.

```
Attempt to load duplicate device
```

Windows is trying to load a device that is already loaded. Check your SYSTEM.INI file for duplicate lines and eliminate them.

`Call to undefined dynalink`

This message results when a Windows program tries to use an incompatible DLL file. You'll probably need to wipe the program from your hard disk and reinstall it from scratch. It's also possible that an old printer driver can cause this problem. The solution is similar; erase the old driver and install an updated version.

`Cannot communicate with modem`

For some reason, Windows cannot access your modem. Check all connections and setup configurations to make sure that your modem is working and properly set up.

`Cannot find file`

The most common cause for this message is that the file in question is either missing or corrupted. Use File Manager to search for the file; reinstall the program in question, if necessary. In some instances, this message may be generated if the APPEND command appears in your AUTOEXEC.BAT file. If this is the case, delete the offending line.

`Cannot format disk`

Windows generates this message when you try to format a disk that is write-protected. Change disks or uncover the write-protect notch (on 5 1/4-inch disks) or slide the write-protect tab into the down position (on 3 1/2-inch disks).

`Cannot install A20 line`

This message is generated when the HIMEM.SYS driver is not working correctly. Sometimes HIMEM.SYS or Windows does not recognize your particular hardware setup. See the Windows documentation for information on how to add switches to make HIMEM.SYS work with different hardware setups.

`Cannot print. SoftRIP error.`

Some printers print an entire page as a graphic image, forming that image in memory before printing. If your system doesn't have enough memory, this message is generated. Close any other open applications to free up additional memory.

`Cannot read from drive x`

Windows is looking for a file on drive *x:*. If no disk is in drive *x:*, insert an old disk to end the Windows look loop. If a disk is in drive *x:*, you either have a bad (or unformatted) disk, or a bad disk drive. If the message refers to drive C: (your hard disk), you either forgot to load SMARTDRV.EXE in your CONFIG.SYS file or your hard disk is going bad.

`Cannot replace xxxx: Access Denied.`

You tried to copy a file to a write-protected disk or to a drive that doesn't have a disk inserted. Make sure the disk is inserted correctly before you resume the operation or change the disk's write-protect status.

`Cannot run DOS application in second instance of Windows`

This message appears when either the WINOLDAP.MOD or WINOA386.MOD files on your hard disk are from an earlier version of Windows. You'll need to reinstall Windows from your installation disks to add the new versions of these files to your hard disk.

`Cannot run program -- No application is associated with this file.`
`Choose Associate from the File menu to create an association.`

If no program file is associated with a data file you're trying to launch, you receive this message. To associate a program file with a data file extension, pull down the File menu, select the Associate option, and fill in the Associate dialog box.

`Cannot run program -- Out of system resources`

Resources include system memory, as well as space taken by everything you see on your screen—icons, fonts, dialog boxes, etc. When too much is going on at one time, Windows runs out of resources. Try closing any open programs or simplifying your screen in any way—minimizing windows, closing dialog boxes, etc.

`Cannot start application`

Windows cannot start the desired application. Check to make sure the correct directory path and file name were specified. It's also possible that sufficient memory was not available to run this application. You should also check to make sure that an APPEND statement is not present in your AUTOEXEC.BAT file; if it is, remove it.

`Cannot start more than one copy of xxx`

Some programs cannot be loaded twice in Windows. If a program is already running, avoid starting a second instance of the program.

`Cannot start Windows in Standard Mode (Low Memory)`

Windows cannot start in standard mode due to a low memory situation. Increase system memory or restart Windows in real mode (if using Windows 3.0) by typing **WIN /R.**

`Change Disk --`
`Cannot Find` *xxx*`. Please insert in drive` *x*`.`

Windows is looking for a particular file on a particular disk. Insert the proper disk in the proper drive. It's also possible that the APPEND command is active. Look for this command in your AUTOEXEC.BAT file; if it's there, remove it.

`Could not print page` *x*

Windows could not print a particular page in your printout. This is often due to low memory or insufficient disk space to print a page with lots of graphics. Try printing this page at a lower resolution.

`Device conflict`

Both a Windows and a DOS application are trying to use your printer at the same time. Stop one of the print jobs and allow the other to complete before resuming the first job.

`Device contention`

Both a Windows and a DOS application are trying to use your printer at the same time. Stop one of the print jobs and allow the other to complete before resuming the first job.

`Device is being used by another application`

This message is generated when a particular device is not loaded into memory. Use the pertinent setup or Control Panel to install the device.

`Directory` *xxx* `does not exist`

You have specified a directory that does not exist. Check the typing of the directory and path name. If you are using File Manager, select the **R**efresh option from the Window menu to refresh the current directory tree.

`Divide by zero`

This message generally results from software bugs. When it occurs, close Windows, reboot your computer, and then restart Windows and the problem application. If this message occurs with frequency, consult the publisher of the software.

`Disk error`

If Windows generates a disk-error message, it's normally because you're trying to use a bad or unformatted disk. If you receive a disk-error message, try another disk.

`Drive x: is inaccessible`

This message is displayed when a specified drive can't be accessed. Make sure you actually have a disk correctly inserted in the drive and that the disk is formatted. If the drive does exist, there may be a problem with your Windows setup.

`Error 20`

You're trying to print a document with a considerable amount of graphics or a large number of fonts to a Hewlett-Packard or HP-compatible printer. Your printer doesn't have enough memory to print the entire page, and your output will be incomplete. Simplify your document or print at a lower resolution.

`Error 21`

See `Error 20`.

`Extremely low on memory, close applications and try again`

This message results when your system doesn't have enough memory to run the application or perform the operation you specified. Just like the message suggests, close some applications and try the operation again. You may also need to exit Windows (to free up some unreleased memory), restart Windows, and then run the application or perform the operation.

`File xxx.xxx open -- Creation access denied`

You tried to create a new file that already existed and is currently open. Try renaming the file.

`File already exists. Overwrite?`

You're trying to create or save a file with a name that already exists. Windows is asking if you wish to overwrite the existing file. If so, answer yes. If no, answer no, and assign a new name to your file.

`File is missing`

When Windows loads, it attempts to load any programs that are included in the Startup program group. This message is generated when one of these files no longer exists or has been entered incorrectly. Open the Startup group and check all programs and associations, removing or editing those that are not correct.

`General printer error`

This message actually tells you that you're low on hard disk space (because Windows uses spare disk space to store information about printing in process). Delete some files from your hard disk and resume printing.

```
Group file is damaged
```

Sometimes Windows will delete or corrupt a program group file. Re-create the file by exiting Windows and typing **SETUP /P** at the DOS prompt.

```
Illegal disk change
```

You're trying to use SMARTDRV.EXE with a removable hard drive. Edit the SMARTDRV line in your AUTOEXEC.BAT file to exclude this particular drive by placing a minus sign after the drive letter, like this:

SMARTDRV.EXE *x-*

```
Incompatible display driver
```

The selected video driver is not supported by this version of Windows. Change your setup to include a compatible video driver, such as standard VGA.

```
Incorrect DOS Version
```

This message is usually generated when you have more than one version of the COMMAND.COM file on your hard disk. Instead of running the correct COMMAND.COM, Windows found an older or noncompatible version and tried to use it to run your DOS program. As you can see, this doesn't work. You want to hunt down and delete all instances of the COMMAND.COM file except those located in your DOS directory and/or your root directory (C:\). Then you can run your DOS program again, successfully this time.

```
Incorrect system version
```

This problem is caused by a certain Windows program called a "grabber." If you have the wrong version of the grabber file on your hard disk, you'll get this message. The solution is to erase the SETUP.INF file from your hard disk, then run the Windows Setup program and select a new video resolution. Close the Setup program, then run it again, this time selecting the correct video resolution. This will install the correct grabber for your system and let you run DOS programs in Windows.

```
Incorrect Windows version
```

Part of an old Windows version still coexists with your current Windows files. You may need to erase the file(s) in question and/or reinstall Windows.

```
Insufficient conventional memory
```

Your system does not have enough memory to perform the desired operation. Try closing some open applications and restarting the operation.

`Insufficient disk space`

Your system is short on hard disk space. Try deleting some unneeded files and then restarting the operation at hand.

`Insufficient file handles, increase files in CONFIG.SYS`

You need to increase the value of the FILES command in the CONFIG.SYS file for Windows to operate properly. See Chapter 3 for more information.

`Insufficient memory to run the application`

You're trying to launch a DOS program that needs more memory. Edit the associated PIF file to increase the KB Required to a larger number (512KB is good).

`Internal stack overflow`

This message is generated when DOS stacks are not configured correctly for Windows use.

`Invalid destination specified`

Windows displays this message when you try to copy a file to a directory or drive that doesn't exist. Check your commands and try this operation again.

`Invalid HIMEM.SYS`

The HIMEM.SYS file loaded into memory is incompatible with your version of Windows. (This happens when there is more than one version of this file on your hard disk.) Check your CONFIG.SYS file to make sure the path of the HIMEM.SYS driver points to the correct directory—most often the WINDOWS directory.

`No association exists for this file`

If no program file is associated with a data file you're trying to launch, you'll receive this message. To associate a program file with a data file extension, pull down the File menu, select the Associate option, and fill in the Associate dialog box.

`No COM ports available`

You're trying to add a new device to your Windows and all of your COM ports are filled. You'll need to uninstall one of your current devices before you can add the new device.

`Not a valid filename`

You typed an invalid file name for a file operation. Try typing a different file name. Remember, all files can have eight characters before the dot, and a three-character extension afterwards.

```
Not enough file handles
```

You need to increase the value of the FILES command in the CONFIG.SYS file for Windows to operate properly. See Chapter 3 for more information.

```
Not enough memory to load
```

You're trying to launch a DOS program that needs more memory. Edit the associated PIF file to increase the KB Required to a larger number (512KB is good).

```
Out of environment space
```

You're trying to run DOS under Windows and there isn't enough memory space to hold the entire DOS environment. Change the properties of the MS-DOS Prompt icon to read:

```
COMMAND.COM /E:512 /C
```

```
Out of memory
```

Windows has trouble running under low memory conditions. When this message is generated, try closing some open applications to free up memory space. If Windows continues to generate this message, exit Windows and reboot your system to free up any unreleased memory.

```
Parity error
```

This message most often results when something is wrong with your system memory. It's also possible that a power supply problem can cause this message. Whatever the cause, rebooting your system and restarting Windows generally clears things up.

```
PCL PRINTING WARNING: SOFT FONT PAGE LIMIT
```

This message is generated when you're using a Hewlett-Packard laser printer (or compatible) and you're using more than 16 fonts per page, which is the limit for an HP printer.

```
Permanent swap file corrupted
```

Windows uses a specified section of your hard disk to create a *swap file,* where data is temporarily stored during operations. This message is generated when something has corrupted your system's swap file. To rebuild your swap file (under Windows 3.1), open Control Panel and double-click on the 386 Enhanced icon. When the 386 Enhanced dialog box appears, select the Virtual Memory option. From the Virtual Memory dialog box, select the Change option to rebuild your swap file.

`Print queue is still active`

You're trying to exit Windows while a print job is still in progress. Select Cancel to return to the print job, and then exit Windows when printing is complete.

`PROGMAN.INI is deleted`

Sometimes Windows will delete or corrupt the file that holds the information about your program groups (PROGMAN.INI). Re-create this file by exiting Windows and typing **SETUP /P** at the DOS prompt.

`Program groups are missing`

Sometimes Windows will lose or scramble your program groups, often on a whim. If this happens to you, you can re-create your original program groups by exiting Windows and typing **SETUP /P** at the DOS prompt.

`Sector not found reading drive X`

Windows encountered a problem reading one of your drives, most probably due to a bad sector on the disk. If the drive is your hard drive, you may be developing a serious hard drive failure. Call a computer technician for advice.

`Setup Error Code S208`

This message results when you don't have enough disk space on your hard drive to install all of Windows. You'll need to delete some files from your hard drive and start over.

`Setup Error Code S209`

The message results when Setup, for some reason, tries to overwrite a file that your computer is currently using. It's possible you have some programs loaded automatically via your AUTOEXEC.BAT file; close these files and then try running Setup again.

`Setup Error Code S210`

This message results when Setup tries to overwrite a file that is write protected. You'll need to un-write protect the file in question. Generally the culprit is in the Windows directory or a subdirectory, and a simple DOS command can make all files in these directories read/write. Just change to the Windows directory and type the following command at the DOS prompt:

ATTRIB -R *.* /S

`Setup Error Code S211`

Your system didn't give Setup enough memory to do its job. Check to see if you have any other programs (including memory-resident programs) running, and then close them and run Setup again.

`Setup Error Code S212`

This message results when you're installing a new version of Windows over a previous version on your hard disk. Sometimes certain older files have the same names as newer files to be installed and this screws up Setup. The best solution here is to totally delete all your old files from your Windows directories and subdirectories, and install your new version of Windows to your now clean hard disk.

`Setup Error Code S213`

See `Setup Error Code 211`.

`Setup Error Code 214`

This message results when Setup cannot read a file on your installation disk. Most often this is caused by a bad or corrupted disk, although a bad disk drive can also be the culprit. You should call Microsoft or your dealer to get a replacement set of installation disks.

`Setup Error Code S020`

You're trying to install Windows 3.1 over an older version of Windows and your old WIN.INI file is too large. Try editing the WIN.INI file to remove unneeded portions, and then run Setup again.

`SHARE is installed`

SHARE is a DOS TSR that Windows often doesn't like, and in this case, won't work with a specific Windows application. Edit your AUTOEXEC.BAT file to remove the SHARE command, and then reboot your system.

`SOUNDCARD ERROR: DRIVER.XXX not installed`

This error occurs when the driver for your sound card is not being installed, cannot be found, or is not listed in your SYSTEM.INI file. Check your sound card installation (perhaps even reinstall it) before proceeding.

`Standard mode switcher is not running`

If this message appears while you're running Setup, chances are you have a bad SETUP.INF file on your installation disk; you'll need to obtain a new set of installation disks. If this message occurs at any other time, you have a bad WIN.COM or DSWAP.EXE file. You'll need to rerun the Windows Setup program to install working versions of these files.

`SUBST installed`

SUBST is a DOS TSR that Windows doesn't like. Edit your AUTOEXEC.BAT file to remove the SUBST command, and then reboot your system.

`System Error`

This is similar to a GPF or UAE for your hardware. When some part of the system stops working, this message is generated. You'll see it often when something is wrong with your disk drives—like you're using an unformatted disk or you forgot to close the disk drive door. Cancel out and fix your problem before retrying the operation.

`The printer on LPT1 is offline or not selected`

This message appears when your printer is not ready to print. It may be off-line or out of paper. Check your printer and press the Retry button to resume the print job.

`The specified path is invalid`

You typed an incorrect directory path for a file operation. Check the path and retype the command.

`This application has violated system integrity`

This is a general protection fault generated by a DOS application within Windows, normally caused by a memory conflict. You'll need to close the application, exit Windows, and reboot your computer before continuing.

`Unable to load KRNL386.EXE`

This message can be generated if the KRNL386.EXE file has been deleted or corrupted. You may need to reinstall Windows to get a new copy of this file into your Windows directory.

`Unable to start Enhanced Mode`

Windows cannot start in enhanced mode due to a low memory situation or hardware incompatibility. Increase system memory, or restart Windows in standard mode by typing **WIN /S.**

`Windows will not use more than the virtual memory specified`
`by the Recommended Size.`
`Are you sure you want to create a larger swap file?`

This message occurs when you use Control Panel to increase the size of Windows' permanent swap file. It's really a bug; Windows will use whatever size swap file you specify, so go ahead with what you were doing.

```
Write protected disk
```

You're trying to perform a file operation on a floppy disk that is write-protected. Change disks, uncover the write-protect notch (on 5 1/4-inch disks), or slide the write-protect tab into the down position (on 3 1/2-inch disks).

```
You cannot format the current drive
```

You're trying to format a floppy disk that is write-protected. Change disks, uncover the write-protect notch (on 5 1/4-inch disks), or slide the write-protect tab into the down position (on 3 1/2-inch disks).

```
You can't run this application while other applications are
running full-screen
```

If you're using Windows 3.0, you can't run a graphical DOS program in a window; it must run in full-screen mode.

```
You must have WINA20.386 in the root directory of the drive
you booted from
```

(Windows 3.0 only.) Windows needs the WINA20.386 file to load. The file should be located in the root directory of your hard drive. If this file is not in your root directory, reinstall Windows to copy this file to your hard disk.

DOS Error Messages...

What They Mean and How To Deal with Them

CHAPTER TWENTY-EIGHT

This chapter lists the most common DOS error messages in alphabetical order. Along with each listing, I include a probable cause of the message and a recommended course of action to take.

For more information on DOS itself, see Chapter 3—or read Chapter 21 to learn how to troubleshoot specific DOS problems. Because this book is not intended to be a comprehensive DOS guide, I recommend reading Que's *Using MS-DOS 6.2*, Special Edition, for a more comprehensive discussion on DOS commands and error messages.

`/B invalid with black and white printer`

You were using the GRAPHICS command with the /B switch to print a screen and included the background color; unfortunately, you do not have a color printer connected to your system. Try the command again, but without the /B switch this time.

`A BAD UMB number has been specified`

In DOS 6, you attempted to use the LOADHIGH command in your AUTOEXEC.BAT file with the /L parameter referring to a nonexistent UMB area. You can either fix this yourself or use MemMaker to find the right UMB area for you.

```
A program was run that took memory that Backup
requires. The program must be removed from memory before
Backup can continue
```

You have installed a memory-resident program that uses too much memory, taking memory needed for Microsoft Backup to run. You must unload the program before rerunning Microsoft Backup.

`Abort, Retry, Fail?`

This message—or its kissing cousin, `Abort, Retry, Ignore?`—appears in conjunction with other DOS messages and gives you three options. You can abort the operation, which cancels all work in process and returns you to the DOS prompt. You can retry the operation, which starts the operation over again, in the hope that two wrongs make a right. Or you choose Fail, which continues the operation from the point at which it encountered an error, but that choice may incorporate the error into the results of the operation. I recommend that you retry things a time or two first, and then if that doesn't work, abort. As a last resort, choose Fail. If none of these work, you'll have to reboot.

`Access denied`

You tried to change or erase a read-only file or a file that is currently open. Either close the open file or use the ATTRIB command to change the file's attributes before you try again.

`Active Code Page not available from CON device`

You used the KEYB command with an unsupported code page. Check your code page and try again.

```
All available space in the Extended DOS Partition is assigned
to logical drives
```

You're trying to format a large hard disk, and there is no room in the extended partition for additional logical drives. Use FDISK to change the size of the extended partition before you continue.

```
All files in directory will be deleted!
Are you sure (Y/N)?
```

This warning appears when you issue the DEL *.* command. DOS just wants you to be sure that you want to erase every file in the specified directory. Press Y to confirm or N to wimp out.

```
Allocation error, size adjusted
```

You're running CHKDSK, and DOS has noted a discrepancy between the size of a file in the directory table and the amount of data allocated to the file; DOS has truncated the file. Use CHKDSK /F to correct the discrepancy.

```
An incompatible DOSKey is already installed
```

The version of DOSKEY that you're running is incompatible with the version of DOS installed on your system. Delete DOSKEY.COM from your hard disk, and copy the DOSKEY.COM file from your original DOS disks to your hard disk. Also, it's possible that you have more than one copy of DOSKEY.COM on your disk; delete one.

```
ANSI.SYS must be installed to perform requested
function
```

You invoked the MODE command to request a screen function that can't be executed unless the ANSI.SYS device driver is loaded, and it isn't. Edit your CONFIG.SYS file to include the line DEVICE=C:\DOS\ANSI.SYS, reboot your system, and then use the MODE command.

```
APPEND/ASSIGN Conflict
```

You tried to use APPEND on an ASSIGNed drive. Cancel the drive assignment before retrying the APPEND command.

```
Attempted write-protect violation
```

You tried to format a write-protected floppy disk. If you really want to format the disk, you must remove the write-protect tab (5 1/4-inch disks) or move the write-protect shutter into the down position (3 1/2-inch disks).

```
ATTENTION: A serious disk error has occurred while writing to
drive
```

SmartDrive detected a hard disk error when trying to write from memory to your hard disk. The data that was supposed to be written to the disk is probably lost. You should check out your hard disk at your earliest convenience.

`Bad call format error`

A device driver was given a header with an incorrect length because a bug in the software program made the call. Call your software publisher's technical-support line for help.

`Bad command error`

A device driver was issued a bad command because a bug in the software program issued the command. Call your software publisher's technical-support line for help.

`Bad command or filename`

You entered an incorrect name for a command, program, or batch file. You may have simply mistyped the name, or perhaps you forgot to enter the complete directory path. Check the spelling and syntax of the command, and try again—but more carefully this time.

`Bad format call error`

DOS received a bad format call because of a bug in the software program's device driver. Call your software publisher's technical-support line for help.

`Bad or Missing Command Interpreter`

If you receive this message on startup, it means that DOS cannot find the COMMAND.COM file. If you're booting from a floppy disk, remove the current disk and replace it with one that contains COMMAND.COM. If you're booting from your hard disk, several problems may cause this error message to appear; see Chapter 8 for some hints. If this message appears in the middle of a DOS session, COMMAND.COM has somehow been erased from your hard disk. Reboot from your Bootable Emergency Disk, and copy COMMAND.COM from the disk back to your hard disk.

`Bad or missing filename`

You receive this message during the booting process if a device driver referenced in your CONFIG.SYS file was not found. Check the file to make sure that the command is typed correctly, and make certain that the file really does reside where it's supposed to.

`Bad or Missing Keyboard definition file`

You tried to use the KEYB command, and DOS couldn't find the KEYBOARD.SYS file. Check to make sure that KEYBOARD.SYS is where it's supposed to be. If not, copy the file from your original DOS disks to your hard disk. If it *is* where it's supposed to be, this message indicates that the file may be corrupted, so go ahead and make a new copy from your DOS disks.

`Bad Partition Table`

You ran FORMAT on a hard disk, and DOS was unable to find a DOS partition. You need to run FDISK before you run FORMAT on any hard disk.

`Bad unit error`

A device driver received an invalid subunit number because of a bug in the software program. Call your software publisher's technical-support line for help.

`Batch file missing`

You were running a batch file, and DOS misplaced the file. This generally happens when you're running a long batch file from a floppy disk and accidentally remove the disk from your drive before the batch file has finished running. Replace the disk, and restart the batch file.

`Baud rate required`

You tried to run the MODE command without indicating the proper baud rate. Rerun the command with this information included.

`Cannot change BUFSIZE`

You tried to change the DOSKEY buffer. You can't do that!

`Cannot CHDIR to path--tree past this point not processed`

For some reason, CHKDSK was unable to go to the specified directory. Because of this, no subdirectories below this directory have been checked. Run CHKDSK /F to correct this error.

`Cannot CHDIR to root`

For some reason, CHKDSK was unable to return to your disk's root directory. Because of this, no remaining subdirectories have been checked. Reboot your computer and try again. If you continue to receive this command, your disk is bad and must be reformatted.

`Cannot Chkdsk a Network drive`

You tried to run CHKDSK on a drive that is assigned to a network. You can't do that!

`Cannot Chkdsk a SUBSTed or ASSIGNed drive`

You tried to run CHKDSK on a drive that has been substituted or assigned. You can't do that!

```
Cannot create a zero size partition
```

You were using FDISK on a hard disk drive and tried to create a partition of zero percent. Sorry to have to be the one to tell you this, but you must assign a minimum of 1 percent (or 1M) to any partition you create.

```
Cannot create extended DOS partition without primary DOS
partition on disk x
```

You were using FDISK on a hard disk drive, and you tried to create an extended DOS partition before you assigned a primary DOS partition. This is backward. You must first create a primary DOS partition, and then you can create an extended DOS partition.

```
Cannot create Logical DOS drive without an Extended DOS
Partition on the current drive
```

You were using FDISK on a hard disk drive and tried to create a logical drive before you created an extended DOS partition. Create your extended DOS partition first, and then create your logical drive.

```
Cannot delete Extended DOS Partition while logical drives
exist
```

You were using FDISK on a hard disk drive and tried to delete an extended DOS partition while it still contained one or more logical drives. Delete the drive(s) first, and then delete the partition.

```
Cannot DISKCOMP to or from a network drive
```

You tried to use DISKCOMP with a drive on a network. You can't do that!

```
Cannot DISKCOMP to or from an ASSIGNed or SUBSTed drive
```

You tried to use DISKCOMP on a drive created with the ASSIGN or SUBST commands. You can't do that!

```
Cannot DISKCOPY to or from a network drive
```

You tried to copy a floppy disk to a drive that is assigned to a network. Sorry, but DISKCOPY can't work with network drives. Use COPY *.* instead.

```
Cannot do binary reads from a device
```

You tried to use the /B switch to copy from a device. Unfortunately, you can't do binary (/B) reads from a device. Use the COPY command with the /A switch (to create an ASCII copy) or by itself.

```
Cannot edit BAK file--rename file
```

You tried to use the EDLIN text editor to edit a file with a BAK extension (a backup file). Surprise! EDLIN won't let you do that. Either quit while you're ahead, or rename the file's extension to something other than BAK.

`Cannot find file QBASIC.EXE`

DOS went looking for QBASIC and couldn't find it. Make sure that you have QBASIC on your hard disk before you try this operation again.

`Cannot find FORMAT.EXE`

You were running a BACKUP procedure with an unformatted floppy disk, and DOS couldn't find the FORMAT command. Copy FORMAT.EXE from your original DOS disks to your hard disk, and try this one again.

`Cannot find GRAPHICS profile`

You tried to use the GRAPHICS command and did not include the path of the GRAPHICS.PRO file. Try the command again, specifying the complete directory path this time.

`Cannot find System Files`

DOS couldn't find the system files in the root directory of the current disk. This can happen if you're trying to issue commands from a floppy disk that has not been made bootable. Try switching to your hard disk or inserting a bootable disk in your disk drive.

`Cannot FORMAT a network drive`

You tried to format a disk that is part of a network, and DOS won't let you do that.

`Cannot format an ASSIGNed or SUBSTed drive`

You tried to format a disk that was created with the ASSIGN or SUBST commands. You need to run ASSIGN or SUBST again to remove the assignments before you can format this drive.

`Cannot FORMAT nonremovable drive x:`

You tried to format a hard disk with the FORMAT /F command. Because the /F switch is for floppy disks only, this was a mistake. Run FORMAT without this switch next time.

`Cannot JOIN a Network drive`

You tried to use the JOIN command on network drives. You can't do that!

`Cannot LABEL a Network drive`

You can't use the LABEL command on network drives either. (And why would you want to, anyway?)

`Cannot LABEL a SUBSTed or ASSIGNed drive`

Guess what? You can't even use the LABEL command on drives created with the SUBST or ASSIGN commands.

```
Cannot load COMMAND, system halted
```

Whoa! This is a big one! Either COMMAND.COM was erased from your disk, or you have a bad sector on your disk where COMMAND.COM was supposed to be. Reboot your computer from the Bootable Emergency Disk, and copy COMMAND.COM from the disk to your hard disk. Then reboot your system from the hard disk. It's also possible you have an incorrect or missing SHELL statement in your CONFIG.SYS file; check the file for accuracy. If these steps don't fix the problem, see Chapter 8.

```
Cannot loadhigh batch file
```

You tried to use the LOADHIGH command in your AUTOEXEC.BAT file to load another batch file (BAT extension). You can't do that!

```
Cannot move multiple files to a single file
```

You used the MOVE command with wild cards for the source file and a specific name for the destination file—in other words, you tried to move multiple source files to a single file destination. You can't do that, so go back and retype the command, either without the wild cards or with a directory destination instead of a file destination.

```
Cannot perform a cyclic copy
```

You tried to use XCOPY /S to copy the current directory and its subdirectories, but you specified one of these subdirectories as the target of the copy. This is called a *circular reference*, and you can't do this. Copy these files somewhere else.

```
Cannot read file allocation table
```

Your FAT is in a bad sector on a defective disk. This is a big deal. See Chapter 8 for help on this one.

```
Cannot recover .. entry,
Entry has a bad attribute (or link or size)
```

CHKDSK has discovered that the parent directory to the current directory is defective and cannot be recovered. Try running the CHKDSK /F command to correct the error.

```
Cannot recover .. entry, processing continued
```

CHKDSK has discovered that the current directory is defective and cannot be recovered. Try running the CHKDSK /F command to correct the error.

```
Cannot RECOVER a Network drive
```

You tried to use the RECOVER command on a drive assigned to a network. You can't do that!

`Cannot setup expanded memory`

Your expanded memory (EMS) card is not functioning correctly. Call a technician to get it fixed.

`Cannot specify default drive`

You were using the SYS command to make a disk bootable and specified the same source and target drives (that is, you typed **SYS A: A:**). Well, you can't do that, so check the command and correct whichever drive was the wrong one.

`Cannot start COMMAND, exiting`

You (or one of your programs) tried to load a second copy of COMMAND.COM, but DOS couldn't do it—probably because you didn't have enough memory or because your FILES command was set too low in your CONFIG.SYS file. If you really want to do this, edit your CONFIG.SYS file to increase the FILES statement. Running two command interpreters at the same time really isn't a good idea, however, so why don't you just give it a rest, huh?

`Cannot SUBST a network drive`

You can't substitute drives that have been assigned to a network—so don't do this again, okay?

`Cannot SYS a Network drive`

You can't transfer system files to a network drive. (Have you noticed that DOS doesn't let you do very much to network drives?)

`Cannot use FASTOPEN for drive x:`

You tried to use FASTOPEN on a drive that isn't allowed, such as a network drive or a floppy disk drive. You also may have tried to use FASTOPEN on more than four disks at one time, which you can't do.

`Cannot use PRINT - Use NET PRINT`

You tried to use the PRINT command over a network. Either use the NET PRINT command, or consult your system administrator.

`Cannot XCOPY from a reserved device`

You tried to use XCOPY with a printer or communications device as the source, which you can't do. If you want to use XCOPY, make sure that you're copying *from* a disk!

`Cannot XCOPY to a reserved device`

You tried to use XCOPY with a printer or communications device as the destination, which you can't do. If you want to use XCOPY, make sure that you're copying to another disk.

`CHDIR .. failed, trying alternative method`

You were running CHKDSK, and it wasn't able to return to a parent directory, so now it's trying to get there by taking a different route. If the new route doesn't work out either, you'll probably get another error message in a few seconds.

`Code page not prepared`

You used the MODE command and selected an incorrect or unprepared code page. Either change the code page or prepare it with the MODE PREPARE command.

`Code page operation not supported on this device`

You used the MODE command and selected an incorrect device/code page combination. Check your selection and correct it as necessary.

`Code page requested xxx is not valid for given`
`keyboard code`

You used the KEYB command and selected an incompatible keyboard code/code page combination. Check your selection and correct it as necessary.

`Code page specified has not been designated`

You used the KEYB command with an unrecognized code page. Either change the code page or prepare the code page with the MODE PREPARE command.

`Code page specified is inconsistent with invoked code page`

You used the KEYB command with an option that's not compatible with your console's code page. Either change the option or change the code page.

`Code page specified is inconsistent with selected code page`

You used the KEYB command with an option that's not compatible with your console's code page. Either change the option or change the code page.

`Code page xxx not prepared for all devices`

You used the CHCP command with a code page that's not supported by a device. Either change the code page or prepare the code page with the MODE PREPARE command.

`Code page xxx not prepared for system`

You used the CHCP command with a code page that's not supported by your system. Either change the code page or prepare the code page with the MODE PREPARE command.

`Code pages cannot be prepared`

You either tried to use a duplicate code page for a specified device or you used the MODE PREPARE command and specified more code pages than DOS supports. Check your CONFIG.SYS file to see how many prepared code pages your device command line accepts.

`Compare process ended`

You were using the DISKCOMP command and DOS encountered a fatal error, which killed the entire process. You may have a bad file or a bad disk.

`Configuration too large for memory`

At startup, DOS didn't load because either the FILES or BUFFERS statements in your CONFIG.SYS file were set too high or the /E switch in your SHELL command was set too high. Reboot from the Bootable Emergency Disk and edit your CONFIG.SYS file. Then fix whatever is wrong and reboot.

`Content of destination lost before copy`

You were using the COPY command and specified the same source and target files, so DOS just overwrote the original contents with nonsense. This is pretty bad because Undelete generally doesn't work with over-written data. You're probably out of luck—be more careful next time!

`Copy process ended`

You were using the DISKCOPY command, and it terminated because of some error. Try using COPY or XCOPY instead.

`Current drive is no longer valid`

For some reason, DOS thinks your current drive really isn't there. This normally happens if you're logged onto a disk drive and you remove the disk or when you choose Fail at the `Abort, Retry, Fail?` prompt. Switch to your hard disk and resume operations.

`Current keyboard does not support this code page`

You selected a code page/keyboard page combination that is incompatible. Change one or the other.

```
Data error
```

DOS couldn't read or write the specified data, probably because your disk has a bad spot. See Chapter 14 for more information on this phenomenon.

```
Device ddd not prepared
```

You tried to specify a device that didn't have a code page prepared. Use the MODE PREPARE command to fix this.

```
Directory already exists
```

You (or a program) tried to create a directory that has the same name as an existing directory. Either rename your new directory or remove the old directory before attempting the procedure again.

```
Disk boot failure
```

Ooooh, another bad one! This error occurred when DOS tried to load the IBMBIO.COM and IBMDOS.COM files into memory, but one of them was missing or corrupted. Try rebooting again; if you still get this message, read Chapter 8.

```
Disk full. Edits lost.
```

You were using the EDLIN text editor, and it couldn't save your work because the selected disk was full. Delete some files from the disk and try again.

```
Disk unsuitable for system disk
```

You were using FORMAT with the /S switch (to make a bootable disk), but DOS detected bad sectors where the system files should be placed. You may try running FORMAT /S again, but if you continue to get this message, the disk is bad and should be discarded.

```
Divide overflow
```

You were running a program that tried to divide by zero, and the program crashed. If this program continues to generate such messages, report the bug to the software publisher's technical-support line.

```
Do not specify filename(s) Command format: DISKCOMP drive1:
drive2: [/1] [/8]
```

You were using the DISKCOMP command and typed an incorrect switch or file name. Try it again, but type more carefully this time.

```
Do not specify filename(s) Command format: DISKCOPY drive1:
drive2: [/1] [/v]
```

You were using the DISKCOPY command and typed an incorrect switch or file name. Try it again, but type more carefully this time.

`DOS memory-arena error`

You were using the DOS Editor and generated a serious memory error. To be safe, reboot your computer.

`DoubleSpace found Crosslink between files X: and X:`

This can happen if your drive is too full (90 percent or more utilized) or if your EMM386 command line in the CONFIG.SYS file has a HIGHSCAN parameter.

To correct the cross-linked entries, run the CHKDSK /F command (or the DBLSPACE /CHKDSK /F command) from the DOS prompt.

`Drive assignment syntax error`

In DOS 6, INTERLNK found a syntax error in its command line. Retype the line correctly.

`Drive not ready error`

DOS tried to read or write to the disk drive, but couldn't. If you're using a floppy drive, make sure that the disk is correctly inserted and the drive door closed. It's possible, too, that the selected drive has not yet been formatted. Check all these possibilities, and then try repeating the operation.

`Drive types or disk types not compatible`

You were using DISKCOMP or DISKCOPY, and the two disks were not the same size or density. Try it again with similar disks.

`Duplicate filename or File not found`

You were using the REN command, and you tried to change a file name to a name that already exists. Either that, or the file to be renamed wasn't where you said it would be. Check what you were doing and try again.

`EOF mark not found`

You were using the COMP command to compare two text files, and DOS couldn't find the normal end-of-file mark. (This means that something was wrong with one of the two files.)

`Error in COUNTRY command`

The COUNTRY command has been inserted into your CONFIG.SYS file but used incorrectly. Edit your CONFIG.SYS file to fix the problem.

`Error in EXE file`

DOS tried to load an EXE file and detected an error. You need to recopy the program from its original disks.

```
Error loading operating system
```

DOS couldn't load itself into memory on startup. See Chapter 8 for information on this and similar problems.

```
Error reading directory
```

You were formatting a disk, but DOS was unable to read the directory because of bad sectors in the disk's FAT. If this happens with a floppy disk, throw it away. If it happens with a hard disk, consult an expert.

```
Error reading (or writing) partition table
```

You were running FORMAT on a hard disk and encountered a corrupted partition table. Run FDISK on the disk, and then try formatting again.

```
Error writing to file on remote system
```

In DOS 6, INTERSVR has detected that the remote system has a write error, most likely because the disk is full. Delete some files and try the operation again.

```
EXEC failure
```

If this error occurs while you're copying files, you probably have a bad destination disk. If this occurs during other situations, your FILES setting in your CONFIG.SYS file is low. Increase the number of FILES to at least 20.

```
Extended Error
```

COMMAND.COM has detected an error but can't provide a normal error message because the disk containing the COMMAND.COM file is missing. Insert the disk containing COMMAND.COM into drive A and try the operation again—see what kind of error message you get this time!

```
FCB unavailable error
```

You loaded SHARE.EXE, and one of your programs tried to open more file-control blocks than were specified with the FCBS command. Abort the operation and edit your CONFIG.SYS file to increase the FCBS setting by four. Then reboot your system.

```
File allocation table bad, drive d
Abort, Retry, Fail?
```

DOS found a problem in the FAT on the specified drive. Retry the operation a few times; if that doesn't work, abort the operation. If this happens on a floppy disk, try copying all files to another disk and then discard the bad disk. If this happens on your hard disk, see Chapter 6 for instructions.

`File cannot be copied onto itself`

You tried to copy a file to a directory that contained a file with the same name. Check your file names and then try again.

`File creation error`

Either DOS or a program failed to add a new file as instructed. The file could be marked as read-only; you can use the ATTRIB command to fix this. It's possible, too, that the directory is full; if so, delete some files before you go much farther. It's also possible that DOS is trying to write to a nonexistent directory.

`File not found`

DOS couldn't find the specified file. It's either not where you think it is (meaning that you need to check and specify the entire directory path) or you mistyped the file name. Check these possibilities and try again.

`Filename device driver cannot be initialized`

You tried to load a device in your CONFIG.SYS file, but something went wrong. Edit CONFIG.SYS to check the spelling of the device, as well as the directory path.

`FIRST disk bad or incompatible`

You used the DISKCOMP command, and the source disk is either unreadable or a different density from the second disk. Change disks and try again.

`Format not supported on drive x:`

You tried to use FORMAT on a drive that doesn't support the device parameters you selected. Check your CONFIG.SYS file for any discrepancies in the DEVICE commands.

`General failure error`

You get this message when something is wrong, but DOS doesn't know what. It often results from using an unformatted disk, trying to access a disk in a drive that has an open door, inserting a disk incorrectly in the drive, or using the wrong density disk in a disk drive.

`Illegal device name`

You used the MODE command, and DOS doesn't recognize the device name. Check your work and try again.

`Incorrect DOS version`

You tried to execute a DOS command or utility from a different version of DOS than that of the current command interpreter. You may have to copy the command from your original DOS disks to your hard disk.

```
Incorrect parameter
```

You just issued a command with at least one wrong parameter. Check the parameters for this command and then try it again.

```
Insufficient disk space
```

You don't have enough free space on your disk to do whatever it is you wanted to do. Delete some unwanted files and try again.

```
Insufficient memory
```

Your system doesn't have enough free RAM to execute the program or command. Try closing some programs and then retry the operation. If this happens to you frequently, you probably need to add more memory to your system.

```
Insufficient memory to store macro. Use the DOSKEY command
with the /BUFSIZE switch to increase available memory
```

You're using a lot of DOSKEY macros and have filled up all the allocated memory space. Use the /BUFSIZE switch with the DOSKEY command to increase the macro memory area.

```
Intermediate file error during pipe
```

This message is generated when DOS can't create a temporary file needed to pipe information between two programs. It generally means that your disk is full, and you should delete some unwanted files.

```
Internal stack overflow
System halted
```

DOS and/or your programs have used up all the memory space reserved for temporary use. You need to reboot your system to get going again. It's likely that this error was a fluke. If you keep receiving this error message, however, increase the value of the STACKS command in your CONFIG.SYS file.

```
Invalid /BAUD parameter
```

In DOS 6, you selected an illegal baud rate for either INTERLNK or INTERSVR. Select another baud rate to continue.

```
Invalid characters in volume label
```

You were assigning a label to a disk and either entered more than 11 characters or used some forbidden characters. Try it again, but get it right this time!

```
Invalid COMMAND.COM, system halted
```

DOS couldn't find COMMAND.COM on your hard disk and halted your system. Try rebooting to see what happens; if you get this message again, you have problems. See Chapter 8 for information.

```
Invalid COMMAND.COM in drive d:
```

For some reason, the version of COMMAND.COM that DOS just tried to access was a different version from the one that it was originally running. This generally happens only when you're booting from a floppy disk and accidentally place the wrong bootable disk in your system. Just be careful and try not to keep so many different versions of COMMAND.COM floating around your desk.

```
Invalid COUNTRY code or code page
```

You used the COUNTRY command in your CONFIG.SYS file and got it wrong. Edit your CONFIG.SYS file to correct the error.

```
Invalid date
```

You entered an impossible date or used an invalid separating character. Try entering the date again, but look at what you're doing this time.

```
Invalid device parameters from device driver
```

You probably have a bad DEVICE command in your CONFIG.SYS file. Edit the file to correct any mistakes.

```
Invalid directory
```

Oops! You messed up when you entered a directory name. Check to make sure that the directory name is the one you really wanted to type and that the directory really is where you think it is.

```
Invalid disk change
Abort, Retry, Fail?
```

You changed the disk in your disk drive before DOS was done with it. Place the correct disk back in the drive, and retry the operation.

```
Invalid drive in search path
```

You specified an invalid disk drive in your PATH command. Edit your AUTOEXEC.BAT file to correct your PATH statement.

```
Invalid drive or file name
```

You typed a nonexistent drive or file name. Check your work and type it again.

```
Invalid drive specification
```

You either mistyped the drive letter or specified the same drive for both source and target in an operation. Check your work and try again.

```
Invalid drive specification
Specified drive does not exist or is non-removable
```

You mistyped the drive letter or specified a hard disk in an operation that only works with floppy disks. Check your work and try again.

```
Invalid environment size specified
```

In the SHELL command in your CONFIG.SYS file, you specified an incorrect argument for the /E switch. Edit the file and check this line; you can't use any number less than 160 or more than 32,768. Also, you can't include commas in the number.

```
Invalid keyboard code specified
```

You were using the KEYB command and selected an invalid code. Check your work and try again.

```
Invalid macro definition
```

You were using DOSKEY and tried to create a macro with an incorrect command. Check your work and carefully retype your macro.

```
Invalid media or Track 0 bad - disk unusable
```

You're trying to format a disk that is damaged. Try running FORMAT a second time; if it still doesn't take, trash the disk.

```
Invalid number of parameters
```

You tried to issue a command and included either too many or too few parameters. (It's a common error to include too many spaces in between parameters.) Check your work and try again.

```
Invalid parameter
```

You just issued a command with at least one wrong parameter. Check the parameters for this command and then try it again.

```
Invalid parameter combination
```

You issued a command and used two parameters that give conflicting instructions to DOS. Check your parameters and try again.

```
Invalid partition table
```

On startup, DOS detected a problem in your hard disk's partition information. See Chapter 8 for help with this situation.

```
Invalid path
```

In the PATH statement in your AUTOEXEC.BAT file, you mistyped a directory name, included some illegal characters, or made your path more than 63 characters long. Edit your AUTOEXEC.BAT file to correct the problem.

```
Invalid path or file name
```

You typed a path or file name that is wrong. Check your work, make sure that everything is where it's supposed to be, and try it again.

```
Invalid STACK parameter
```

You used the STACKS command in your CONFIG.SYS file, and something is typed wrong. Edit the CONFIG.SYS file, and correct any mistakes.

```
Invalid switch character
```

You loaded VDISK in your CONFIG.SYS file, but you included a switch other than the /E switch. Edit your CONFIG.SYS file to correct this mistake.

```
Invalid time
```

You entered an impossible time or used an invalid separating character. Try entering the time again, but look at what you're doing this time around.

```
Invalid Volume ID
```

You were formatting a disk and entered an incorrect volume label. The format is good, fortunately, but if you still want to assign a volume label, you'll have to use the LABEL command.

```
Lock violation error
```

You loaded SHARE.EXE or network software, and a program tried to access a locked file. You can retry the operation, but you'll probably have to abort the operation because it's illegal.

```
Memory allocation error
Cannot load COMMAND, system halted
```

One of your programs messed up that area of memory where DOS is loaded. You must reboot your system. If this problem reoccurs, you have a bug in your software that should be reported to the software publisher's technical-support line.

```
MIRROR cannot operate with a network
```

In DOS 5, you can't use MIRROR if your hard disk is assigned to a network. Unload MIRROR from your AUTOEXEC.BAT file or unassign your hard disk from the network. (Not a problem under DOS 6, which doesn't use MIRROR.)

```
Missing operating system
```

Your system can't find DOS at startup. See Chapter 8 for some ideas on how to deal with this perfidious problem.

```
MSBACKUP program files must be located on your hard disk.
You cannot start MSBACKUP from a floppy disk.
```

In DOS 6, you tried to use Microsoft Backup from a floppy disk (perhaps from your Bootable Emergency Disk), and it can only run from a hard disk. Copy the program file to your hard disk, and then run the program.

```
Must enter both /T and /N parameters
```

You've entered the FORMAT command and forgotten to specify either the /T or /N parameters. Check your work and try again.

```
Must specify COM1, COM2, COM3, or COM4
```

You used the MODE command and forgot to specify the COM port. Re-enter the command, but include the COM port this time.

```
No free file handles
Cannot start COMMAND, exiting
```

You tried to start a second copy of COMMAND.COM, but there wasn't enough memory available. Try increasing the number of FILES in the CONFIG.SYS file.

```
No paper error
```

Your printer is out of paper or isn't turned on. Check the thing, fix the problem, and then retry the operation.

```
No room for system on destination disk
```

You're trying to make a bootable disk with the SYS command, but there isn't room on the disk for the system files. If you really want to make this disk bootable, you'll have to reformat it with the FORMAT /S command.

```
No serial ports were found
```

In DOS 6, you specified the /COM switch while using INTERSVR, but no serial ports were available. It's possible that a memory-resident program took control of the available port, your hardware is configured incorrectly, or there really aren't any available serial ports!

```
No system on default drive
```

You're trying to use the SYS command, but the system files aren't on the source disk. Try running SYS from another bootable disk.

```
No target drive specified
```

You issued the BACKUP command but forgot to specify the target drive. Retype the command, and include the target drive this time.

```
Non-DOS disk error
```

The FAT on the specified disk is unusable. This normally happens when you try to use a floppy disk formatted for use on another operating system (using a 3 1/2-inch disk formatted on a Macintosh, for example).

```
Non-System disk or disk error
Replace and strike any key when ready
```

This happens when you start your system and there is a non-bootable disk in drive A. Remove the disk and reboot.

```
Not enough memory
```

Your system doesn't have enough free RAM to execute the program or command. Try closing some programs and then retry the operation. If this happens to you often, you probably should add more memory to your system.

```
Not ready...
```

The specified device is not ready and can't receive and/or transmit data. Check all your connections, make sure that the floppy disk is formatted and inserted correctly, and then retry the operation.

```
Out of environment space
```

You're trying to add strings to your environment with the SET command and the environment can't be expanded. Use the SHELL command to expand your environment space.

```
Out of memory
```

You're using the DOS Editor and you ran out of memory. Close some programs and try again.

```
Packed file is corrupt
```

One of two things has happened. The first is, for some reason, a program file could not load into the first 64K of memory. Use the LOADFIX command to load the program into memory above 64K. The second possible cause is a damaged program file that may need to be reinstalled.

```
Parameter format not correct - parm
```

You entered a command with a parameter that used an incorrect form. Check for the proper use of the slash character (/), as well as colons used with drive designations.

```
Parameters not compatible with fixed disk
```

You tried to load a device driver for a hard disk that does not support generic IOCtl functions. (Don't ask what these are—it's too complicated for us normal folks!) Check with the manufacturer for instructions on how to proceed.

Parameters not supported

You tried to issue a command with incorrect parameters. Check the possible parameters and try again.

Parameters not supported by drive

You tried to issue a command with incorrect parameters. Check the possible parameters and try again.

Parse Error

COMMAND.COM has detected an error, but can't provide a normal error message because the disk containing the COMMAND.COM file is missing. Insert the disk containing COMMAND.COM into drive A and try the operation again—see what kind of error message you get this time!

Path not found

You specified an incorrect directory path. Check your work, make sure that everything is where it's supposed to be, and try again.

Path too long

Your PATH statement in your AUTOEXEC.BAT file exceeds the 63-character limit. Edit your AUTOEXEC.BAT file to shorten your PATH statement.

Program too big to fit into memory

You tried to start a program that won't run on your current system. Try closing some programs to free up memory for the new program. If the problem persists, you should add more RAM to your system. You also may be running an older program under DOS 5 or 6. If so, run SETVER so that the old program can run with your new DOS.

Read fault error

DOS couldn't read the specified data from the disk. Make sure that the disk is inserted properly, and then retry the operation.

Required parameter missing

You left out part of the parameter list needed to execute a command. Check your work and retype the command, complete with the required parameter.

Same parameter entered twice

You typed a command and duplicated a switch. Check your work and try again.

SECOND disk bad or incompatible

You used the DISKCOMP command, and the target disk is either unreadable or of a different density from the first disk. Fix the problem and try again.

`Sector not found`

The specified disk sector couldn't be accessed. Normally this indicates a bad disk.

`Sector size too large in file filename`

The specified device driver is bad. Copy a new version of the driver to your hard disk, or contact the driver's publisher for instructions on how to proceed.

`Seek error`

The specified disk track couldn't be accessed. Normally, this indicates a bad disk.

`Sharing violation`
`Abort, Retry, Ignore`

With SHARE.EXE loaded, you (or your program) attempted to access a file that was already being used by another program. Press **R** (for Retry) until the program is available, or press **A** to abort the procedure.

`SOURCE disk bad or incompatible`

You were copying files and the source disk was damaged or of the wrong format for its drive. Check the disk and try again, or give it up.

`Specified COM port number not recognized by BIOS`

You specified a port number that is legal but not supported by your ROM BIOS. You either need to replace the BIOS with a newer version or use a different port.

`Syntax error`

You entered a command incorrectly. Check the proper syntax and parameters, and re-enter the command.

`TARGET disk bad or incompatible`

You were copying files, and the target disk was damaged or of the wrong format for its drive. Check the disk and try again, or give it up.

`Target disk may be unusable`

You were copying files, and the target disk was damaged or of the wrong format for its drive. Check the disk and try again, or give it up.

`Target disk unusable`

You were copying files, and the target disk was damaged or of the wrong format for its drive. Check the disk and try again, or give it up and use a good disk.

```
TARGET media has lower capacity than SOURCE
Continue anyway (Y/N)?
```

You're using DISKCOPY, and the target disk can't hold as much information as the source disk, usually because of a few bad sectors. If your source disk is filled to the brim, you may lose some data if you proceed. It's your choice whether you want to chance it or use a different target disk.

```
There are no serial ports or parallel ports available for
communication
```

In DOS 6, INTERSVR cannot find any free ports. Free up a port so that INTERSVR can communicate with INTERLNK.

```
There is not enough room to create a restore file
You will not be able to use the unformat utility
Proceed with Format (Y/N)?
```

You're trying to FORMAT a disk, and there isn't enough room to create a restore file. If you never think you'll use the UNFORMAT utility, go ahead and use the disk. If you want to be safe, throw this disk away.

```
This program requires Microsoft Windows
```

You tried to execute a Windows program from the DOS prompt. You must first start Windows (by typing **WIN** at the DOS prompt), and then load the program from within Windows.

```
Too many block devices
```

Your CONFIG.SYS file contains too many DEVICE commands. Edit your CONFIG.SYS file to remove any unnecessary devices.

```
Too many parallel ports, port ignored
```

In DOS 6, INTERLNK cannot automatically scan this many parallel ports; only the earlier ports will be used.

```
Too many parameters - parms
```

You issued a command with too many parameters. Check your work and try again.

```
Too many serial ports, port ignored
```

In DOS 6, INTERLNK cannot automatically scan this many serial ports; only the earlier ports will be used.

```
Top level process aborted, cannot continue
```

DOS generates this message when another error was detected. You chose the Abort option, and DOS could not successfully reload COMMAND.COM. You'll need to reboot your system to get going again. If this error persists, you may have a bad hard disk. See Chapter 6 for hints on how to reformat your hard disk.

`Unable to create destination`

In DOS 6, MOVE was unable to create the destination file. It's possible that the destination drive or directory is full.

`Unable to create directory`

DOS couldn't create a directory. Either another directory by the same name already exists, a file by the same name already exists, the directory name contains illegal characters, or the root directory is full. Figure out which of these problems is yours, and then take steps to fix it.

`Unable to initialize serial port COMn`

In DOS 6, INTERSVR was unable to initialize the specified serial port, probably because two devices are using the same port address. Check your port assignments and try again.

`Unable to load MS-DOS shell, Retry (y/n)?`

DOS couldn't load the DOS Shell. You probably didn't have enough free memory to load the shell. Try unloading some other programs to free up memory. Next, try rebooting your PC and then try to start the DOS Shell. If this doesn't do it, your DOSSHELL.EXE file might be corrupted. Recopy the file from your original DOS disks to your hard disk.

`Unable to open source`

In DOS 6, MOVE was unable to open the specified source file. You may have an illegal character in the file name, or you're trying to move an entire *directory* instead of a single file, which you can't do.

`Unable to read source`

In DOS 6, an error occurred while using the MOVE command. You may have to use the COPY and DELETE commands to execute the operation.

`Unable to write BOOT`

You're using the FORMAT command and DOS can't write to the BOOT tract or DOS partition of the selected disk. This means the disk is bad, and you should throw it away.

`Unable to write destination`

In DOS 6, an error occurred while using the MOVE command. You may have to use the COPY and DELETE commands to execute the operation.

`Unrecognized command in CONFIG.SYS`

You mistyped something in your CONFIG.SYS file. Edit the file and correct any mistakes.

`Unrecognized switch`

You tried to use a switch that is illegal with this particular command. Check your work and try it again with a different switch.

`Unrecoverable read error on drive x side n, track n`

DOS couldn't read the disk in question. The disk might need to be reformatted or discarded.

`Unrecoverable transmission errors, maximum retries exceeded`

In DOS 6, INTERSVR is getting a lot of errors in the communication cable to INTERLNK. Make sure that all connections are tight, that the cable is good, and that it isn't too close to any sources of electrical interference.

`Unrecoverable write error on drive x side n, track n`

DOS couldn't write to the disk in question. The disk might need to be reformatted or discarded.

`WARNING: Unable to use a disk cache on the specified drive`

In DOS 6, you tried to use SmartDrive to cache a drive that can't be, such as a network drive or a CD-ROM drive. Edit the SMARTDRV.EXE line in AUTOEXEC.BAT to remove this drive reference. (This isn't a problem with DOS 6.2 or later; these versions can cache network and CD-ROM drives with SmartDrive.)

`Write failure, disk unusable`

DOS found bad sectors on the disk in question. Throw it away, and use another disk.

`Write fault error`

DOS couldn't write to this disk. Make sure that the disk is inserted properly. If it is, you could have a bad disk.

`Write protect error`

The specified disk is write-protected. If you really want to use the disk, remove the write-protect tab (5 1/4-inch disks) or move the write-protect shutter into the down position (3 1/2-inch disks).

`Wrong DOS`

You can't use UNFORMAT with this version of DOS. You need to upgrade to DOS 6!

`X contains n non-contiguous blocks`

CHKDSK found noncontiguous blocks on the specified drive. You need to run a defragmenting program, such as DOS 6 DEFRAG, to optimize the performance of your disk.

`xxxxxxx code page cannot be initialized`

Either PRINTER.SYS or DISPLAY.SYS did not load. Check your CONFIG.SYS file for errors in these commands.

```
You have started the Interlnk server in a task-switching
environment. Task-switching, key combinations, and some disk-
writing operations are disabled.
To restore these functions, exit the server
```

In DOS 6, INTERLNK won't allow certain operations to happen, such as the DOS Shell's capability of switching tasks, so it disabled them. Sorry.

In DOS 6, you tried to use SmartDrive to cache only the DoubleSpaced drive. Sorry, but it doesn't work this way; the entire drive, compressed portion, and noncompressed portion must be cached together.

Common System Settings

CHAPTER
TWENTY-NINE

Throughout this book, we've talked about a lot of different system settings. I thought it might be a good idea to take all the common system settings and put them in one place.

That one place is this chapter.

The Least You Need to Know About System Settings

Generally, system settings—such as IRQ and DMA assignments—are a little too technical for the average user. However, when you're installing a new peripheral for your system, you may be asked to select one or more of these settings. So, if you know a little bit about this stuff, you may be able to fake your way through it.

The settings listed in this chapter are *common* settings. The settings for your particular system may be different.

Determining Your System's Settings

How do you determine what the settings are for your system? Well, one way to do this is to run the Microsoft Diagnostics utility included with DOS 6. This DOS-based utility generates reports about all the pieces and parts of your system.

To launch Microsoft Diagnostics, type the following line at the DOS prompt:

MSD

Microsoft Diagnostics then reports information on the following:

- Computer
- Video
- Memory
- Network
- Operating System Version
- Mouse
- Other Adapters
- Disk Drives
- LPT Ports
- COM Ports
- IRQ Status
- TSR Programs
- Device Drivers

You can view this information on-screen, or opt to print a report.

Common System Settings

The following tables list some of the most common system settings you may run into.

Standard IRQ Assignments

IRQ	PURPOSE	COMMON DEVICES
0	CMOS clock (system timer)	
1	Keyboard controller	
2	Cascade to second IRQ controller	Mouse, scanner, network adapter
3	COM2 or COM4	Mouse, modem, network adapter, video, scanner
4	COM1 or COM3	Mouse, modem, CD-ROM, scanner
5	LPT2	Sound card, mouse, modem, scanner
6	Floppy disk controller	Tape drive
7	LPT1	Network adapter, mouse, sound card
8	Real-time clock	
9	*Unused*	SCSI adapter, scanner
10	*Unused*	Network adapter, mouse, sound card, SCSI adapter
11	*Unused*	Mouse, sound card, scanner
12	Motherboard mouse port	Mouse, video, SCSI adapter, scanner
13	Math coprocessor	Mouse
14	Hard disk controller	SCSI adapter
15	*Unused*	Mouse, SCSI adapter

Standard DMA Channel Assignments

CHANNEL	PURPOSE
0	Unused
1	Unused
2	Floppy disk controller
3	Unused
4	First DMA controller
5	Unused
6	Unused
7	Unused

Standard Serial Port Addresses and Assignments

PORT	I/O ADDRESS	IRQ
COM1	3F8h	IRQ4
COM2	2F8h	IRQ3
COM3	3E8h	IRQ4
COM4	2E8h	IRQ3

Standard Parallel Port Addresses and Assignments

PORT	I/O ADDRESS	IRQ
LPT1	3BCh	IRQ7
LPT2	378h	IRQ5
LPT3	278h	None

The Great Trouble-shooting Road Map

Here it is—the fastest way to work through all your computer problems! Just follow me and Mr. PC down the road until you come to the path that describes your particular problem. Read through the list of the most likely causes and then turn to the chapter referenced. If you don't encounter any road blocks, congratulations—your system is working

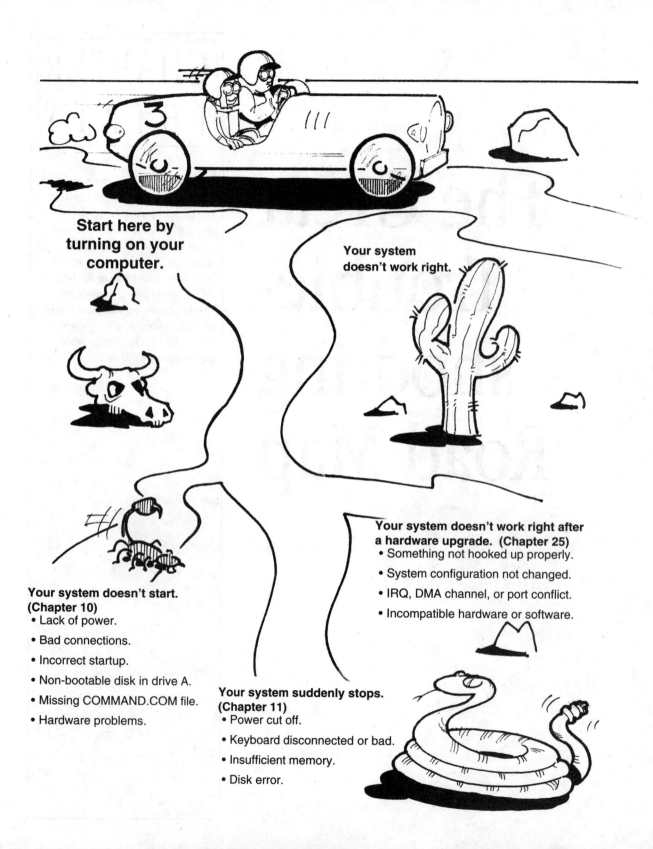

Start here by turning on your computer.

Your system doesn't work right.

Your system doesn't work right after a hardware upgrade. (Chapter 25)
- Something not hooked up properly.
- System configuration not changed.
- IRQ, DMA channel, or port conflict.
- Incompatible hardware or software.

Your system doesn't start. (Chapter 10)
- Lack of power.
- Bad connections.
- Incorrect startup.
- Non-bootable disk in drive A.
- Missing COMMAND.COM file.
- Hardware problems.

Your system suddenly stops. (Chapter 11)
- Power cut off.
- Keyboard disconnected or bad.
- Insufficient memory.
- Disk error.

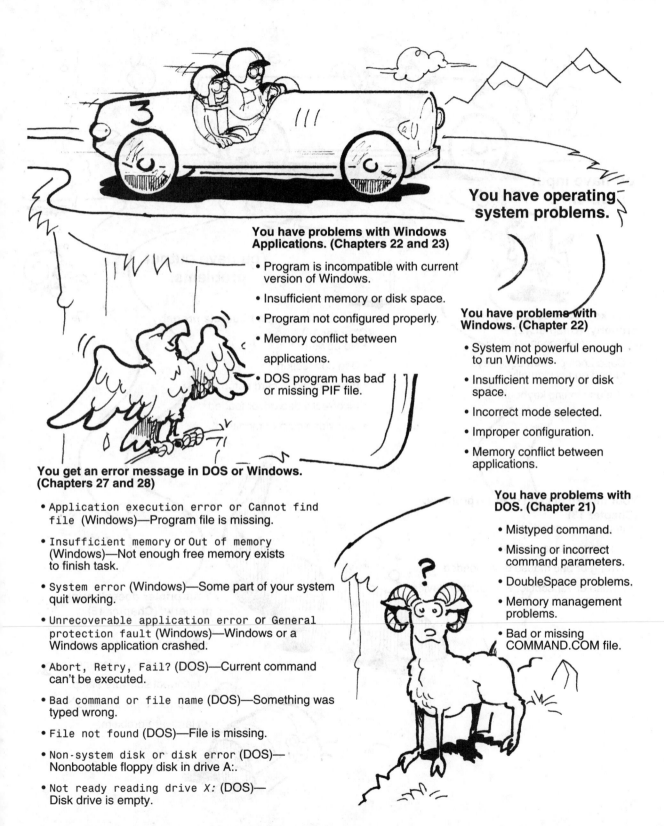

You have operating system problems.

You have problems with Windows Applications. (Chapters 22 and 23)

- Program is incompatible with current version of Windows.
- Insufficient memory or disk space.
- Program not configured properly.
- Memory conflict between applications.
- DOS program has bad or missing PIF file.

You have problems with Windows. (Chapter 22)

- System not powerful enough to run Windows.
- Insufficient memory or disk space.
- Incorrect mode selected.
- Improper configuration.
- Memory conflict between applications.

You get an error message in DOS or Windows. (Chapters 27 and 28)

- `Application execution error` or `Cannot find file` (Windows)—Program file is missing.
- `Insufficient memory` or `Out of memory` (Windows)—Not enough free memory exists to finish task.
- `System error` (Windows)—Some part of your system quit working.
- `Unrecoverable application error` or `General protection fault` (Windows)—Windows or a Windows application crashed.
- `Abort, Retry, Fail?` (DOS)—Current command can't be executed.
- `Bad command or file name` (DOS)—Something was typed wrong.
- `File not found` (DOS)—File is missing.
- `Non-system disk or disk error` (DOS)—Nonbootable floppy disk in drive A:.
- `Not ready reading drive X:` (DOS)—Disk drive is empty.

You have problems with DOS. (Chapter 21)

- Mistyped command.
- Missing or incorrect command parameters.
- DoubleSpace problems.
- Memory management problems.
- Bad or missing COMMAND.COM file.

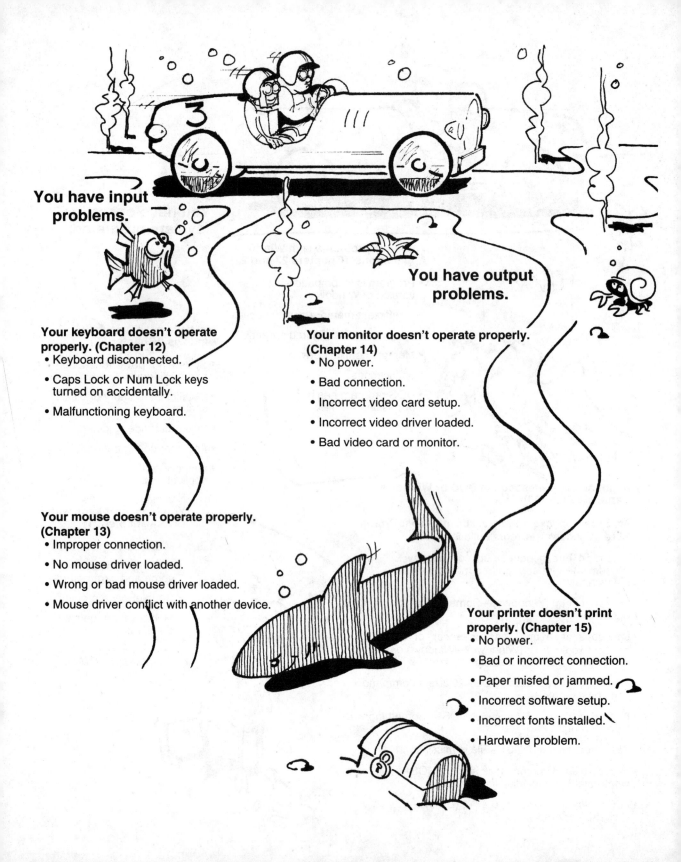

You have input problems.

You have output problems.

Your keyboard doesn't operate properly. (Chapter 12)
- Keyboard disconnected.
- Caps Lock or Num Lock keys turned on accidentally.
- Malfunctioning keyboard.

Your monitor doesn't operate properly. (Chapter 14)
- No power.
- Bad connection.
- Incorrect video card setup.
- Incorrect video driver loaded.
- Bad video card or monitor.

Your mouse doesn't operate properly. (Chapter 13)
- Improper connection.
- No mouse driver loaded.
- Wrong or bad mouse driver loaded.
- Mouse driver conflict with another device.

Your printer doesn't print properly. (Chapter 15)
- No power.
- Bad or incorrect connection.
- Paper misfed or jammed.
- Incorrect software setup.
- Incorrect fonts installed.
- Hardware problem.

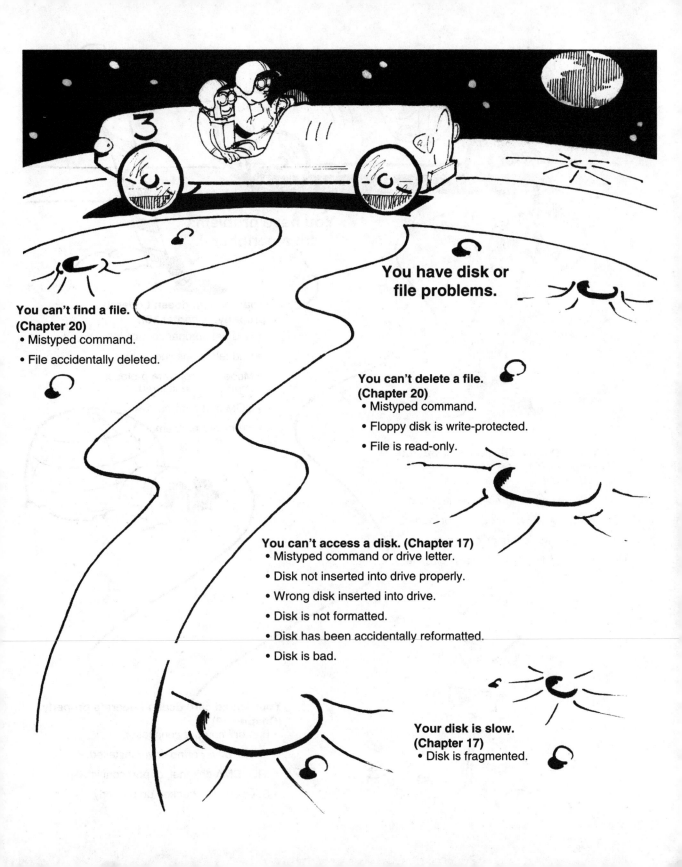

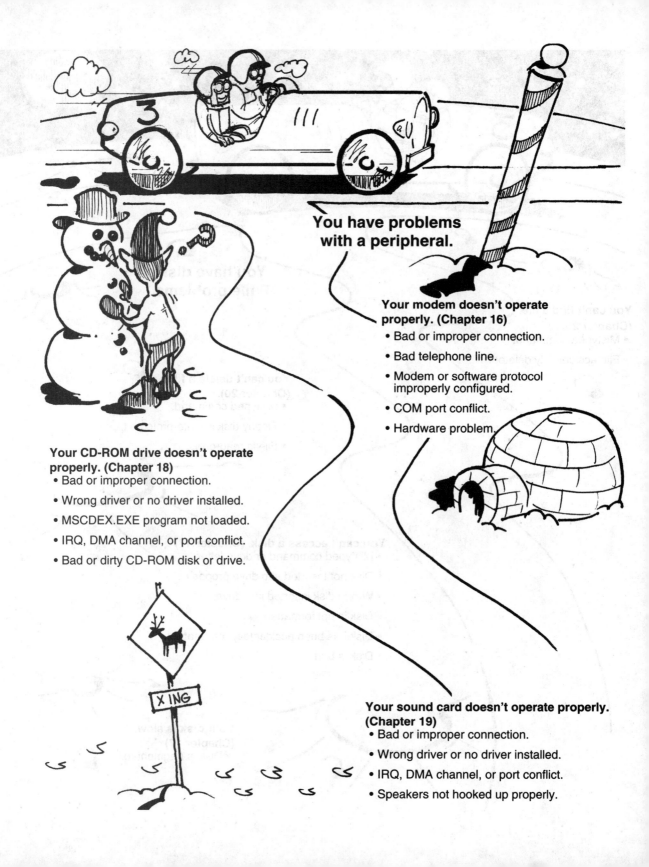

You have problems with a peripheral.

Your modem doesn't operate properly. (Chapter 16)
- Bad or improper connection.
- Bad telephone line.
- Modem or software protocol improperly configured.
- COM port conflict.
- Hardware problem.

Your CD-ROM drive doesn't operate properly. (Chapter 18)
- Bad or improper connection.
- Wrong driver or no driver installed.
- MSCDEX.EXE program not loaded.
- IRQ, DMA channel, or port conflict.
- Bad or dirty CD-ROM disk or drive.

Your sound card doesn't operate properly. (Chapter 19)
- Bad or improper connection.
- Wrong driver or no driver installed.
- IRQ, DMA channel, or port conflict.
- Speakers not hooked up properly.

You have problems with a software program.

Your program won't load. (Chapter 23)
- Mistyped or incorrect command.
- Conflict with other programs.
- Insufficient system requirements (that is, not enough memory).

Your software upgrade doesn't work right. (Chapter 24)
- Poorly altered AUTOEXEC.BAT or CONFIG.SYS files.
- Memory conflict with existing program.
- Old document files are incompatible with new program.

Your program crashes. (Chapter 23)
- Conflict with other programs.
- Low memory.
- Software bug.

Congratulations! Your system is working OK!

The OOPS! Glossary

America OnLine   A major on-line service, composed of special-interest forums.

applet   A small program in Windows that performs a common task.

application   Another word for computer software program.

audio   Sound.

AUTOEXEC.BAT   A file that contains several lines of commands that load devices, start programs, and set system parameters.

back up   A way of creating duplicate files for archival storage.

batch file   A user-creatable file that contains a series of DOS commands. A batch file executes similarly to regular program files and carries a BAT extension.

baud rate   Rate at which the transmission speed of modems is measured.

BBS   Bulletin board service. A small on-line service used for communicating by modem-equipped computer users.

BIOS   The basic input/output system. The part of DOS that actually interacts with computer hardware.

board   A device that plugs into your system unit and provides auxiliary functions. (Also called a *card*.)

boot   Computerese for turning on your computer system. Used as follows: "I'm booting up my system now." You also can *reboot* your computer (turn it off and then on again).

bootable disk A disk that can be used to start your system because the disk contains certain system files. See *system disk*.

byte A measurement of space (on-disk or in memory); one byte is pretty much equal to one character. Approximately one thousand bytes is called *one kilobyte* (K) and one million bytes (more or less) is called *one megabyte* (M).

C prompt The prompt issued by the DOS command interpreter when it is waiting for you to input a command.

card A device that plugs into your system unit and provides auxiliary functions. You can add video cards, modem cards, and sound cards to your system. (Also called a *board*.)

CD-ROM Compact disk—read-only memory. CD-ROM disks contain large volumes of information and are read by lasers.

central processing unit Also known as the CPU. See *microprocessor*.

CGA Low-resolution (320 × 300 pixels) color display standard.

command The way you talk to DOS. You can issue one of many DOS commands to make DOS perform a specific function.

command interpreter The part of DOS that lets you input specific commands; often called the *DOS prompt* or *command line*.

compression A way of squeezing data so that a disk can hold more data than before.

CompuServe A major on-line service, composed of special-interest forums. (Que has a forum on CompuServe.)

computer That big beige thing on your desk that's causing you all the problems.

cursor The on-screen pointer.

cyberspace Where all on-line communications take place.

delete Erase. Kill. Zap. Get rid of.

density The amount of data stored on a disk. Can be high-density or low-density.

directory An index to files you store on your disk. Your disk is divided into multiple directories, and each directory contains multiple files.

disk A device that stores data in magnetic format. A portable disk.

DOS The most popular operating system for IBM-compatible computers.

DOS Shell The menu-driven shell program that buffers you from the command interpreter. (Not included with versions of DOS after 6.2.)

DOS utilities Special mini-programs that perform specific tasks in DOS, such as formatting disks.

DoubleSpace The disk-compression utility provided with DOS 6 and 6.2.

DriveSpace The disk-compression utility (similar to DoubleSpace) provided with DOS, starting with version 6.22.

EGA Medium-resolution (640 × 400 pixels) color display standard.

error message An on-screen message that DOS issues to tell you that you did something wrong or that a command was not able to be executed correctly.

FAT File allocation table. A special section of your disk that stores tracking data to help DOS locate files.

file The data you store on your hard disk. All computer data is organized into files, and all files have file names.

File Manager The file-management applet in Windows.

file name The name assigned to a file. Each file name consists of two parts, the root (up to eight characters long) and the extension (up to three characters long).

floppy disk The portable data-storage device, available in two sizes (3 1/2-inch and 5 1/4-inch). Floppy disks are inserted into the floppy disk drive on the front of your system unit and are read by your system.

format The process that prepares a disk for use.

function key One of the special keys labelled F1 to F12, located either on the left side or top of your computer keyboard.

graphical user interface A shell for an operating system that uses graphical elements instead of character-based elements. Also known as the GUI (pronounced "gooey").

hard disk The data storage device located inside your PC system unit.

hardware The parts of your computer system you can touch (as opposed to the part you can't touch, which is your software).

IBM-compatible All personal computers that are compatible (that is, can share software and operating systems) with the original IBM PC.

information superhighway
Either the next generation of the Internet, or the entire conglomeration of today's various on-line services and BBSs.

install How you get software from its box to your hard disk.

Internet A network of networks; the major gateway to millions and millions of other computer users.

keyboard The thing that looks like a typewriter that you use to type instructions to your computer.

kilobyte One thousand bytes, more or less. (Actually, it's 1,024 bytes.) Also known as K, as in 640K.

megabyte Approximately one million bytes. Also known as M.

megahertz One million hertz. (A hertz is a measurement of frequency; in the case of computers, the speed of a microprocessor is measured in megahertz, abbreviated MHz.)

MemMaker The memory-management utility included with DOS 6.

memory Temporary storage for data and instructions via electronic impulses on a chip.

memory-resident program
Utility or accessory that, after it's loaded into your system's memory, stays there, in the background, doing its job. Also called terminate-and-stay-resident (TSR) program.

microprocessor The chip inside your system unit that processes all the operations your computer can do.

Microsoft The company that developed and publishes the MS-DOS operating system, the Windows operating environment, and dozens of other best-selling programs, including Excel and Word for Windows.

Microsoft Anti-Virus The anti-virus utility provided with DOS 6.

Microsoft Backup The backup utility provided with DOS 6.

Microsoft Undelete The undelete utility provided with DOS 6.

modem A device that lets your computer communicate with other computers over telephone lines.

monitor The thing that looks like a TV screen, which displays all your computer text and graphics.

motherboard The big board that makes up the bulk of the insides of your system unit. The motherboard holds your main microprocessor and memory chips and also contains slots to plug in additional boards (cards).

mouse The hand-held device with a rollerball and buttons that you use to navigate through menu-driven and graphical programs.

MS-DOS The Microsoft-specific version of DOS.

multimedia The combination, usually on a computer, of interactive text, graphics, audio, and video.

multitasking The capability to run more than one application at a time. Windows is multitasking; DOS isn't.

on-line communications Any and all communications between one computer and another over phone lines via modem.

on-line service A data center that facilitates modem communication between multiple computers.

Oops! The sound you make when something goes wrong with your computer.

operating system The core system software that lets you (and your software programs) communicate with your hardware.

OS/2 A higher-end operating system from IBM, not discussed in this book.

path The listing—including all directories and subdirectories—of exactly where a file is located.

PIF Program Information File. A file that instructs Windows how to handle a specific DOS program from within Windows.

pixel The unit of measurement used in measuring the quality of screen displays.

port A fancy name for those connectors that stick out of the back of your system unit. Also refers to the system assignment of specific devices.

printer The piece of computer hardware that lets you create hard-copy printouts of your documents.

Program Manager The Windows program organizer and launcher.

protocol The configuration settings for a modem.

RAM Random-access memory. A type of temporary memory used in your computer.

read How data is absorbed from a disk to your system's memory.

resolution The size of the images on a screen; how the quality of screen displays is measured.

root directory The main directory on a disk.

screen saver A utility program, such as After Dark, that prolongs the life of your monitor by blanking the screen—or providing a continuously moving image—while your monitor is not in use.

set up How you configure your system (or individual software or hardware).

shell A friendly face for a difficult environment.

software The programs that run on your computer.

startup files The files that DOS reads when it first starts up that hold information on system configuration. The two files are AUTOEXEC.BAT and CONFIG.SYS.

subdirectory A subsidiary directory located off a main directory.

surge suppressor A device that protects your system from unwanted power line surges.

SVGA SuperVGA. High-resolution (minimum of 800 × 600 pixels) color display standard.

switch There are two types of switches—hardware and software. A hardware switch is a physical switch on a card that toggles various functions. A software switch is an optional parameter added to the end of a DOS command that toggles various options.

syntax The "grammar" you use when issuing a DOS command. You have to issue the command and all its parameters in the correct order—or syntax—for it to execute correctly.

system disk A disk containing the operating system and all files necessary to start your computer.

system files The two files whose presence are necessary for DOS to start; normally hidden from user view or editing. The two files are IO.SYS and MSDOS.SYS.

system unit   That part of your computer system that looks like a big beige box. The system unit contains your microprocessor, system memory, hard disk drive, floppy disk drives, and various cards.

telecommunications   How your computer talks to other computers, using a modem.

undelete   Unerase. Bring back from the dead. Save your skin.

UNIX   A higher-end operating system, common among Internet users, not discussed in this book. (For more beginning-level information on UNIX, check out Que's very good *Introduction to UNIX*, 2nd Edition.)

upgrade   To add a new or improved peripheral or part to your system hardware. Also to install a newer version of an existing piece of software.

VGA   High-resolution (640 × 480 pixels) color display standard.

virus   A bad, nasty, evil computer program that can cause untold damage to your data.

wild card   A character used to represent other characters. There are two wild cards used in DOS commands and operations—the * and the ? characters.

Windows   An operating environment from Microsoft that runs on top of DOS and provides a graphical user interface.

write   How data is placed on a disk.

Index

C

S